Seeds of Faith, Branches of Hope

The Archdiocese of Newark, New Jersey

By
Reverend Christopher Ciccarino

Acknowledgments

SPONSOR
The Archdiocese of Newark, New Jersey

SENIOR AUTHOR
Reverend Christopher Ciccarino

WRITERS
Monsignor William Noé Field
Reverend Eugene Field

PRODUCTION SUPERVISION / COORDINATION
James G. Goodness
Archdiocesan Office of Communication

EDITORIAL CONSULTANT
Loretta Pastva, SND

RESEARCH / PHOTO SECTION
Seton Hall University
Elizabeth Kepniss

PHOTOGRAPHY
Frantisek Zvardon
Archdiocesan Archives

FRONT COVER PHOTOGRAPHY
Randy Brockway

PUBLISHER
Éditions du Signe – B.P. 94 – 67038 Strasbourg – France

PUBLISHING DIRECTOR
Christian Riehl

DIRECTOR OF PUBLICATION
Dr. Claude-Bernard Costecalde

PUBLISHING ASSISTANT
Audrey Harrer

DESIGN AND LAYOUT
Sylvie Reiss & Juliette Roussel

PHOTOENGRAVING
Editions du Signe - 104420

ISBN: 2-7468-1137-5
Printed in China by Sun Fung Offset Binding Co., Ltd.

Table of Contents

TODAY

The Archdiocese of Newark Today

The Newark Archdiocese is geographically the smallest Archdiocese in the United States. It comprises 511 square miles in the counties of Bergen, Essex, Hudson and Union, New Jersey. The total population is 2,809,607. The Catholic population is 1,319,556, which makes it the seventh largest archdiocese in the U.S.

The Archdiocese has 235 parishes, 139 elementary schools and 37 high schools. It is served by one university and three colleges. Total enrollment of all levels of Catholic education is about 75,000. There are 72,000 students in elementary and secondary religious education programs.

The Archdiocese is served by 722 diocesan and 227 religious priests, 251 permanent deacons, 104 brothers and 1,276 sisters. There are 11 Catholic hospitals in its area. (Statistics as of September 2001)

Mary, under her title of the Immaculate Conception, is the patroness the Archdiocese of Newark.

Archdiocese of Newark
OFFICE OF THE ARCHBISHOP

MYSTERIUM ECCLESIAE LUCEAT

My Dear Friends in Christ,

This year we, the people of the Church of Newark, celebrate a special moment – a look back at our first 150 years as a diocese. Our story is one of joy and celebration, of challenges and sadness, of generosity and witness to the Gospel of Jesus Christ.

This history looks at our life from many perspectives: the bishops and priests who have led the Church of Newark through the years; the growth of the diocese from our early days as mission parishes to a Church of at least 1.3 million men, women and children of varied ethnic and cultural backgrounds; the countless contributions of laypeople and religious to the Church; the changing attitude toward Catholics from a past marked by prejudice to our present-day acceptance and leadership in society, yet with lingering prejudices.

Most of all, though, this is a story of people – of loyal and devoted Catholics like you, many of whom brought their traditions and depth of faith from distant lands to seek a new life and strengthen the Church here in New Jersey. Through portraits of each parish in the Archdiocese – portraits written by you — this history reflects that continued depth of faith. In many instances, they reflect the continuing tide of change and renewal by new immigrant groups that marks our Church. Change is part of the fabric of this state and this Archdiocese, and we welcome new Catholics wishing to join the life of our Church in the years to come.

In the two years since I have been part of the life of the Archdiocese of Newark, I have come to know many of you and it is my desire to know so many more of you in the years ahead. I have been most fortunate to share in your celebrations, your joys and sadness, your hopes and your challenges, and your moments of witness. I have also learned that as an Archdiocese we are who we are because the Catholics who came before us believed strongly in the Church and its teachings.

The Church today faces some significant problems that I know we will overcome through reliance on the essential truths that our faith has revealed to us. If this first volume of our history teaches us one thing, it is this: just as strong, devout Catholics who came before us have written our past, strong, devout Catholics like you, your children and all who join this Church of Newark will shape our future.

With every good wish, I remain,

Sincerely in the Lord,

✝ The Most Reverend John J. Myers
Archbishop of Newark

Preface

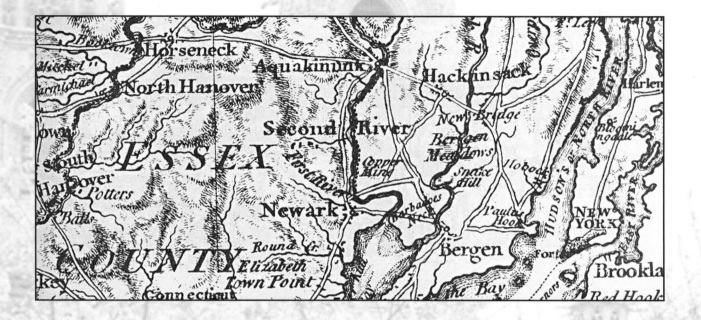

Nestled between two broad rivers, where the heights of the Alleghenies fade into foothills and meet the sea plains rising from the Atlantic, at the center of the eastern coast of what is now the United States, rests a small peninsula which today is the home of the State of New Jersey. Well before the arrival of the Europeans, this land served as a fertile crossroads for the many cultures of the first peoples in this portion of North America. From the early spring morning in 1524 when Giovanni da Verrazzano sighted "a coast which was very green and forested… with some pleasant promontories and small rivers," to the present day, New Jersey has attracted countless others from across the world to her shores. The peoples who both arrived here and lived here have brought with them their talents, their cultures, their industry, and – for so many – their abiding trust in God.

Immigrants brought their devotions with them when they came to this country. Here Italians celebrated the Feast of Maria SS. della Lavina Society in 1914 with a march down Bloomfield Avenue.

Faith in the New World

There are as many different stories of faith as there have been persons in New Jersey. The present work hopes to follow the journey of one group of those persons whose story of faith is as intricate as it is engaging. They brought with them an ancient Faith to a New World, where, despite beginning as

Archbishop Theodore McCarrick celebrates Mass at the Pope John Paul II Pavilion as part of a pastoral visit to the nurshing home in 1998.

Fr. Anthony F. Granato with Religious Education / Special Education children at St. Anthony, East Newark.

a distrusted minority, they grew and developed and thrived and have made a singular contribution to the life and history of New Jersey. This volume intends to recount the broad lines of this people's story from the advent of the Catholic Faith in the New World to the first days of the Third Millennium.

The First Catholics

Unrecognized and unknown, the first Catholics of New Jersey included the immigrant German ironworkers of Macopin, the French glassblowers who came over from Philadelphia, and the Anglo-Irish farmers, widely scattered between the Delaware and the Hudson. Lacking even one church, prey to the difficulties which all immigrants face, and bearing the additional burden of religious antipathy, these men and women planted a seed which now, almost three centuries later, has yielded

a vast harvest. Within the present Archdiocese of Newark itself the hundreds of parishes, schools, religious houses, hospitals, social services, and institutions which serve almost one and a half million Catholics, as well as citizens of all faiths, stand as an eloquent testimony to the faith of these first Catholics.

Of course, the testimony to the infant Catholic community in written accounts, records, memoirs, and artifacts is scattered and scarce. The available materials have been greatly augmented with the growth of the community over time and gradually the portrait of this people has become increasingly distinct and vivid to the present day. However this was not always the case. As far as can be told, this journey began much more modestly.

Lily Cup chalice of silver gilt, presented to Seton Hall University, 1890 by the St. Patrick, Newark, Rosary Society

Indian signatures (or "marks") on 1667 deed that conveyed Newark to the first settlers.

(Copy in State Library, Trenton)

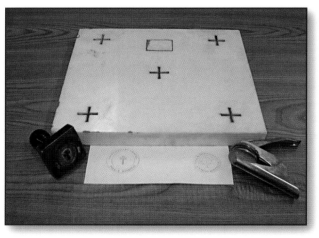

Altar stone, stamps and seal from Sacred Heart Chapel, Pollack Hospital, Jersey City

A New World

ASIDE FROM THE BRIEF VISIT OF VERRAZZANO IN 1524, THE FIRST
CATHOLICS CAME TO NEW JERSEY, SO FAR AS IT CAN BE ASCERTAINED,
TOWARD THE END OF THE 17TH CENTURY. WHEN THEY ARRIVED, THEY FOUND
NEW JERSEY ALREADY A PLACE WHERE EUROPEAN CULTURES MET AND
MIXED WITH EACH OTHER AS WELL AS WITH THE NATIVE AMERICANS.

First Settlers

The first Europeans to establish permanent settlements in New Jersey were the Dutch. Indeed, it wasn't until almost a century after Verrazzano's initial voyage that Europeans returned to New Jersey and Henry Hudson, under Dutch patronage, sailed into Newark Bay. The Netherlands had been born of the battle of the Calvinist Dutch for independence from the Holy Roman Empire. Limited land and economic need had always spurred the Dutch to draw their living from the sea and their successful struggle for independence saw them develop colonies in Africa, the Far East, and both North and South America.

The Dutch colonization of North America began on the island of Manhattan with the town of New Amsterdam, in what was to become the capital of New Netherlands. The first outpost of New Netherlands west of the Hudson River was the trading station of Bergen, established in 1618. In 1626, Fort Nassau was built on the east bank of the Delaware River, near the present Gloucester. (The building of Fort Nassau is usually attributed to Captain Cornelius Jacobsen Mey, whose name is retained in the present "Cape May.") A significant

Johnson's mill and farm house erected in about 1680 on Bound Creek near the Elizabeth Border. The second mill in town, it ground flour during the Revolution.

number of settlers established themselves in New Amsterdam, and slowly began to cross the Hudson River. Following their bitter conflict with Spain for independence, the Dutch brought with them to the New World a deep aversion to Catholicism, and prohibited its practice in New Netherlands.

The Dutch were not the only Europeans to settle in New Jersey. They were soon joined by the Swedes, who established a series of outposts stretching up both banks of the Delaware River. New Sweden faced great difficulties. Both the Dutch and the English claimed the Delaware Valley, support from Sweden was very sporadic, and relationships with the Native Americans were tense at best.

Excerpt of Nicholas Visscher's 1636 map of the Puritan world from Cape Cod to New Jersey

English Newcomers

The English were actually the last of the European powers to arrive on the scene. There were, however, several early English explorers or explorers with English patrons (notably John

The surly actions of Edmond Andros, Governor of New York, stirred resentment wherever he went. His actions against Jerseymen in 1680 induced even gentle Newarkers close to seething rebellion.
Painting by Howard Pyle.

Section of a map drawn in 1740 for use by proprietors in major court action against alleged squatters. Squatters' rights were at first ignored or tolerated, but as land grew valuable, pressure for rents increased, leading to the Horseneck riots and other clashes.

Cabot, who arrived in North America on June 24, 1497, less than five years following Columbus' initial voyage). However, the turbulence brought to Great Britain by the Reformation and then her long struggle with Spain absorbed much of the energies of the English during the sixteenth century.

During the seventeenth century, at home England underwent several upheavals as King and Parliament struggled for supremacy. Religious and political disquiet spurred both the exploration and colonization of the New World. Gradually, English trappers and traders (followed by settlers), mainly from New England, began to make their way into the regions of New Netherlands and New Sweden.

Of course, all of the Europeans who came to New Jersey came to a land that was already inhabited. Though not so well known as many tribes of surrounding territories, the first people of New Jersey, the Lenape, had a significantly developed cultural and social system – which would be almost completely disrupted by their contact with the European nations.

The good will of the Native Americans was vital to the survival of almost all of the initial European settlements in North America. They received the Europeans in peace and shared their skills, knowledge, and – above all – food. Commerce rapidly developed between the Dutch and Swedes and the Lenape. In exchange for the food, furs, and pelts from the Lenape, the Europeans offered finished products, metal utensils, textiles, and liquor. While this trade was quite profitable for the Europeans, the ongoing contact had a deeply corrosive effect on the Lenape. Previously unknown diseases, especially smallpox, decimated the native population while differing ideas of land ownership combined with a burgeoning colonist population to bring the first peoples of New Jersey to near extinction.

Thus the English settlers, who followed their traders and fur trappers to New Netherlands, New Sweden, and the lands of the Lenape, found there a generous country with a variety of peoples. As the Native population declined, English settlers and English influence eclipsed the Dutch and Swedes

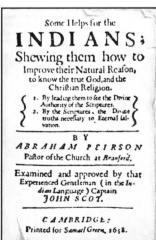

Some Helps for the
INDIANS;
Shewing them how to
Improve their Natural Reason,
to know the true God, and the
Christian Religion.

1. By leading them to see the Divine
Authority of the Scriptures.
2. By the Scriptures, the Divine
truths necessary to Eternal Sal-
vation.

BY
ABRAHAM PEIRSON
Pastor of the Church at *Branford*.

Examined and approved by that
Experienced Gentleman (in the In-
dian Language) Captain
JOHN SCOT.

CAMBRIDGE:
Printed for *Samuel Green*, 1658.

Advertisement for Indians

HISTORY OF THE ARCHDIOCESE OF NEWARK

The Colony of New Jersey

ON MARCH 12, 1664, CHARLES II GAVE TO HIS BROTHER JAMES, THE DUKE OF YORK, LETTERS PATENT CREATING HIM PROPRIETOR OF FRESH TERRITORIES IN THE NEW WORLD.

These territories included some lands both north of New England and also the land from "the West side of the Conecteutte River to the East side of Delaware Bay" – that is, the whole of New Netherlands. Colonel Richard Nicholls was made the Duke's deputy governor and given 450 soldiers to make good the Duke's claim. Nicholls arrived in Boston in July of 1664, and by August 29th of that year had peacefully taken possession of New Amsterdam. He dispatched Sir Robert Carr to the other side of the Hudson, and, in short order, the English conquest of New Netherlands was complete. The English thus found themselves in possession of almost the whole Atlantic seaboard of North America.

In June of 1664, while Colonel Nicholls and his expedition were actually still at sea, the Duke of York had decided to make over a part of his hoped-for acquisitions to two of his friends, Lord John Berkeley and Sir George Carteret, who had stood by him during the English Civil War. "In commemoration of Carteret's heroic defense of Jersey in the Civil War this territory received the name of New Jersey." When Nichols was informed, he wrote the Duke, strenuously objecting to the transfer of his land, for he considered the lands of New Jersey the "best part of the conquest."

New Colony Agreements

The "Concessions and Agreements of the Proprietors of New Jersey" laid down the fundamental directions for the new colony. Very significantly, it was provided:

> That noe person qualified as aforesaid within the said Province at any time shale in any waies be molested punished disquieted or called in Question for any difference in opinion or practice in matters of Religious concernments, who doe not actually disturbe the civill peace of the said Province, but that all and every such person and persons may from time to time and at all times truly and fully have and enjoy their Judgements and Consciences in matters of Religion throughout all the said province.

The new proprietors of the colony were very eager to promote as much settlement in the province as possible, and, for a brief time, Catholics, Quakers, Unitarians, and Englishmen of all religious faiths actually enjoyed theoretically more liberty in New Jersey than in their mother country.

As time passed, western New Jersey came under the influence of the Quakers. The Quakers, having themselves experienced religious discrimination, provided that in their portion of New Jersey:

> [I]t is consented, agreed and ordained, that no Person or Persons whatsoever in said Province, at any Time or Times hereafter, shall be any ways upon any pretense whatsoever, called in Question, or in the least punished or hurt, either in Person, Estate, or Privilege, for the sake of his Opinion, Judgement, Faith or Worship towards God in Matters of Religion.

Medallion of a Papal Chamberlain.
Archdiocesan Archives

As generous as the provisions governing New Jersey were in theory, they still needed to be carried out in practice. The person to whom this duty fell was Sir Edmund Andros, who took control of New Jersey on behalf of the Duke of York.

A Catholic from Bergen

Andros arrived in New York in 1674, with wide writ to set up the "Dominion of New England" on behalf of his patron. Included within the Dominion was the whole of New Jersey. Upon his arrival, Andros discovered that his ill-defined authority, combined with a less-than-tactful personality, met with great resistance throughout the colonies of the Dominion. Andros returned to England in 1678 to clarify his instructions and the nature of his authority with the Duke of York. Thus fortified, he returned to the New World, and, in 1680, Andros convened the Assembly of the colony. It was to this assembly that William Douglas, a gentleman from the town of Bergen in East Jersey, had been elected on May 22, 1680. However, Douglas was a Catholic.

Few details are known about Douglas' personal life. It seems likely that he came to Bergen in the late 1660's. He was, evidently, well regarded within the community for it is recorded that he sat on at least two juries in the colony during the early 1670's. That he served as a juror indicates that he was a man both of some means and of good repute. Likewise, his election to the Assembly as one of two deputies from a town known for its non-English and non-Catholic sympathies may be taken as an indication of the esteem with which he was held.

While Douglas and his fellow deputy from Bergen, Hans Diedewicker, were late in arriving at Elizabethtown for the start of the Assembly, they were welcomed by the Governor and the other deputies and both were duly sworn in and seated in the Assembly. At the time of his swearing-in Governor Andros

The Jesuit Missionaries gave religious rings and crosses to their Indian converts.

and the rest of the Assembly were well aware that Douglas was a Catholic, for indeed it is recorded that Douglas expressed concerns (quickly assuaged) about the oath which he was to take. Douglas took the Oath of Office and was seated in the Assembly on June 3, 1680. The Assembly, with Douglas participating, elected a Speaker, Clerk, and began its business – Governor Andros returning to New York. However, on June 10th, the clerk of the Assembly, Isaac Whitehead, wrote and informed Governor Andros that the deputies of the Assembly found "occasion to purge themselves of such a member as cannot be allowed of by law, namely, William Douglas, the aforesd member upon examination ouning himself to be a Roman Catholick."

> *"Congress shall make no law... prohibiting the free exercise [of religion]."*
>
> 1ST AMENDMENT, U.S. CONSTITUTION

Early Religious Freedom?

Whatever transpired at the Assembly leading to Douglas' expulsion after just one week is obscure. Given the "Concessions and Agreements of the Proprietors," the "Charter or Fundamental Laws," as well as the religious sympathies of the Duke of York, it is not known to which law Whitehead referred in his letter to the Governor. It would seem likely that, had there been a specific statute forbidding political participation in New Jersey by Catholics, then William Douglas would never have been elected nor sworn into office. However, the facts of both his election to and eviction from the Assembly still stand. After his ignominious expulsion from the Assembly, history falls silent about the career of Douglas, who left the colony. Thus, despite formal guarantees of religious liberties, the very first known record of a Catholic in the English colony of New Jersey ended on a melancholy note.

It was shortly after William Douglas' difficulties that the first extant records of the visit of a Catholic priest to New Jersey are recorded. In 1683 Edmund

Andros was succeeded as governor of New York by Colonel Thomas Dongan, an Irish Catholic. Dongan's appointment as governor, and his subsequent becoming the Earl of Limerick, reflected a new religious situation in the mother country. James, Duke of York, had become a Catholic in 1670, and, when he ascended the throne as James II, Catholicism again found a place in England.

With the new Governor came Rev. Thomas Harvey, of the Society of Jesus. He was thereafter to be joined by Rev. Henry Harrison, Rev. Charles Gage, and two Jesuit lay brothers. The Jesuits established themselves at a chapel on Governor's Island and began seeking out Catholics in New Jersey, visiting families in both Elizabethtown and Woodbridge.

An Uneasy Prominence

The prominence which Catholics in the New World and in Great Britain received during the reign of James II was uneasy and short-lived. In November 1688, the Glorious Revolution swept James from his throne and installed his daughter Mary (a non-Catholic) with her consort, the firmly Protestant William the Silent of the Netherlands, in his place. The accession of William and Mary intensified the penal laws against Catholics in England. These penal laws were to be echoed fiercely in British possessions in the New World.

In New York, Dongan was removed from office, a warrant was issued for his arrest, and the Assembly declared that Catholic priests coming into the province would be deemed "incendiaries, disturbers of the public peace, and enemies of true Christian religion." Furthermore, all Catholics were prohibited from voting for members of the Assembly or any other office. In New Jersey, the General Assembly, meeting in 1698, granted religious freedom in East Jersey to those who "profess faith in God, and in Jesus Christ, His only Son," but added the exception that "this shall not extend to any of the Romish religion." Likewise, when the proprietors gave up their rights over New Jersey and it became a

royal colony, the first royal governor, Lord Cornbury, was instructed to ensure that all members of his council were to take the test contained in the "Act for Preventing Dangers which may happen from Popish Recusants." Cornbury was also directed by Queen Anne that he was to "permit a liberty of conscience to all persons (except papists)." These instructions were renewed to each governor. Oaths of office for military and civil officers declared various Catholic beliefs "impious, heretical, superstitious, and idolatrous."

Various forms of strictures against Catholics were actually to remain in force during the entire 18th century, through the Revolutionary War and the founding of the new Republic, until they were finally removed by an act of the State Legislature in 1844.

In this window from Queen of Peace Church, North Arlington, George Washington recognizes the patriotic and important assistance of Catholics in the accomplishments of the Revolution and the establishment of the government. Upper window shows original Stars and Stripes flag entwined with the Colonial flag and the great tree grown from the acorn at the base.

First Missionaries

IF THE 18ᵀᴴ CENTURY SAW THE ENACTMENT OF STERN OFFICIAL MEASURES
AGAINST THE BUDDING CATHOLIC COMMUNITY OF NEW JERSEY, IT ALSO SAW
THE BEGINNING OF THE FIRST EFFORTS OF CONSISTENT AND ON-GOING
PASTORAL CARE FOR THE CATHOLICS OF THE COLONY. THE FIRST
MISSIONARY PRIESTS TO SERVE THE NEEDS OF CATHOLICS IN THE COLONY OF
NEW JERSEY WERE GERMAN JESUITS, BASED MAINLY IN PHILADELPHIA.

First Catholic Center

A small group of Catholic families, skilled glassblowers, had established themselves a short distance from Salem, New Jersey, and the "Wister glass house" thus became the first Catholic mission center in New Jersey. The first regular missionary was Rev. Theodore Schneider, S. J., who is recorded as arriving in New Jersey in 1744. In fact, he traveled throughout eastern Pennsylvania, Delaware, and western New Jersey. Fr. Schneider, originally from Bavaria, had been rector of a German university, and spent a full 20 years on the New Jersey mission. Due to stringency of New Jersey law against Catholic priests and, having some medical skills, Fr. Schneider usually traveled in the disguise of a physician, bringing with him his

Old St. Joseph Church, Philadelphia, 1734, the only Catholic Church for Pennsylvania, New Jersey and New York for 80 years.

own hand-copied Roman Missal. During his journeys, "Dr. Schneider" said Mass for little congregations, blessed marriages and grave sites, baptized many, heard numerous confessions, and, on occasion, dodged the bullets of those who were less than happy to see a Catholic priest in New Jersey.

"Father Farmer"

Beginning in 1758, and continuing for 28 eventful years, the missionary priest from this period who is best known is Rev. Ferdinand Steinmeyer, who was called "Father Farmer." Fr. Farmer crisscrossed New Jersey ministering to Catholics as it was transformed from a colony to an independent member of a Confederation to the third state to ratify the new federal constitution.

Father Farmer had originally hoped to have been sent to mission in China, but his superiors instead sent him to the equally exotic North America, where he worked for six years in Lancaster, Pennsylvania, before moving to Philadelphia and beginning to serve the New Jersey Mission. Each spring and autumn, Fr. Farmer would travel a circuit, starting his journey from his base in old St. Joseph's Church in Philadelphia, crossing the Delaware River into Salem County, New Jersey, and working his way on foot, horse, stage, and boat through the colony, ending in Elizabethtown and New York City. Thus, most Catholic communities in New Jersey were visited at least twice a year. On occasion, other priests, both from Philadelphia and from New York, especially old St. Peter's Church on Barclay Street – a congregation which was largely organized by Fr. Farmer – were also able to visit the Catholics of the colony. Among

With sections dating to the 1740s, the "little red farmhouse" is the oldest building at Ringwood Manor State Park. It may have been used as a Mass house by Fr. Farmer. Tom Lynch/The Beacon

Washington), Catholics in the new United States of America found themselves still viewed with suspicion and disdain. This prejudice was inscribed in nine of the new state constitutions of America, including that of New Jersey, where Catholics were prohibited from holding public office. Notwithstanding these obstacles and prejudices, Fr. Graessl ministered for six years in New Jersey prior to his death. Indeed, he had become so well regarded by his fellow priests that his name had been submitted to Pope Pius VI as a possible candidate to work with and eventually succeed Bishop Carroll. This suggestion was in fact accepted, and the Holy Father appointed Fr. Graessl to serve as Bishop Carroll's coadjutor – however this news from Rome arrived shortly after Graessl's death by yellow fever in Philadelphia.

John Carroll

those priests to accompany Fr. Farmer on one of his journeys was Rev. John Carroll, who was to become the first Roman Catholic bishop in the United States when the Diocese of Baltimore was established in 1789. [As Superior of the Mission in the United States, Carroll was empowered to celebrate the Sacrament of Confirmation, which he did in Macopin, northern New Jersey in the fall of 1785. This was the first time the Sacrament of Confirmation was celebrated in New Jersey.]

Father Farmer was also known as a philosopher and astronomer, and was so regarded as a scholar that, despite his Catholicism and his status as a priest, he was selected as one of the first trustees of the University of Pennsylvania. As the years went on, Fr. Farmer's flock grew and his health declined. Fr. Farmer began to correspond with a young priest who was a former Jesuit, Rev. Lawrence Graessl, who accepted Fr. Farmer's invitation to join him on the New Jersey Mission. Fr. Graessl arrived in the United States in November 1787, only to learn that the celebrated Fr. Farmer had passed away four months prior to his coming.

Fr. Graessl picked up the work of Fr. Farmer, finding the new language and new customs of the young nation profoundly challenging. Despite playing a significant role in the Revolutionary War, a role which was recognized by many (including George

If Bishop John Carroll, the first bishop of Baltimore and the first Catholic bishop resident in the United States, was unable to take advantage of Fr. Graessl's gifts as his coadjutor, he did have some reason for hope as he surveyed the situation of the Catholic Church in America in the first years of the new Republic. The Catholic population, though still quite small, was growing, and increasingly

The map of Fr. Farmer's mission station in New Jersey (John Spiegel)

included some prominent members of society – not least of whom were the Carroll family themselves. Catholic churches began to appear in some of the cities. Catholic clergy, including a small but growing group of those born in the colonies, began to minister to organized Catholic congregations. Catholic higher education began with the founding of Georgetown College in 1789.

Bishop Carroll's diocese comprised the entire United States at that time. The missions of New Jersey continued to be served by Jesuits from Philadelphia and from New York. Fathers Ennis, Bulger, and Neal succeeded Farmer and Graessl. Their work was supplemented by three trips of Bishop Carroll through the State to celebrate Confirmation, help resolve disputes, and take stock of the situation of the state's approximately one thousand Catholics.

Diocesan Reconfiguration

In 1808, the Diocese of Baltimore was raised to the dignity of an Archdiocese, and the country was divided into four further dioceses, each with a resident bishop. New Jersey found itself split, with the western portion of the state being cared for by the Diocese of Philadelphia and the eastern portion by the Diocese of New York.

The Rev. M. A. Corrigan, D.D., president of Seton Hall College, 1868

Both of the new bishops, Michael Eagen of Philadelphia and John DuBois of New York, took some interest in the spiritual welfare of the state, but the needs of the Catholic communities in Pennsylvania and New York remained central for these bishops. Six years after the creation of the Dioceses of New York and Philadelphia, Bishop Eagan visited New Jersey to dedicate the first Catholic church built in New Jersey – St. John's in Trenton. The first church to be built in the present Archdiocese of Newark would be St. John's in the city of Newark, which was dedicated in 1828. The founding pastor in Newark was Rev. Gregory

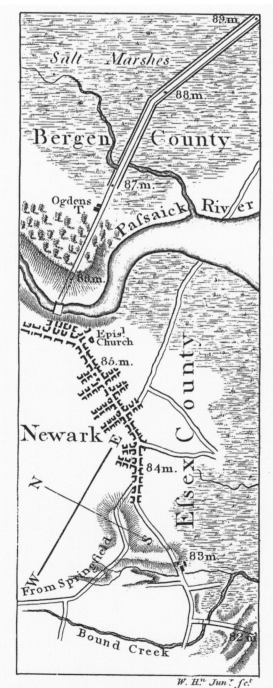

Road from Philadelphia to NEW YORK.

14

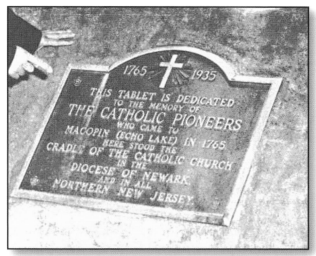

Tablet memorializing St. Joseph Church, Macopin (now Echo Lake) as the cradle of the Catholic Church in New Jersey

Bryan Pardow, a priest of New York, who began with a little congregation of just thirty Catholics. Twenty-five years later it was to become the See City of the new Diocese of Newark.

Inventions Attract

The period from the raising of the first Catholic churches in New Jersey to the establishment of the Diocese of Newark saw a tremendous series of changes within the state and the state's Catholics. Far-scattered communities were knit together by the construction of railways.

Ample port facilities, steam engines, new canals, and natural resources laid the foundations for New Jersey's industries in the early nineteenth century and attracted an increasing number of immigrants – many of whom were Catholic. Catholics in

The Morris Canal, fully completed from Newark to Phillipsburg in 1831, transformed the town into bustling center of business activity.

New Jersey were heartened by changes to New Jersey's constitution in 1844 which allowed them to hold elected office in the state. Yet, despite many promising signs of progress, the developing Catholic community still faced a great number of challenges.

In addition to the general antipathy that had always greeted Catholic immigrants, as Catholics and their churches became both more numerous and more prominent in the state, there was also a significant new negative reaction against them. "Nativist" sentiment, also fed by events in Philadelphia and New York, and a rising tide of immigration, crystallized in New Jersey during the 1830's and 1840's with the establishment of the "Know-Nothing" Party in 1846. Tension between Catholics and non-Catholics would remain for many decades.

The Doctrine of St. Thomas on the Right of Property and of Its Uses by Rev. Msgr. Januarius De Concilio (then rector of St. Michael, Jersey City), copyright 1887. The book was dedicated to Bishop Wigger.

Cathedral Basilica of the Sacred Heart

THE CATHEDRAL BASILICA OF THE SACRED HEART IS CONSIDERED ONE OF THE MOST SPECTACULAR CATHEDRALS IN THE COUNTRY. SITUATED ON THE HIGHEST PEAK IN NEWARK NEXT TO BRANCH BROOK PARK, THE FRENCH GOTHIC STRUCTURE, BUILT UNDER THE INSPIRATION OF NOTRE DAME OF PARIS, COVERS 40,000 SQUARE FEET, AN AREA EQUAL TO THAT OF LONDON'S WESTMINSTER ABBEY. IT IS LARGER THAN THE RENOWNED ST. PATRICK'S CATHEDRAL IN NEW YORK CITY.

Building History

Sacred Heart Cathedral was built over a 55-year period, beginning at the turn of the century. The land was purchased in 1871 for $60,000 by Bishop James Roosevelt Bayley whose transfer left his dream unfulfilled. The cost of the edifice, which was begun by Bishop Winand Wigger, was initially estimated at $1 million, but rose to $18 million. Most of the funds were raised through large donations and church collections. First used for Bishop Thomas Walsh's installation on May 1, 1928, it was dedicated on October 19, 1954 by Archbishop Thomas Boland.

Unique Features

The Cathedral Basilica features hand-carved decorations of wood, stone and marble imported from countries around the world. Its stained-glass windows, crafted in Munich, Germany, are among the finest in the world. The 14 bells in the west tower were cast in Padua, Italy, and tested by Vatican bell experts. The sanctuary's carved woodwork and pews are Appalachian oak. Both a state and national historical landmark, the structure boasts massive bronze doors imported from Rome and an altar carved from Italian Pietra Santa marble.

The five ambulatory chapels arching the main sanctuary are designed to reflect the ethnic groups that made up the Roman Catholic Church in New Jersey at the time of the construction of the Cathedral. They include the Irish Chapel honoring St. Patrick, the Italian Chapel honoring St. Lucy Filippini, the German Chapel honoring St. Boniface, the Slovak-Magyar Chapel honoring St. Stanislaus and the Chapel of St. Anne, which honors saints of Hispanic, African and Asian heritage. Behind the altar is the most impressive chapel of all. The

Sacred Heart Cathedral, original church 1891-1913

Sacred Heart Cathedral during its construction

Sacred Heart Cathedral Convent at 107 Park Avenue, first used 1920

The congregation participates in singing at Cathedral liturgies.

Lady Chapel, dedicated to Our Lady of Grace, has an altar crafted from Cararra marble and three brilliant chandeliers of hand-cut crystal.

A little-known fact about Sacred Heart Cathedral Basilica is that four of the former bishops of Newark are buried in its crypt.

The 34-foot rose window in the gallery over the main entrance is the second largest such window in the Western Hemisphere. The granite exterior was lighted on Christmas Eve, 1986, making the Cathedral visible on the night horizon. With its 232-foot twin towers, taller than Notre Dame in Paris, and its great copper spire soaring 260 feet skyward, the Cathedral Basilica represents a beacon of hope to all who look upon it.

Cathedral Music

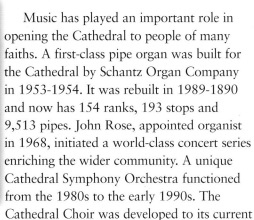

John Miller, Cathedral music director, at the magnificent cathedral organ

Music has played an important role in opening the Cathedral to people of many faiths. A first-class pipe organ was built for the Cathedral by Schantz Organ Company in 1953-1954. It was rebuilt in 1989-1890 and now has 154 ranks, 193 stops and 9,513 pipes. John Rose, appointed organist in 1968, initiated a world-class concert series enriching the wider community. A unique Cathedral Symphony Orchestra functioned from the 1980s to the early 1990s. The Cathedral Choir was developed to its current high caliber in the 1990s. A comparably excellent Spanish Choir was added. These choirs serve for both parish and diocesan liturgies. Since 1997 the concert series flourishes under the direction of John Miller, Cathedral organist. Recordings give the Cathedral's music ministry an even wider scope.

Historic Events

A historic highlight of the Cathedral was the visit of Pope John Paul II on October 4, 1995, to preside at Evening Prayer. The first Pope to visit New Jersey, his presence in the church was a tribute to all who sacrificed to make its completion a reality. It was during his visit that the Holy Father designated the Cathedral a Minor Basilica, one of only 40 churches in the United States so honored.

The Cathedral Basilica, built on the model of Notre Dame of Paris, features several rose windows among its other wonderful stained-glass windows.

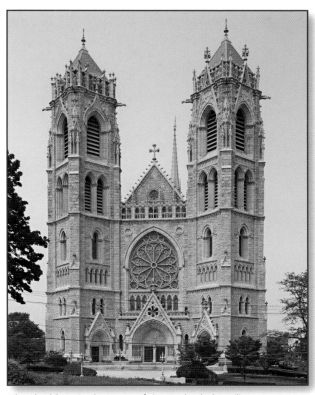

The double-spired towers of the Cathedral Basilica of the Sacred Heart stand on the highest point of Newark.

The Great Jubilee of 2000 was inaugurated locally when Archbishop Theodore E. McCarrick opened the Cathedral's west tower door. This symbolic gesture linked Newark's thousands of Holy Year pilgrims with millions worldwide.

In the wake of September 11, 2001, Sacred Heart reached out its arms. World Trade Center workers, firefighters and police who perished in the terrorists' assault were remembered in memorial Masses.

Today Archbishop John J. Myers leads the Archdiocese of a million and a half Catholics entering the new millennium with a rich spiritual heritage.

"*Good Doctor Bayley*"

THIS THEN WAS THE ATMOSPHERE – HOPEFUL YET CHALLENGING – WHEN
THE MATURING CHURCH IN NEW JERSEY REACHED AN IMPORTANT
MILESTONE IN 1853: THE ESTABLISHMENT OF THE DIOCESE OF NEWARK
UNDER HER FIRST BISHOP, THE MOST REVEREND JAMES ROOSEVELT BAYLEY.

The Bayleys of New York

New Jersey's first Catholic bishop descended from
very distinguished families whose roots stretched
back into colonial times. James Roosevelt Bayley's
grandfather, Dr. Richard Bayley, was one of the first
physicians in America and professor of Anatomy at
Columbia Medical College. One of Dr. Bayley's
daughters, Elizabeth Ann, was to go on to convert to
Catholicism, found the Sisters of Charity, and become
one of America's earliest saints. Dr. Bayley's youngest
son, Guy Carleton Bayley, married Grace Roosevelt
in 1813, and on August 23, 1814, their first child, a
son, James Roosevelt Bayley was born.

Dr. Richard Bayley, father of Elizabeth Ann Bayley Seton

James Roosevelt Bayley grew up in the beautiful
surroundings of Mamaroneck, New York. His family
was highly regarded in a prominent town, with his
father serving as town clerk and school inspector,
and they were very friendly with the De Lanceys,
Jays, Van Cortlandts, and Posts. His family was also
religious, with his father assisting as a vestryman at
St. Thomas, the town's Episcopal parish. By all
accounts, Bayley's childhood, as that of his sister and
two brothers, was a happy one, though he lost his
mother at the age of thirteen. He studied for a time
at the Mount Pleasant Classical Institution in
Massachusetts, matriculated at Amherst College in
the fall of 1831, and completed his college course at
Washington College in Hartford, Connecticut. Like
his father and grandfather before him, James Bayley
contemplated a career in medicine following his
graduation. Bayley related that he spent only one
year studying medicine and then decided to study for
the Episcopal ministry. He did not attend a
seminary, but studied privately with the distinguished
Rev. Dr. William Farmar Jarvis. He delighted in
Jarvis' vast library, which Bayley described as
"perhaps the most valuable private collection in this
country," consuming his many patristic, historical,
and literary works.

In the fall of 1839, James Roosevelt Bayley was
ordained a deacon at Dr. Jarvis' parish, Christ
Church, in Hartford. After spending a year as a
deacon, Bayley was ordained to the Episcopal
priesthood by the Right Reverend Benjamin
Onderdonk, on February 14, 1840. He was called
to serve as rector at St. Andrew's in Harlem which,
so near to New York City, had become his family's
adopted parish.

Bishop James R. Bayley's bench

Statue of St. Elizabeth Ann Seton, Seton Hall University, South Orange, New Jersey

Exercising his ministry surrounded by relatives and friends, the young Reverend Bayley began also to attend to deeper religious questions which had begun to form during his studies with Dr. Jarvis. Jarvis' high churchmanship, his respect for antiquity, and his being steeped in the writings of early Church Fathers all led Bayley to ponder deeply the roots of his Episcopal faith. Undoubtedly, the example of his famous aunt, Mother Elizabeth Ann Seton, and her conversion in 1804, as well as the conversions of several other relatives, must have given Bayley much food for thought and prayer. Bayley's spiritual questioning gave his family much concern, as did his increasing and cordial relations with New York City's Catholic clergy. In fact, in the fall of 1841 Bayley resigned the rectorship of St. Andrew's and undertook a journey to Rome, which, his grandfather believed, would dissuade him from the claims of the Roman Catholic Church.

A Journey Begun

While Bayley did not tour extensively, he did visit France and several sites of interest in Italy before arriving in Rome on February 23, 1842. After several days of experiencing Rome and her antiquity, Bayley undertook a spiritual retreat directed by Father Bartholomew Esmonde, S.J. During the spiritual exercises, Bayley made a general Confession and received conditional Baptism. At his retreat's conclusion, James Roosevelt Bayley was confirmed and received First Holy Communion at the hands of Filippo Cardinal Franzoni on Thursday, April 28, 1842. No doubt,

ESSEX COUNTY

St. Patrick Pro-Cathedral, Newark

St. Patrick Pro-Cathedral is one of the oldest churches in New Jersey. Built in 1850, it became the pro-cathedral of the newly established Diocese of Newark in 1856. It served as the diocesan cathedral until the opening of Sacred Heart Cathedral Basilica in 1954. For many decades in the 19th and early 20th centuries, it was the residence of the Bishops of Newark. An outstanding example of the neo-gothic style and recently restored, its centerpiece is the magnificent *cathedra*, or Bishop's chair, carved in walnut by the premier cabinetmaker of 19th century Newark, John Jeliff.

The first parishioners were predominantly Irish immigrants. For more than 150 years the parish has welcomed newcomers from a myriad of nations. Today it serves a congregation drawn from every continent in the world as well as students from nearby universities. The pro-cathedral is on the National Register of Historic Places of the United States Department of the Interior and the Register of Historic Places of the New Jersey Historical Association.

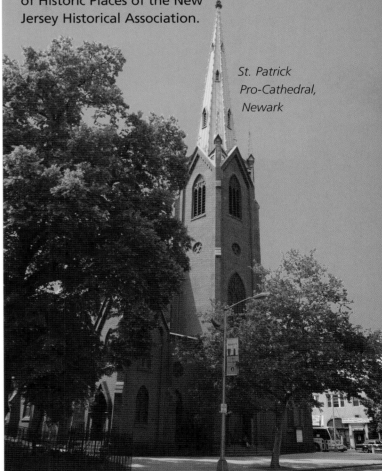

St. Patrick Pro-Cathedral, Newark

Blessed Sacrament / St. Charles Borromeo, Newark

Blessed Sacrament was established as a parish in the Clinton Hill section of Newark in 1902. Ground was broken on a new three-acre tract for a frame church on August 14, 1903. While the chapel was being built, Mass was celebrated at 34 Homestead Park. The first pastor, Fr. Frederick C. O'Neill, was assigned in 1905 and guided the parish for 45 years. As the parish continued to grow, the little frame church became too small. Seven years later, ground was broken for a new church on Palm Sunday 1912. On October 5, 1913, Fr. O'Neill celebrated the first Mass.

In the meantime, Fr. O'Neill established another parish, breaking ground on November 12 on property at Custer and Peshine Avenues, and by April 1910, the new parish of St. Charles Borromeo was completed. During the 1980s and '90s, changing neighborhood demographics brought a loss of membership. Blessed Sacrament and St. Charles Borromeo were merged on May 10, 1999. Today, the parish boasts many ministries and societies, including Holy Name Society, Rosarians, Youth Group and Angels in Motion. It offers healing services, Bible classes and hot meals with an elaborate food pantry program.

Bishop James Bayley's passport, issued in New York

Bishop James Bayley's passport, issued in France

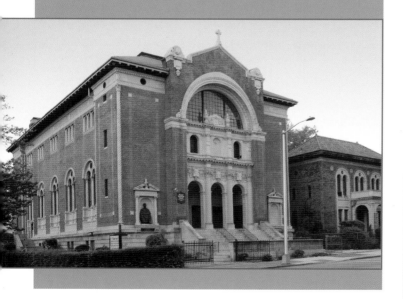

Bishop Bayley's lace-skirted alb and maniple

Bayley believed that, in some sense, his spiritual pilgrimage was complete. In fact, a new journey had begun, a road that would lead him to New Jersey and her small but growing Catholic flock.

Bayley remained in Rome for a brief time, was received by Pope Gregory XVI, and then spent another eighteen months in Europe for travels and further study. When he arrived back in the United States in November of 1843, he discovered a bewildered family and that his conversion had become a running subject for the newspapers. Undismayed, James Bayley decided to pursue ministry in the Catholic Church and was sent by the bishop of New York, John Hughes, for a brief course of study at St. John's College, Fordham. On March 2, 1844 James Roosevelt Bayley was ordained to the Catholic priesthood by Bishop Hughes at old St. Patrick's Cathedral on Mott Street.

The day of his ordination, Bayley discovered that he was to be sent back to St. John's College – not as a student, but as its vice-president and professor of Rhetoric. In addition, Bayley assisted

in two parishes, one in New Rochelle and one in Port Chester. Less than two years later, the College was turned over to the care of the Jesuits, and Bayley became a pastor on Staten Island. In his parish less than six months, James Bayley found himself appointed

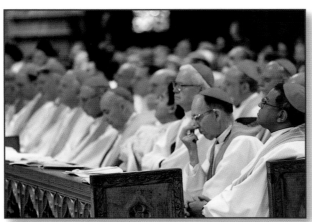

A gathering of hierarchy is always an impressive and colorful occasion.

Epiphany / Holy Trinity, Newark

Secretary to Bishop Hughes. At this time, the Catholic population of New York and the whole United States was expanding rapidly, doubling in the period from 1840 to 1850. As Secretary, Father James Bayley gained firsthand experience of both the many challenges and strengths of this community. Entrusted with increasing responsibilities, he was asked by Bishop Hughes to assist the financially troubled *The Freeman's Journal* as overseeing editor, and also served as administrator of the Diocese of New York when Bishop Hughes was absent.

In order to provide for the needs of these newly-arrived Catholic immigrants, the Bishops of the United States, assembled in the First Plenary Council of Baltimore (where Father Bayley was one of 41 theologians assisting the Council), requested that the Holy See expand the number of dioceses in the United States. Ten new dioceses were created – among them the Diocese of Newark, New Jersey.

Her new bishop was James Roosevelt Bayley

Nine years after his ordination to the priesthood, on October 30, 1853, James Roosevelt Bayley was consecrated bishop by Archbishop Gaetano Bedini in old St. Patrick's on Mott Street in New York.

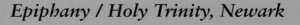

Official document in consecration of a church

The two communities of Holy Trinity and Epiphany were formally combined in October 2002. In July the same year, the parishioners of Epiphany processed with their statues from St. Casimir to Holy Trinity in Newark.

Epiphany was established as a "personal parish" in 1992 to serve the needs of the ever-growing Portuguese-speaking population (approximately 20,000 throughout the Ironbound section of the city at that time). A personal parish is not based at a specific location, but on nationality, rite or language. It can be placed within another parish territory to meet specific requirements while maintaining its independence.

The new parish was initially designated to be at St. Casimir, a church within a Polish community. Although the two groups shared the same building for services and functions, for the most part, they remained separate.

Holy Trinity parish was established in 1887 to serve Lithuanian immigrants. The first services in their own church was in 1901. On New Year's Day, 1981, an electrical fire demolished the church. The lower hall of the parish center was then converted into a church where services continue today. In October 2002 Holy Trinity's small Lithuanian community welcomed the larger number of Portuguese parishioners who accepted the enthusiastic invitation.

Immaculate Conception, Newark

In 1922, Fr. Cataldo Alessi of St. Anthony, Belleville, established the mission of Immaculate Conception to serve the Italian immigrants of North Newark. When the parish was formally incorporated in 1925, two stores were converted into a church, which served the parish until the present church was built. The next pastor inaugurated several spiritual societies and a sacramental preparation program. Plans for a new church followed soon after but the cornerstone wasn't laid until 1965. The following year the parish hosted a theater group, a Boy Scout troop and the Legion of Mary. Two stores were converted to St. Joseph Center for religious education.

The population of the area has changed over the years. In 1997 a Spanish Mass was added and in 2000, a second. The Spanish community has become involved in parish life and given the Immaculate Conception Community new hope for the future.

Immaculate Heart of Mary, Newark

Immaculate Heart of Mary Parish was founded as San Jose in 1926, being served by the Franciscan Fathers (TOR) and the Missionary Sisters of the Blessed Sacrament and Mary Immaculate (MSSMI). In 1967 the parish was renamed Immaculate Heart of Mary. Serving the Spanish-Portuguese and Latino-American communities, it is a warm and friendly parish. The Religious Education program now serves more than 500 children and adults. Among many parish organizations, societies, committees, programs and activities are perpetual Eucharistic adoration, monthly retreats, the Daughters of Mary, Secular Franciscans, Ladies of the Immaculate Heart of Mary, Cursillistas, Charismatic Prayer Group, Youth Group and support groups. The church also offers the parochial services of servers, pastoral care of the sick, Women's Commission and choirs. Social services include Sunday breakfast, the Charity Bazaar, English and computer classes and psychological services. Since 1998 a house in front of the rectory has become a place of social service with a juvenile center.

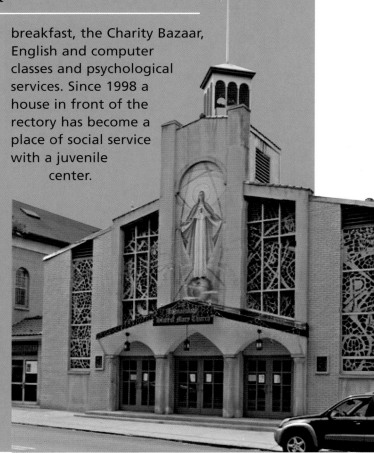

Our Lady of Fatima, Newark

The parish of Our Lady of Fatima was founded in 1958 by Archbishop Thomas A. Boland to serve the Portuguese Ironbound community of Newark and neighboring areas. The first pastor was Fr. Jose Capote. The parish church was inaugurated in December, 1958.

The parish complex includes the church, rectory, Parish Center and a nursery. The parish serves a population of 10,000, most of whom are Portuguese people of first and second generations. There are six Sunday Masses.

The nursery serves children from two to four years of age and the parish runs a day care program for the elderly, a catechism (CCD) program with 900 youth, Girl and Boy Scout programs, a marching band, a Cursillo Movement charismatic prayer group and other associations with a religious and social character. The parish records a yearly average of 250 Baptisms, 140 First Communions, 160 confirmations, 50 weddings and 40 funerals.

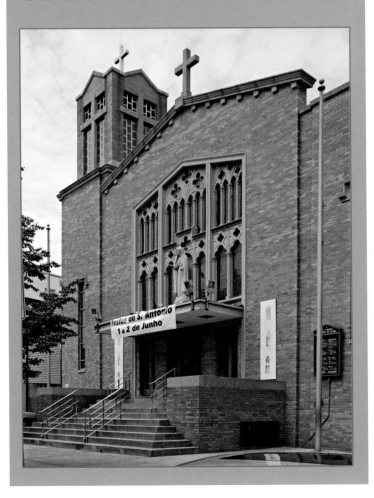

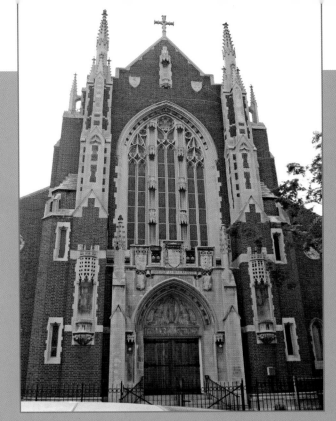

Our Lady of Good Counsel, Newark

In 2002 Our Lady of Good Counsel Parish celebrated its 100th anniversary. It has survived because it accommodated to the changing needs of the neighborhood. Schools were expanded for increased enrollment after WWII. The parish school went from a two-year commercial to a four-year academic high school and, at the request of Archbishop Thomas J. Walsh, met and continues to meet the needs of a greater area, serving as a parochial regional high school.

The present church is the third in the parish's history, continuously increasing membership necessitating ever-larger liturgical space. The church basement is now a day care center.

With a change in ethnic makeup, the parish provided Sunday and daily Eucharist, religious instruction, sacraments and societies in Spanish, while continuing to serve the English-speaking members. The parish facilities are used to host community meetings, English language classes and meetings of self-help groups. Before the Archdiocesan Pastoral Center was built, the parish often hosted Archdiocesan events of the larger Hispanic community.

Over the 100 years, there have been many changes in society, neighborhood and church. The parish has remained faithful and constant in Gospel proclamation and celebration by adaptation and service.

Our Lady of Mount Carmel, Newark

Our Lady of Mount Carmel, founded in 1890 and incorporated as *La Chiesa Cattolica Italiana della Madonna del Carmine,* is the oldest Italian parish in Newark. Erected by Bishop Wigger and Fr. Conrad Schottfer, it has counted St. Frances Xavier Cabrini as its first religious teacher. As pastor, Fr. Giuseppe Ali, an Arab priest trained in the Franciscan Seminary in Bethlehem, brought many customs with him from the Holy Land. Msgr. Ernesto D'Aquila, a great organist and musician, raised the cultural level of the parish, which by 1934 was large enough to support a parochial school. The saintly Fr. Leonardo Viccaro brought about a revival in the spiritual life of the parish. Fr. Richard Calligaro united the people and built the present church and rectory. The people of Mount Carmel are, however, most proud of their parish because of the real difference it has made in their lives and in the lives of their children. Among those children are proudly numbered Auxiliary Bishop of Newark Arthur J. Serratelli. The parish counts itself fortunate to have had the priestly services of the late Bishop James McHugh, a great defender of life, and to have had as its pastor, Bishop of Brooklyn Nicholas DiMarzio. Taking Our Lady's hand, the parish walks bravely into the future.

Two days later, on All Saints Day, Bishop Bayley was escorted by three fellow bishops and by thousands of New Jersey faithful to St. Patrick's Church in Newark, which had been designated as the cathedral of the new Diocese of Newark. Before the new bishop lay the formidable challenge of organizing his new diocese.

40,000 in 33 Churches The Flock Expands

Bayley estimated the Catholic population of New Jersey at about 40,000 souls. These Catholics had thirty-three churches and another twenty-odd missions, served by 28 diocesan priests (of whom, only seven, excluding Bayley himself, were Americans by birth). The religious of the diocese numbered two Benedictine priests at St. Mary's in Newark and nine Sisters of Charity working in both Newark and Jersey City. Aside from an orphanage and several parochial schools, there were no further Catholic institutions in the state. Indeed, one of Bayley's first tasks was to ascertain the actual properties and debts for which the new Diocese was responsible, disentangling deeds, copy books, and ledgers from the offices of the Archdiocese of New York, the Diocese of Philadelphia, as well as many individual pastors. His wide experiences, including his work at St. John's, as secretary to Archbishop Hughes, and his own energetic nature stood him in good stead – the day of his installation, Bayley issued his first circular letter to his clergy on the subject of the administration of parishes without trustees.

Bishop Bayley immediately set to work organizing his diocese which, in addition to the previous Catholic population, began to experience a great surge in

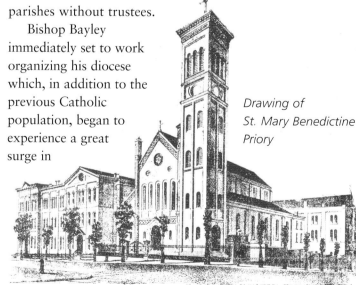

Drawing of St. Mary Benedictine Priory

24

In years past, at the perpetual profession of a Felician Sister, she wore a crown of thorns in imitation of her divine spouse.

immigrants from Catholic countries. To care for his expanding flock, Bayley set about recruiting additional clergy and enlisting the aid of several religious congregations. During Bayley's administration a dozen communities of religious sisters, brothers, and priests would begin apostolates in New Jersey. The clergy of the diocese saw their obligations and duties regularized and clarified in the first diocesan synod, held in 1856. The number of churches more than doubled while school enrollment stood twenty times higher when the Bishop left for Baltimore in 1872 than when he began in the autumn of 1853. The first Catholic hospitals in the state, St. Mary's in Newark and St. Mary's in Hoboken, were opened in 1867, to be followed by three others all opened during Bayley's time.

Sisters of St. Joseph ministered in the original Holy Name Hospital, Teaneck

Catholic College Opens

As a former college administrator, one project that was very near to Bayley's heart was the establishment of a Catholic institution of higher learning in New Jersey. The Bishop believed that the one thing which would be instrumental for Catholics to advance in mid-nineteenth century America was education. He began working towards this goal during the winter of 1854 and twenty-two months later, in September 1856, Seton Hall College opened its doors on the grounds of the former Chegaray estate in Madison.

Queen of Angels, Newark

Queen of Angels Parish, originally St. Peter German Parish, was burned down by Nativists during Protestant Crusade of the 19th century. Queen of Angels Parish was founded in 1930 as the first Catholic African-American congregation in Newark. For several decades it was seen as a model of religious, social and civil rights activism. The church was integral in developing the March for Understanding, in which 25,000 citizens marched peacefully through the heart of the inner-city. It was also the birthplace of what is now the largest non-profit housing corporation in the country. In 1968, during Martin Luther King, Jr.'s visit to Newark, Queen of Angels was one of the churches he visited.

Queen of Angels mission today is pastoral. It serves as the home of many community-based outreaches that improve the lives of people in the neighboring areas. Its school ministers to almost 300 students from Pre-K to the 8th grade in a Catholic, state-of-the-art facility. The youth of the parish are deeply involved in promoting peace and non-violence. Queen of Angels is one of the signs of hope in the Renaissance City of Newark.

Sketch of Seton Hall College after announcement of its opening

Written announcement of Seton Hall College opening

St. Benedict College as it appeared in 1892 next to St. Mary Church. Benedictine monks founded the college in 1868 in a time of growing Catholic demands for parochial education.

The thousands of Irish and German immigrants who came to the United States during this period filled the churches that Bishop Bayley was building and swelled the ranks of his clergy and religious. They also were the subject of a considerable Nativist backlash that peaked soon after Bishop Bayley arrived in Newark. Landlords refused to allow German Catholic tenants to have Mass said in their homes, Irish domestics were dismissed for frequenting Catholic churches, while marches were held by the American Protestant Association and the

public schools in many places took on a decidedly sectarian air. St. Mary's Church in Newark was severely damaged in an anti-Catholic riot in September of 1854, which left two dead. The state "Know-Nothing" party convention was held in Newark a month later a few blocks from the ruined church. Six Nativist state senators and fifteen assemblymen were elected to the New Jersey legislature that year, the highpoint of Nativist political power. In a famous incident in the town of Elizabeth, the women of St. Mary's of the Assumption Church, led by Mary Whelan, child in arms, stood between the mob and their church, and saved it from destruction. Perth

ESSEX COUNTY

Sacred Heart (Vailsburg), Newark

Sacred Heart Parish, Newark, was born on October 11, 1892, but baptismal and confirmation records point to an earlier relationship of the parish to St. Mary Orphanage. No history of Sacred Heart would be complete without an account of the tremendous contributions of the Sisters of Charity of St. Elizabeth. It might be said that the first parishioners of Sacred Heart were the residents of St. Mary Orphanage.

When Fr. James McManus began the parish, worship was held in the orphanage chapel. In 1910 a combination church/school was constructed under his leadership, and for the first time the Mass was celebrated in a place the parishioners could call their own.

The pastorate of Fr. Henry G. Coyne was a time of tremendous growth. A convent was built and the four-story school moved

to erect the present Italian Renaissance church dedicated on June 9, 1929. During World War II more than 1200 parishioners served in the Armed Forces, including two priests who ministered in the parish. Sacred Heart was the setting for Archbishop Thomas Boland's installation.

School enrollment has nearly doubled in the past three years to 600 children. A catechetical program is available for children and adults through the RCIA. The parish social service program enables parishioners to continue the mission of Jesus to serve those in need.

The Irish left their homeland by the hundreds of thousands in the wake of the potato famine of the 1840s. Immigrants wait for ships to take them to Canada and the United States.

Amboy, Jersey City, Hoboken and other towns also saw considerable anti-Catholic activity. In spite of these difficulties, several economic depressions, and the fury of a civil war, the Church in New Jersey gradually matured and grew in stature and respect, viewed from both within the Catholic community and also without.

In 1864, Blessed Pope Pius IX expressed his intention to convene an ecumenical council for the Church, which was opened in St. Peter's Basilica on December 8, 1869. Among those attending was James Roosevelt Bayley of Newark. Bishop Bayley was to spend more than a full year absent from the diocese, which he left in the care of the Very Rev. Michael Corrigan, his vicar general and the

president of Seton Hall College. While his letters attest that the heat of the Eternal City and the fatiguing nature of the gatherings were not particularly enjoyable, nor did he desire to be so long away from his people, Bayley did take an active role in the Council. One of the central topics discussed there was the dogma of papal infallibility, namely that the Pope, when he teaches faith and morals to the whole Church *ex cathedra*, is preserved from error. In this the Bishop of Newark found himself among the group called "inopportunists," that is, those who adhered to the doctrine, yet thought that the time was not right for solemn definition of this dogma. Ultimately, however, James Roosevelt Bayley was one of 25 Americans present to give their assent to the Dogmatic Constitution *Pastor Bonus*, which articulated this belief. The anxious bishop returned to his diocese in August 1870 to much jubilation. Unfortunately, he was to remain in New Jersey for less than two years. The death of Archbishop Martin Spalding of Baltimore on February 7, 1872 left the nation's oldest see without a head. Blessed Pope Pius IX appointed a reluctant James Roosevelt Bayley to the Archdiocese of Baltimore on July 21, 1872. A new chapter opened in both the life of Archbishop Bayley and the Church in New Jersey.

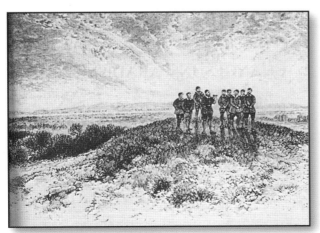

Having set a boundary between Newark and Elizabeth, the town delegates asked God's blessing on their work. (From Atkinson's History of Newark.)

The Most Rev. Michael Augustine Corrigan, D.D.

St. Aloysius, Newark

St. Aloysius Parish in the Ironbound section of Newark was originally St. Thomas Mission attached to St. James, Newark. This church on Chapel Street and the Bowery received a pastor in 1879 and became a parish on the northeast portion of the St. James boundary. The church was dedicated on May 8, 1881. A great majority of the parishioners at the time and for some years following were Irish-Americans and Irish immigrants. In the Fifties and Sixties other ethnic groups joined the parish. Today St. Aloysius Parish is composed of English-, Spanish- and Portuguese-speaking people, the greatest growth coming from the Spanish- and Portuguese-speaking communities.

St. Ann, Newark

St. Ann Parish was started as a German parish in 1886 with the naming of the first pastor. The official opening came two years later when the foundation stone of a new church-school was laid. The school opened by Christmas of that year—without windows. By 1889 the school enrolled 150, the Caldwell Dominican Sisters forming the staff.

In 1932 the foundation stone for the present French Gothic church seating 600 was laid. Four years later the original church was remodeled into the parish school. During the Second World War many people came from neighboring areas to pray to St. Ann for loved ones giving their lives in the Services.

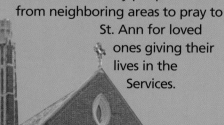

In the Fifties and Sixties, the composition of the parish changed as the neighborhood became more culturally diverse with a predominance of Hispanic people. In the mid-Eighties, the statue of Jesus, el Gran Poder (Jesus of the Great Power) was brought from Ecuador, and St. Ann was formally constituted a National Shrine. The school was closed in 1990 after the departure of the Dominicans in 1988.

With the exodus of African Americans, St. Ann became Ecuadorian and Puerto Rican with a mix of other Latin American nationalities. In 1991 the school building was sold. The former convent had already become St. Rocco Shelter for Women and Children and the old Lyceum had become St. Ann Shelter for Women.

The church was leased for five years to the Syrian Antiochian Church, although a succession of Spanish-speaking priests continued to serve the Spanish Catholic community. In 1996 a separate Eastern Rite Diocese of the Syrian Antiochian Church was formed and St. Ann was named to serve the Spanish community. Devotion to Jesus, el Gran Poder remains strong and St. Ann continues as an active parish with a food pantry serving the neighborhood.

St. Antoninus, Newark

"The Little Parish on the Hill" in Newark was born in May 1875 on the first floor of a three-story frame building. Two months later a converted wooden barn was dedicated to St. Antoninus. With Dominicans in charge, parish enrollment grew. A new basement-church was dedicated in 1912. In 1940, the parish's 1500 members had the joy of seeing the "upper" French-Gothic church completed.

Vibrant spiritual and social activity characterized 1940-1960, and a convent for the Sisters of Charity, who taught in the adjoining school, was built. During the following 15 years, many families moved to the suburbs and the church suffered the effects of the race riots in New Jersey. After 100 years of service the Dominican Sisters withdrew.

In 1975 a charismatic group took up residence at St. Antoninus, creating spirit-filled Sunday worship that revitalized the parish. The church was renovated in 1990 and has since augmented its charismatic activities.

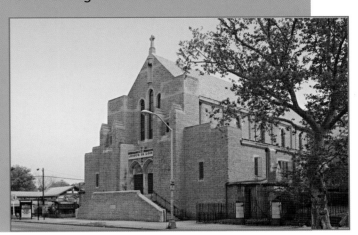

St. Augustine, Newark

St. Augustine Church was incorporated as a German parish on October 21, 1874. Fr. Charles A. Vogl became the first pastor of its 75 families. The church was dedicated the following year on May 23. The school opened to 100 students in September the same year with the Paderborn, Germany, Sisters of Christian Charity in charge. The rectory was built the next year. The succeeding pastor, Fr. Ruppert Mueller, built the church hall in 1891. In 1892 the church and school were severely damaged in a fire on Christmas Day. The new brick school, built in 1893, stands today as the Queen of Peace Women's Shelter run by the Missionaries of Charity.

Construction on a new church with stained-glass windows by Franz Mayer of Munich began in 1922, a temporary tower housing the 3000-pound bell that marked the golden jubilee of the parish in 1924. From the early 1960s to 1973, repair work was done on the buildings. The school closed in the late 1970s, and the Augustine Recollects took over administration of the parish, initiating a mission to Haitians during their tenure. The Scalabrini Fathers ministered until 1985, when administration returned to archdiocesan priests under Fr. Paul Goñi. The Missionaries of Charity moved into the convent, vacant since the school's closing, and the school became a shelter. The parish was visited several times by Mother Teresa of Calcutta, who dedicated the former rectory as a retreat house for the sisters, who also opened a soup kitchen.

Although the parish hall was demolished in 1997, the parish at its 125th anniversary in 1999 flourishes as it serves its predominantly Puerto Rican and Dominican parishioners.

St. Benedict, Newark

In 1854 the Benedictine community opened a parish and school in the Ironbound area of Newark to serve the needs of the German people of the area. Incorporated under the title of St. Joseph, a small church was built. Unfortunately, it was destroyed by a severe storm the night before its dedication. The community did not lose heart, but regrouped to start over. Staffing problems within the Benedictine Order delayed the building effort until 1857. Finally in 1863, the Benedictines were able to assign a permanent pastor. By this time, the Diocese had used the name St. Joseph for another parish. The parish was renamed after the Order's founder, St. Benedict, and quickly became a center for the German and Hungarian immigrant population. A school was opened by 1866, staffed by the Benedictine Sisters of Elizabeth. The present church was begun in 1881 and dedicated the next year.

The Benedictine priests and sisters

continued to serve the people of the area until their shrinking numbers forced their withdrawal in the early Seventies. The parish has since been served by priests of the Archdiocese, and the school, staffed by lay teachers. The Seventies also saw a new wave of Portuguese immigrants. Today the Portuguese make up more than 80 percent of the parish, which they have enriched and enlivened with their presence. A small but growing Brazilian community has also recently arrived in the area. The 150th anniversary of the parish in 2004 will find St. Benedict serving the new immigrant population as it had the German settlers at its start.

St. Casimir, Newark

When St. Casimir Parish was founded in 1908, new immigrants were pouring into the United States from Europe to create a better life for themselves and their families in the land of opportunity. With the indomitable spirit of the Polish immigrants to the "Ironbound" section of Newark, St. Casimir quickly grew into the impressive parish complex it is today, including its magnificent church--the "Basilica of the Ironbound," the newly renovated and updated St. Casimir Academy, a rectory and a convent.

As the parish approaches it 100th anniversary, it looks proudly upon the past and its history of service to its original Polish-American parishioners. It treasures its present service to their descendants, the new Polish immigrants and the community-at-large, especially those being formed in St. Casimir Academy. Finally, it joyfully

anticipates its future service to the People of God in building up this little portion of God's Kingdom on earth.

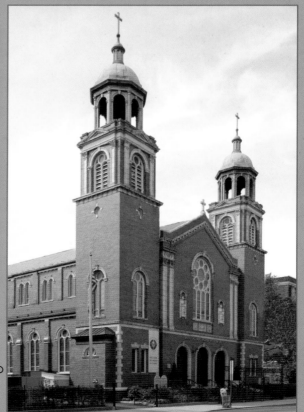

St. Columba, Newark

St. Columba Parish has served the people of the Lincoln Park / South Broad Street area since 1871. The early parishioners gave generously of their meager earnings and the small, original church was replaced on January 15, 1899 with a beautiful edifice. The Sisters of Charity who came to the parish in 1882 afforded the children an excellent education. In 1908 both the school and the convent were completed. The school, now a charter school under the direction of New Community Corporation, educated the parish children until 1999. From the first pastor, Fr. Reilly, to the latest, all left a strong legacy of faithful service. Although community's ethnic roots and language changed through the years, the commitment of the diocesan priests did not falter.

In 1985, St. Columba welcomed the Scalabrini Fathers, who with their deep faith brought new hope and encouragement to the parishioners and worked to develop the parish. The Sisters of Charity continue to be a strong support to the church and community with whom they share life through presence, prayer and participation. The church is faithfully served by the teachers in the Religious Education classes, members of the choir, faithful lectors, the advisory board and the many people who volunteer their time and talent to keep St. Columba Church the strong symbol of the beautiful people it serves.

St. Francis Xavier, Newark

The groundbreaking for the first building of St. Francis Xavier Church was in November 1905. The first wooden chapel was dedicated in March 1906 as a mission chapel of St. Michael. A decade later the congregation was established as a parish and entrusted to the care of its first pastor. Throughout the hundred years of its history, St. Francis Xavier Parish has kept its missionary orientation, eloquently manifested in its dedication to its great missionary patron.

Around 1914, the year when St. Francis was canonically founded as a parish, the congregation counted approximately 60 mainly Irish and German families. Today five ethnic groups come together in the parish: American, Italian, Portuguese, Hispanic and Filipino.

St. James, Newark

St. James Church began in 1853 when the property was purchased, and then on June 18, 1854, the cornerstone of the first brick church was laid. In July 1863, the cornerstone of a beautiful brownstone church was laid. Three years later on June 17, 1866, the new church was dedicated. This historic building stood until 1980.

At its founding, St. James was an immigrant parish for a huge Irish community. The parish school enrolled 1200 students. Over the years immigrants have arrived from Italy, Germany, Portugal, and, most recently, Brazil, with 1,000 Brazilians in attendance at worship each week. The latter are served by the Redemptorist Missionaries. In July 2002, the Redemptorists took over the pastoral care of the parish. Two Franciscan sisters also work with the Brazilian population in the parish.

St. John, Newark

St. John, the first parish established in the Archdiocese, once served waves of immigrants. Now it ministers to the business world and to homeless and the hungry people of the downtown area. For the commuters, it offers weekday Masses at two sites along with personal services as needed. Adhering to the liturgical calendar, on holy days it celebrates Masses throughout the day. In collaboration with the downtown Clergy Association, on holidays it offers spiritual programs. For the homeless and hungry, its soup kitchen's volunteer cooks and servers daily provide breakfast to an average of 165 people and a hot, full dinner to about 285. It also addresses other needs of the poor. The parish also offers its gallery to artists for showcasing their works. With one official parishioner and 45 dedicated people who claim it as their own, the parish depends on its 14,000 donors who know of its work. Adhering to a strict budget to fulfill its ministry, it receives no aid from the Archdiocese or the state. It gets the work done.

St Lucy, Newark

St. Lucy Parish (1891) lodges in the inner city of Newark's old First Ward. Consisting of a church, convent, elementary school (1906), community center and plaza, the church's purpose is to embrace and serve its parishioners and the inner city community, aiming to nurture their religious, social, cultural and educational well being, minister to their spiritual and temporal needs and maintain the vitality of the parish.

The Sacred Heart calls worshipers

From about 1880 to 1925, the First Ward was a densely populated Italian neighborhood. By 1950 almost every conceivable ethnic group in the city was represented in the Ward.

Then massive housing projects in the heart of the neighborhood of the church destroyed the community and displaced thousands. Additionally, the Newark riots of the 1960s further intensified the socio-economic and physical downard turn of the city. The poor gradually abandoned the inhospitable projects and the area became an urban nightmare of decay.

The project buildings have since been demolished. Through the darkest years, St. Lucy endured with only a few scattered members. In an effort to revive the neighborhood, St. Lucy spearheaded the development of 104 units for the elderly and in 1981 subsidized low-rise, low-income family housing. Today a "living community" of neighbors works side by side. With 325 registered local parishioners and a mailing list of 2500, St. Lucy remains a flourishing and vital parish.

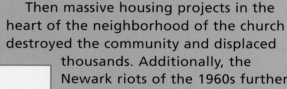

St. Mary of the Immaculate Conception, Newark (NEWARK ABBEY CHURCH)

On Sunday, January 31, 1842, Fr. Nicholas Balleis, OSB, celebrated the first Mass of St. Mary of the Immaculate

Conception Church in a small wood frame building at Court and Howard Streets in Newark. Four years later, Fr. Balleis, who served as pastor from 1842 to 1855, hired a firm to move the building to the corner of High and William Streets. There the small building served German immigrants until 1854, when it was badly damaged during a riot by Orangemen and Know-Nothings.

In 1856 the care of the parish was given to the Benedictines of Latrobe, Pennsylvania, who set in motion plans for a new church building and a bit later opened St. Mary Elementary School. Later St. Benedict Prep School would be opened on the grounds of St. Mary (later Newark) Abbey.

Since its founding, St. Mary Parish has served successive waves of immigrants. Its German parishioners gradually gave way to newcomers from Africa. The current congregation comprises large numbers of recent arrivals from several countries of West Africa. St. Mary School, under the principalship of a Sister of St. Joseph, is a strong educational presence in Newark and in 2000 moved into a new building on William Street.

St. Michael, Newark

St. Michael was officially incorporated on April 24, 1878, and on June 16, the cornerstone was laid. The first Mass was November 17 and the church was formally occupied for worship on Christmas Day, although dedication was deferred to February 23, 1879. Soon after, a rectory was added and two years later, a combination school and convent were built. In 1893 a much larger school and a convent were erected, and in 1933, a high school was added.

To provide for the needs of the Hispanics who came to the area, the Vocationist Fathers opened a Spanish Center in 1962. On June 28, 1964, it became Our Lady of Perpetual Help Church. In 1974 OLPH became

a national Spanish parish with Fr. Mario Muccitelli named its first pastor before St. Michael was entrusted to the Vocationist Fathers in 1977. St. Michael and our Lady of Perpetual Help merged in 1980. Today St. Michael serves a mostly Hispanic community.

"*Learning Enough for 5 and Sanctity Enough for 10*"

When Archbishop-elect Bayley departed for Baltimore, early in the morning of Wednesday, October 9, 1872, he left his people in New Jersey under the care of his close friend, the Very Rev. Michael Augustine Corrigan. Father Corrigan, the vicar general of the diocese since October 1868 and president of Seton Hall College since June of that year, had turned thirty-three in August.

Second Generation Irish

In many ways, Michael Corrigan exemplified the rise of Catholic immigrants in New Jersey during the 19th century. A second generation Irishman, Corrigan's parents arrived in New Jersey from Counties Meath and Cavan towards the end of the 1820's. Of their nine children, five survived to maturity, the eldest son, Michael, being born on August 13, 1839. Sent by his parents for schooling to St. Mary's College in Wilmington, Delaware, he went on, with Bishop Bayley's recommendation, to study at Mount Saint Mary's College. He was graduated in 1859, and was sent by Bishop Bayley to study in Rome. Given the maturation of the Church in the United States, Blessed Pope Pius IX had encouraged the American bishops to establish a national "college," or house of formation and studies in the Eternal City. When the North American College opened its doors on December 8, 1859, Michael Augustine Corrigan was one of four New Jerseyans in the founding class of thirteen.

The experience of studying in Rome had a profound effect on Michael Corrigan. He wrote home that "Rome grows on me more and more, but pagan admiration dies away and Christian veneration grows stronger…" He was, by all accounts, a prayerful, well-liked, and hard-working student. The

Archbishop Michael A. Corrigan, Rome 1890

Commerce boomed on the Passaic River in the 1850s

Rector of the College, William McCloskey, persuaded Bishop Bayley to allow Corrigan to remain an extra year in Rome to complete a doctorate. Corrigan returned to New Jersey in August, 1864, and was immediately appointed director of Immaculate Conception Seminary at Seton Hall. A year later, he became vice-president of the College.

Seton Hall Grows

As with the rest of the Church in New Jersey, Seton Hall had developed considerably since its initial founding by Bishop Bayley. The College had moved from Madison to South Orange, New Jersey, where, though the locale was still rural, it was considerably closer to the Bishop and Cathedral in Newark. Students arrived from states beyond New Jersey and over a dozen foreign countries. The number of students had grown to over ten times the initial class and the faculty, of which the great majority were lay, including some gentlemen of note

The Old Ward Mansion, Corner of Washington and Bleeker Streets, Newark. First an orphanage, then the motherhouse of the Sisters of Charity of Cincinnati. Razed in 1873 to make room for St. Mary Academy.

The Morris Canal is laden with coal barges in this photo of the late 1860s. Foreground, the Canal passes under the New Jersey Railroad aided by a lock clearly visible beyond the track.

such as Orestes Brownson and Warren Revere. Vice President Corrigan, in addition to his administrative duties, also served as Professor of Dogmatic Theology and Sacred Scripture.

In 1868 the President of Seton Hall College, Rev. Bernard McQuaid, was named the founding bishop of Rochester, New York. To succeed him, Bishop Bayley turned to Father Corrigan. Corrigan was to remain as president for the next four years. While he was no longer director of the seminary, he did continue his teaching activity and also lectured on moral theology, liturgy, Latin, and ecclesiastical and secular history. His reputation as a sound and careful scholar, a conscientious and energetic college president, and a pious and holy priest, was noticed and he was nominated by the bishops of the Province of Cleveland to become Bishop of Cincinnati. Corrigan avoided the signal honor, much to the relief of Bishop Bayley, who wanted the young cleric to be appointed his coadjutor, or assistant bishop with right of succession. While Corrigan was not appointed coadjutor, when Bishop Bayley was elevated to the Archdiocese of Baltimore, Michael Augustine Corrigan was appointed as the second bishop of Newark. Six months shy of his 34th birthday, he was the youngest bishop in the United States of America.

Civil War

The generation that had passed from the beginning of Bishop Bayley's service to the Church in New Jersey to the beginning of that of Bishop

Corrigan had witnessed broad and profound changes in both the state of New Jersey and the situation of her Catholics. The nation had concluded a deeply divisive and bloody civil war. A new wave of immigration, chiefly from Southern and Eastern Europe, was beginning to arrive at the shores of New Jersey and fill her towns. The Catholics of the state had become an established presence, far too numerous and prominent for the overt sort of anti-Catholic prejudice and disorders that had marked the state at the beginning of Bishop Bayley's time. The modest Catholic population that welcomed its first resident bishop 20 years prior was now a community served by 106 diocesan and religious priests and several hundred women and men religious working in 105 churches and missions, two colleges, one seminary, three hospitals, dozens of parochial schools, secondary and industrial schools, orphanages, and other religious works.

The post-war expansion that the nation, New Jersey, and New Jersey's Catholic community shared in was seriously shaken by the economic panic of 1873. An adverse balance of trade, an overextension of credit, and considerable political corruption all combined with the failure of several important investment houses in September 1873 to tip a volatile American economy from perceived prosperity to extended privation. The effects of the Panic would last almost the entire length of Bishop Corrigan's service in the Diocese of Newark. In his diocesan journal for November 16th of that year, Bishop Corrigan lamented the thievery of sacred vessels from churches due to the hard times...

Catholic Rituals Speak Faith

A procession outside the Cathedral Basilica is led by the cross, central symbol of Christ's saving sacrifice.

The moment of consecration in Sacred Heart Cathedral Basilica, when the bread and wine become the body and blood of Christ to bring Jesus' sacrifice to the people.

The veneration of the Gospel Book demonstrates reverence for God's sacred word proclaimed in the assembly.

Before Communion, the congregation express their peace with one another.

Sacred song lifts the mind and heart to God.

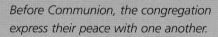
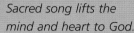

The time of hardship saw a decrease in number of immigrants, yet some groups, particularly the Germans and Italians, saw a marked increase. Knowing how rapidly immigrant groups could lose their faith, Corrigan set about organizing new ethnic parishes.

New Churches Open

Notwithstanding the economic difficulties, the seven brief years of Corrigan's service saw the number of new Catholic churches and missions in New Jersey open at the rate of over twelve per annum, a pace hitherto unknown and never again equaled. Watching over it all was Bishop Corrigan, who crisscrossed the state continuously, personally visiting each parish. Dedications, confirmations, lectures, pastoral visits filled his time. The size of the Catholic community in New Jersey – growing larger now than all other denominations combined – was now such that, even with Corrigan's whirlwind schedule, perhaps the time had come for the diocese to be divided into more manageable parts. The Holy See concurred, splitting the state of New Jersey into two dioceses, one in Newark and one in Trenton. However, Bishop Corrigan was not permitted to enjoy the intimacy of a smaller diocese. On Tuesday morning, September 28, 1880, Bishop Corrigan received the cable that Pope Leo XIII had named him as the coadjutor, with right of succession, to Cardinal McCloskey of New York. He who had been the youngest bishop in the United States, and the last bishop of the whole state of New Jersey, now found himself the nation's youngest archbishop.

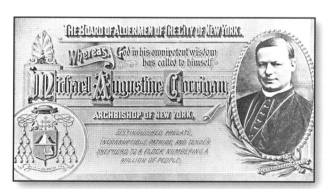

Tribute to Archbishop Michael Corrigan presented by the aldermen of New York upon the occasion of his death.

St. Rocco, Newark

St. Rocco Parish was established on November 6, 1899, when the church was legally incorporated. The first place of worship for its principally Italian immigrants was a small church on Bedford Street in Newark. During the long administration of Fr. Umberto Donati (1916-1941), the present church was built. It opened as a basement church in1927. It took 10 more years to complete the upper church, a basilica-like structure with Byzantine architectural overtones--a testament in stone and glass to the faith and dedication of the early parishioners. The fully domed church, the only one of its kind in Newark, and a reproduction of St. Blasius Church in Lendinara, Italy, is on the National Register of Historic Sites since 1980.

St. Rocco School opened in June 1955. The parish has both a Food Pantry and a Clothing Pantry. It is dedicated to its youth, the homeless and the disadvantaged. Today Hispanic, African-American, continental African and Haitian members make up the parish. St. Rocco represents the hope and potential of Newark—that people of all races and backgrounds can come together to achieve common goals.

St. Rose of Lima, Newark

Once heavily populated by Irish immigrants from Roseville, St. Rose of Lima Parish, founded in 1888, saw succeeding groups of Italians, Hispanic and black residents arrive. At one time St. Rose was probably the largest parish in Newark, its main church seating 1000. With the basement church in use, almost 12,000 worshipers were accommodated at 12 Masses celebrated by five fulltime priests.

After 114 years, St. Rose of Lima has undergone a total metamorphosis now serving three distinct groups: African Americans, African Caribbeans and recent African immigrants, chiefly from Nigeria and Liberia. While these subgroups often worship together, their heritages come through clearly in social events and liturgical preferences.

The Hispanic parishioners originate in more than 15 Central and South American countries, Puerto Rico and the Caribbean Islands. The predominant ethnic group is from the Dominican Republic. Their needs are served by a bi-lingual associate pastor and a religious sister from the Dominican Republic. Religious education classes are held on Saturday mornings for Spanish speakers. The Nigerian sisters conduct classes for English-speaking adults and children. The associate conducts two series of inquiry classes for adults, one in English and one in Spanish.

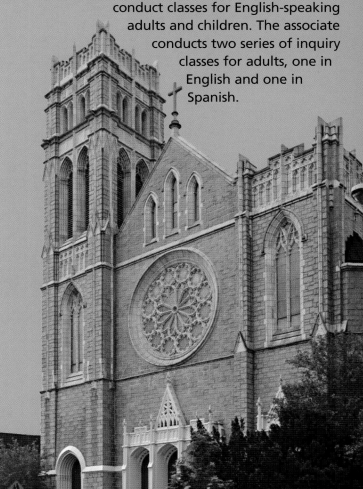

St. Stanislaus, Newark

The chronicles of St. Stanislaus Parish note that at a meeting in 1888, Bishop Winand Wigger agreed to establish a new parish in Newark. The first pastor, Fr. John Machnikowski, celebrated a Polish Solemn Liturgy in 1889. A wooden Baptist church on Belmont Avenue was purchased and the blessing was held on September 28, 1890. Within a short time, several pastors followed one another: Frs. Anthony Klawiter, Kajetan Labudzinski, Valentine Chlebowski, Boleslaw Kwiatkowski and Chester Kurcharski. In 1896 Fr. Vitus Masnicki was appointed pastor. After the debt on the wooden church and rectory was paid, the school, hall and convent were built in 1899 to accommodate the needs of about 6,000 parishioners and 425 children.

The present church was built in 1901. Fr. Erasmus Ansion was succeeded by Frs. Francis Rolinski, Joseph Olszewski, Albert Kiczek, Taddeus Zaorski, Joseph Domozych, and Theodore Czermak. In 1983 Fr. Bogumil Chrusciel was appointed pastor. His concern was to look after the spiritual and material temples of the parish. The roof and steeples were replaced. The interior of

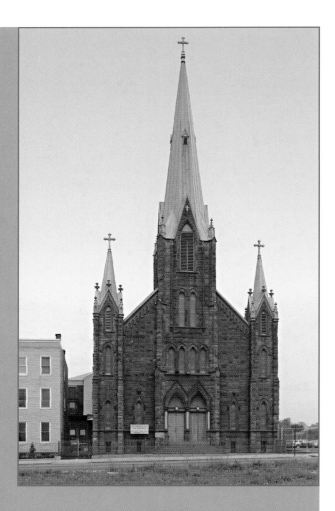

the church was repaired and beautified and the rectory renovated. Today St. Stanislaus continues a beautiful chapter of history of service to God.

St. Thomas Aquinas, Newark

In the 1950s a new parish was conceived as a spiritual need for the growing Catholic population of the Weequahic area. The first pastor, Fr. Philip McCabe, moved speedily to shape it. A new church, consecrated by Archbishop Boland and dedicated to St. Thomas Aquinas, was born in 1957 on Ludlow Street. Elevated to the rank of Domestic Prelate in 1964, Msgr. Philip McCabe served the parish until his untimely death in 1971. Many dedicated parishioners and Sisters of Charity from St. Charles Borromeo continued to help in various apostolic works of the parish. In 1998 Fr. Paul E. L. Comesanas was named pastor, becoming the first pastor of Hispanic origin.

St. Anthony, Belleville

St. Anthony was founded as a mission of Sacred Heart, Bloomfield, in 1899, with Fr. Vincenzo Sanzone, a missionary, serving the religious needs of the predominantly Italian population of the Silver Lake area in Belleville. The first church was built in 1901 as an Italian National Church. St. Frances Xavier Cabrini taught catechism at St. Anthony some time between 1912 and 1915.

To accommodate the growing population, property was purchased at the corner of Lake and Franklin Street, and Bishop Thomas Walsh laid the cornerstone of the new church. The elementary school, staffed by the Religious Teachers Filippini, was completed in 1955. About 1960 a lay Confraternity of Christian Doctrine (CCD) was developed to teach public school children religion and prepare them for the sacraments.

St. Anthony celebrated 100 years as a Faith Community in October 2001. Since 1995, its patron saint, Anthony, has been honored at an annual street Festival in June. Fifty priests have served the parish during its 100-year history, and the Italian and Filipino communities who worship at St. Anthony have brought a rich diversity of gifts to the parish family.

St. Peter, Belleville

The English Gothic church of St. Peter, Belleville was founded in 1838 as the fourth oldest church in the Archdiocese. In 2003 it celebrates its 165th anniversary.

St. Peter seeks to call and challenge each parishioner to hear the universal call to holiness and to serve the Church. Inspired by the Word of God, parishioners pledge time, talent and treasure to further the mission of Jesus Christ through teaching, serving, forgiving, comforting and challenging. The Pastoral Council unites the energy and talents of the community. All parishioners are called to stewardship and commissioned to evangelize.

St. Peter's diversity makes it truly Catholic, reflecting the universality of the Church. Irish immigrants built the original church in 1838 and later greatly contributed to the construction of the present Gothic church, completed in 1914. Irish-Americans continue to make up a large portion of the community. The Italian immigrants who came later also form a vibrant part of the parish. Today's immigrants hail largely from the Latin American nations of Ecuador and  Peru. They join the already established Puerto Rican and Cuban communities at the well-attended 1:00 PM Spanish Sunday Mass. The Spanish community has a body of leaders, Presencia Nueva, who meet regularly to implement outreach and ministry to the large number of Hispanics in the area. A representative from the Spanish leadership reports to the parish Pastoral Council monthly. Most recently large numbers of Filipinos have joined the parish. Vietnamese, Indians and Nigerians are also part of the parish makeup.

St. Peter's thriving parochial school reflects its catholicity, embracing more than 300 children, the majority of whom are Hispanic studying together with children of Afro-American, Asian and European origin. It is a model of cooperation, respect and creativity of spirit.

Sacred Heart, Bloomfield

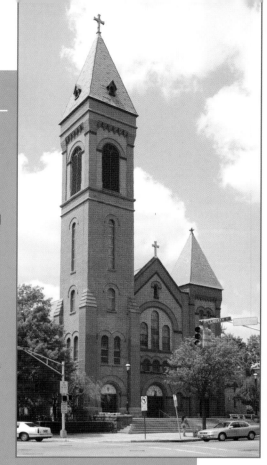

In celebration of its 125th anniversary on March 15, 2003, Archbishop John J. Myers dedicated Sacred Heart Church upon completion of the first major restoration and renovation since 1953. Since 1878 Sacred Heart Parish has embraced all who walk through her doors. Fr. Joseph M. Nardiello, born in 1845, was commissioned by Bishop Michael Corrigan to establish a new parish in Bloomfield. The parish, dedicated to the Sacred Heart, was incorporated on July 1, 1878. With enthusiasm and determination, Fr. Nardiello established a school in 1879, which, even today, is staffed by the Sisters of Charity of Convent Station.

A permanent church was completed and dedicated on October 16, 1892. The same church was expanded in 1953 and renovated in 2003. Among its unique features is its cornerstone. Fashioned in Glen Ridge quarry, it contains a slab of marble from Capernaum, side altars of Honduran mahogany, 1892 stained-glass windows and original baptismal font from 1892.

Sacred Heart continues to serve as a channel of God's grace for those who seek spiritual strength, nourishment and healing.

St. Thomas the Apostle, Bloomfield

St. Thomas the Apostle Parish traces its origin to a giant tent under which the original 300 families of parishioners worshiped while awaiting completion of the combined church-school building. It was a humble beginning for a parish that would ultimately grow to a community of more than 4000 families in four decades. The parish was canonically established on January 16, 1939, and the tent has come to symbolize the pioneering spirit and dedication of those early parishioners who proudly refer to themselves as "tenters." The formal dedication of a new church, separate from the church, was March 26, 1960. The beautiful edifice, along with other parish buildings and grounds, continue to be the pride of its parishioners and the admiration of its visitors.

While St. Thomas has a diverse population, parishioners work together to promote unity, create a warm spirit and serve the Gospel. The parish strives to be inclusive of all, offering many ministries and organizations. Community services and outreach programs touch the lives of people beyond the parish. The parish elementary school, its Religious Education Program and senior and junior Youth Programs allow the parish to reach all its young people.

Sunday Eucharist, backed by well prepared liturgies and various choirs and music programs, is the "source and summit" of parish life. The challenge of the Stewardship Way of Life gives promise of fostering even more spiritual growth among the people.

St. Valentine, Bloomfield

At a meeting of the St. Valentine Society on April 26, 1898, a resolution was passed to establish a Roman Catholic Parish in Bloomfield to be named St. Valentine. The parish was incorporated on February 16, 1899, and the first pastor, Fr. Konstanty Lazinski, assigned the next month.

St. Valentine was established to serve the needs of the growing Polish population in Bloomfield. Over the past 103 years, the parish has changed along with the population. It reaches out to all ethnic groups in its Gospel proclamation.

Its third and present church was renovated about 15 years ago. The church together with its rectory and school building, form a vital presence in the Township. Through its programs and societies, St. Valentine continues to preach and proclaim the resurrection of the Lord Jesus and the Good News of the Kingdom.

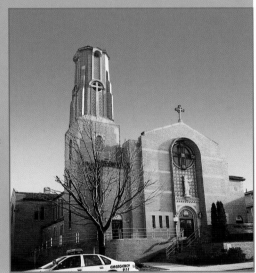

St. Catherine of Siena, Cedar Grove

St. Catherine began as a mission of Our Lady of the Lake, Verona. In the spring of 1950 some 334 Catholic families in Cedar Grove petitioned Archbishop Thomas J. Walsh for a church of their own. Permission was granted, and on September 12, 1951, a certificate of incorporation was signed. The church was built on the site of the Grissing farm. Fr. Raymond Quinn, the founding pastor, offered the first Mass on December 7, 1952. On the seven-acre tract of land were soon added a school, a rectory and a convent staffed by Caldwell Dominican Sisters.

Today St. Catherine is a vibrant, faith-filled community of more than 2300 families with a school enrollment of 280 students. The parish brings together people of all ages and walks of life to build the Kingdom of God. Parishioners accept stewardship of the parish with its fully implemented Pastoral Council of Ministries grouped under the four ministerial clusters that capture the mission of the church: Word, Spiritual Life, Parish Life and Christian Service.

St. Aloysius, Caldwell

St. Aloysius Parish, Caldwell, was founded in 1891. Throughout its more than 111 years, the parish has served the West Essex area of the Archdiocese. The parishioners have given of themselves to make the parish what it is today: a community of faith, prayer and service. In the history of the parish, it is recorded that the early parishioners built the first church in three months. Much of the work was done in the evenings after their own day's work. That same spirit fills the parish community today. The desire to build up their own faith commitment to the Lord, to share that faith with others through worship and witness, to share with those in need, and pride in their parish community typify the parishioners of St. Aloysius.

Holy Name of Jesus, East Orange

The cornerstone of the present Church of the Holy Name of Jesus was laid in the fall of 1929. The Boston architects of the church, who had designed the Shrine of the Immaculate Conception, Washington, DC, consider Holy Name one of the most beautiful churches they have ever built. Many current parishioners belonged to the parish before the erection of the new church. Others have moved in since. All can rightly point to the beautiful edifice and claim it as their own.

The roots of the parish go back to 1910. The parable of the mustard seed might very fittingly be applied to the foundation and growth of Holy Name Church. Like the mustard seed, the parish had a very humble beginning, but thanks to God and the loyalty and co-operation of the people and the zeal of the pastors, it has now grown into one of the outstanding parishes of the Archdiocese of Newark.

Holy Spirit and Our Lady Help of Christians, East Orange

Our Lady Help of Christians Parish was first organized in 1882. The parish was carved from the territory of St. John, Orange, the Mother Church of the Oranges. The first Mass was celebrated in a rental hall in 1882 upon an improvised altar of planks and barrels. A wooden church, which was quickly erected the next year, was dedicated in 1897. It was somewhat unique for its time in that it has no interior columns and a sloping floor to give an unobstructed view of the altar. Our Lady Help of Christians School began in 1883 under the direction of two Sisters of Charity. The school soon outgrew its original building and the parish purchased Ashland School in 1907. The Sisters of Charity remained until 1979, when Sr. Patricia Hogan, a Caldwell Dominican, became the principal.

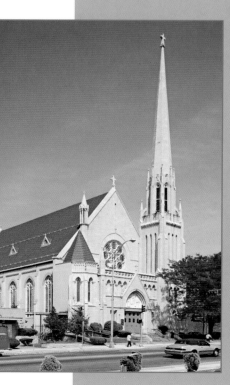

Holy Spirit Parish began in 1931 as a mission to the African-American community. Its first location was in Newark, but it soon relocated to Orange, where a small Protestant church was purchased for its use. As the population of the Oranges changed, both parishes experienced hard times. In the early Eighties, it was decided to merge Holy Spirit Parish and Our Lady Help of Christians to continue to provide for the needs of a changing community. The two parishes were brought together at the East Orange site of Our Lady Help of Christians, which was larger and home to the school. Holy Spirit Church was sold to a Protestant congregation.

Today the combined parish ministers to a largely Haitian congregation in Creole and to the African-American congregation in English. The school continues to thrive with a student population of nearly 500.

St. Joseph, East Orange

St. Joseph, East Orange, is among the most recently founded churches in the Archdiocese of Newark. In 1916 there were some 200 Italian families in the southern section of East Orange and adjacent Vailsburg territory. Bishop John J. O'Connor appointed an Italian priest to serve the people. The first Mass for some 50 families was celebrated in a store known as The Catholic Mission, on Crawford Street. Two years later on May 4, 1918, the first property was acquired for the newly organized parish. The transformation of an old carpenter shop led to naming the church after St. Joseph. The original rectory over the church is now the convent of the Filippini Sisters.

In 1925 two adjoining lots were purchased on which an auditorium was built to provide classrooms for the catechetical instruction of the children and other parochial activities.

Further parish growth prompted the building of the present church, which was dedicated on December 13, 1931. Four Sisters of the Maestre Pie Filippini community occupied the former rectory. This necessitated the construction of a new rectory, dedicated April 28, 1940. The sisters taught 500 children. The marvelous development of the area is a credit to Fr. Neri. Through his influence, streets were beautified, roads opened and lighting facilties improved.

In 1941 the parish enrollment had increased from 1500 to 5000. Since its silver jubilee in 1941, St. Joseph opened a school, which in 1962 had 533 students. It has responded to the call of Vatican II for lay participation in liturgy and ministry. In the late 1960s, the sanctuary was renovated, a new organ acquired and all debts were relinquished.

Sacred Heart of Jesus, Irvington

As the Polish population of Newark expanded after World War I, some families moved to Irvington. As their number increased, the parishes of St. Stanislaus and St. Casimir were no longer able to care for all of them. On October 20, 1925, Fr. Metislaus Sankau was named founding pastor of a new Irvington parish. Masses were held in St. Leo Hall until it was decided to dedicate the new parish to the Sacred Heart of Jesus with the mission to nurture Catholic family life and strengthen awareness of the Polish heritage. The first census showed 250 families.

In 1926 a plot of land (where the school was later built) and a house for the first rectory were purchased. By spring 1926 funds were available to realize the dream of a new multi-purpose building to provide a church, a school and a convent. August 1, 1926, saw the groundbreaking and the cornerstone was laid a few weeks later. The first Mass was celebrated on December 19 with the blessing of the church taking place in January, 1927. The school opened in 1929 with the Felician Sisters in charge.

By 1940, the parish had 600 families and 2 assistants. Five years later, the church building had difficulty accommodating the parish's 1100 families. Permission was granted in 1950 to build a larger church, leaving the original building exclusively for school use. August 1953 saw the Blessed Sacrament transferred to the new church.

In July 2001, the parish school was joined to St. Leo School, Irvington, becoming St. Leo-Sacred Heart Interparochial School. Today the parish includes a strong Polish and Polish-American community as well as Haitian, Nigerian and Spanish communities. Welcoming all ethnic and racial groups, Sacred Heart is a light of hope in the city of Irvington.

St. Leo, Irvington

Like creation, all beginnings are shrouded in uncertainly and mystery. Before 1878 the few scattered Catholics of Irvington, with no place of worship of their own, trod by foot or rode by horse and buggy to the Collegiate Chapel of Seton Hall at South Orange.

On June 23, 1878, Fr. Walter Fleming was appointed the first pastor of a new parish in the Village of Irvington. He built the original small wooden church dedicated under the title of St. Leo. It served mainly a Germanic congregation. When Fr. Tichlet came to Irvington in 1923, he immediately saw the need for a larger church because the congregation of St. Leo had grown enormously since World War I. The new church of Weymouth granite was dedicated September 12, 1926.

In the 1960s, African-Americans joined the parish after the Newark riots, followed by Hispanics in the mid-1970s. Haitians came in 1996, while Nigerians and people from various Island nations help round out the mission statement: "We celebrate our oneness in the Body of Christ. We embrace the cultural diversity of all people and dedicate ourselves to being a community of Christian worship, service and love." And together, the parish of St. Leo joyously sings a new church and a newly renovated church, celebrating 125 years in June 2003.

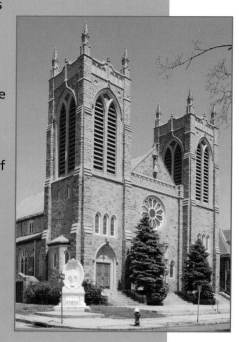

St. Paul the Apostle, Irvington

On June 4, 1948, the first Mass of St. Paul the Apostle was held in the skating rink of the well known Olympic Park. About two years later, the parish had its own church on Nesbit Terrace in Irvington. Today it also has a school and a convent on the premises.

The parish remains a rainbow of nationalities even after 50 years. Through the years of Fr. Eugene R. Gallagher's guidance, the parish developed a family atmosphere that characterizes the parish today. Parishioners hope to continue it in the future.

St. Thomas More, Fairfield

St. Thomas More Church, Fairfield, was established in 1963 with fewer than 300 registered families. Presently more than 1500 households are registered. As the church has increased in members, it has grown in love and community. Full meaning is brought to each liturgical service and sacramental celebration, giving all a deeper understanding, appreciation and love for the Catholic Christian faith. The parish is blessed with many parishioners actively involved in various ministries. They give generously of their time and talents and share their faith and love of God to help create of St. Thomas a true parish family with Christ as its head.

To the Dawn of a New Century

IMPRESSIVE AS THE ACCOMPLISHMENTS OF THE CHURCH IN NEWARK WERE DURING THE YEARS AFTER THE DIOCESE WAS FOUNDED, IT WOULD BE INACCURATE TO BELIEVE THAT ALL WAS ALWAYS AN UNBROKEN, UPWARD SPIRAL TOWARDS HOLINESS OF LIFE AND CHRISTIAN LIVING.

The men and women who make up the Church in any age are people with flaws – often deep – and those flaws are often magnified in the bishops, priests, and religious who serve the Church.

Again and again, Bishop Bayley would note in his journal next to the name of a priest he visited, *nemen potes* ("he drinks…"). Complaints against foreign clergy who were difficult to understand in the pulpit, against pastors who were highhanded, against priests who were not competent (or downright dishonest) in financial matters appear with regrettable regularity in the correspondence and records of Bishop Corrigan. Different ethnic groups in the community often felt overlooked or forgotten. Religious women and men were often both a grace and a burden. Gossip, scandal, and backbiting marked the life of some parishes. And yet, acknowledging its growing pains and fallible humanity, as the Diocese of Newark entered the final decades of the nineteenth century, it did so as a community which was maturing significantly.

An Unexpected Twist

Following the custom of time, after Bishop Corrigan was transferred to the Archdiocese of New York, the bishops of the province met to recommend suitable candidates to the Holy See for the now-vacant Diocese of Newark and the newly created Diocese of Trenton, which now shared the state of New Jersey. At the top of their list for Newark was Michael Joseph O'Farrell, the pastor of St. Peter's Church in New York City. At the top of their list for Trenton was Winand Michael Wigger, the pastor of St. Vincent's Church in Madison, New Jersey. The bishops of the province were thoroughly bewildered when the cable from Rome on July 19, 1881 brought word that Fr. Wigger was the new bishop of Newark and Fr. O'Farrell was to be the first bishop of Trenton!

Bishop Winand M. Wigger

Winand Wigger had been born in New York City on December 9, 1841, the second of four sons of immigrant parents who had come from Westphalia the previous decade. His family had been prosperous and fit in well with the German community of New York. Though not in the best of health as a youth, Winand was an accomplished student and also a skilled musician. Even as a boy, he was attracted to the priesthood, and after graduating college, applied to the seminary of the Archdiocese of New York. He was turned down on account of his health, but, undaunted, Wigger applied to Newark and was accepted by Bishop Bayley. His theological studies were with the Vincentians in Genoa, where he attended the Brignole Sale Seminary and his health was aided by the weather of the Italian Riviera. Remembered there as an *ottimo giovane* (a "fine young man"), Winand Wigger returned to the United States in June of 1865. The steamship on which he was traveling, the Atlanta, suffered an outbreak of cholera among the passengers in steerage and, for two weeks, the young priest remained on board ministering to sick and dying passengers.

Wigger was assigned to the Cathedral, St. Patrick's in Newark, where his first pastor was the redoubtable Msgr. George Hobart Doane. Late one evening in 1855, Doane, the son of the Episcopalian Bishop of

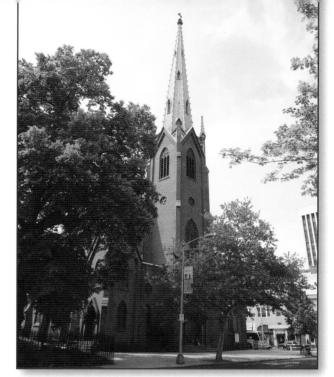

St. Patrick Pro-Cathedral

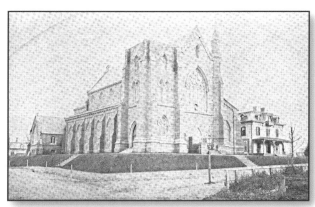

St. John Church in 1873

Founders of St. John, Orange

St. John, Orange, Junior Traffic Police

New Jersey, arrived from Trinity Episcopal Church in Newark at the door of St. Patrick's, and requested to speak with Bishop Bayley, declaring he would not leave the rectory until he had done so. Bayley received him into the Catholic Church in September of that year and ordained him to the priesthood in 1857. Doane would serve as secretary to Bayley, pastor of St. Patrick's Pro-Cathedral, a New Jersey chaplain during the Civil War, as well as Chancellor, Vicar General, and Administrator of the Diocese. When Wigger was bishop, he and Doane would have some conflicts, but during Wigger's first priestly assignment they became fast friends.

Wigger spent only two years at St. Patrick's before he was asked to return to Rome to complete a doctorate. When he came back to the United States for good, in 1869, he was made the pastor of St. Vincent's Church in Madison. Wigger was delighted with his new parish, where he showed himself as a conscientious and meticulous pastor, watching over his people, the parish finances, school, and temperance society with great attention. He did so well in his duties that Bishop Corrigan asked him to undertake the arduous task of pastoring St. John's Church in Orange.

Fiscal Challenges

Orange, like much of the nation, had experienced a great boom in the years immediately following the Civil War, and a beautiful Gothic church had been built by Rev. Edward Hickey to accommodate the burgeoning Catholic population of the town. Though a very popular pastor, Father Hickey was not at all an adept financier and his parish debt swelled to almost $300,000, an enormous sum at the time. Winand Wigger was asked to replace Hickey as pastor and bring some order to the church's finances. Wigger attempted to, raising $2000 a month for debt relief while he was there, but the strain on his personal health was too much. After less than a year, Bishop Corrigan sent him on to Summit, where Wigger would become the founding pastor of St. Teresa's. Once the parish was

The Little Stone Church (St. Teresa of Avila) whose cornerstone Bishop Bayley laid in 1863

A Swift Mover

By all accounts, Wigger's appointment as Bishop of Newark, though unexpected, was well received by his brother priests and religious and laity. He was consecrated by his predecessor, Archbishop Corrigan, in the cathedral where he had been curate, on October 18, 1881. If some in the Church thought that, perhaps, Wigger's lack of administrative experience might oblige a period of relative quiescence in Newark as he learned the state of the diocese and formed ideas of how it should be managed, that was not to be the case. The day following his consecration, while receiving parish delegations, the new bishop declared, "In the Church of God there is no distinction of race, color, or tongue." The new bishop indeed had firmly fixed ideas of what was to be done and how, and moved swiftly, perhaps on occasions even precipitously, to accomplish them.

His first controversy involved the rector of the cathedral, Msgr. George Doane. Wigger felt that, as bishop, it was he who was truly the pastor of his cathedral and therefore he wanted to receive the pastor's salary. Doane, who served faithfully for all of the bishops of Newark in positions of trust and confidence since almost beginning of the diocese, was known and well respected by clergy and laity alike. Deeply grieved by the actions of his one-time curate, the disagreement cast a shadow over the beginning of Bishop Wigger's administration.

established there, Wigger was asked to return to his first pastorate at St. Vincent's in Madison. Here he was to labor until becoming the Bishop of Newark in 1881. A very telling remark about Wigger's character was made by his parishioners when they were visited by the Bishop of Rochester, Bernard McQuaid, who had been their former pastor: "We like him [Wigger] very well indeed; but he has one great fault – he never calls upon his wealthy parishioners; he goes around all the time visiting among the poor."

ESSEX COUNTY

St. Philomena, Livingston

The growth of the Catholic faith in Livingston increased and two sub-parishes were organized. The first Mass was in 1891. Priests from neighboring towns came to Livingston once a month to offer Mass in private homes. By 1925 a group called the Catholic Mission Society of Livingston leased Newman Hall for worship where orange crates served as the altar. In 1928 the community held the first Mass in a new mission church. It was named St. Philomena.

By 1949 the parish had grown to 400 families and needed a school, which opened in 1952. In 1972 the first Mass was offered in a new church. Under Msgr. William J. Daly who served 21 years, St. Philomena School became an Academy, renamed in 1988 Aquinas Academy.

Presently 1782 families make up the St. Philomena family, with 406 students in the Early Childhood Center and Aquinas Academy. The parish also sponsors a successful Catechetical Program, a Sharing program and a thriving Youth Ministry. RCIA, Adult Enrichment Series and an Out Reach Program keep the parish vital and growing.

St. Raphael, Livingston

Founded July 6, 1961, St. Raphael Parish serves the communities of the eastern part of Livingston and a portion of the western part of West Orange. The first pastor, Fr. Richard D. Wall, set in motion groundwork to create a new parish. Completion of a new church and school was concluded by Fr. Francis M. Mulgarden. The formal dedication of the church was January 30, 1965, the Archbishop of Newark, Thomas A. Boland, officiating.

After July 9, 1965, when Fr. Martin F. Sherry assumed direction of the parish, the community continued to grow with ever-increasing numbers of parishioners of different ages and national backgrounds. On August 15, 1979, Fr. G. Thomas Burns was appointed to the parish, which now consisted of 750 registered households. In July 2001 Msgr. Thomas A Donato took leadership of the parish, which had doubled in the preceding 20 years.

Today's parishioners sense that their gifts and abilities are valued, their personal involvement is crucially necessary and that together they are growing in a greater awareness of their life in Christ and Christian responsibilities.

Immaculate Heart of Mary, Maplewood

In January 1954, Immaculate Heart of Mary was established in Maplewood, carved out of Sacred Heart, Vailsburg; St. Leo, Irvington; and Our Lady of Sorrows, South Orange. While Sunday Mass was celebrated in the Seton Hall University auditorium, building began on a new church. On June 8, 1957, the church was blessed and the first Mass offered. The parish school, with the first two grades, opened in 1957, the Sisters of Charity staffing it. By 1959 the school had six grades.

After 21 years as pastor, Msgr. William Naedele retired and in June 1996, Fr. Dominic G. Fuccile was appointed, building a new and vibrant spirit in the parish. A Pastoral Council was formed as parishioners took on new roles of leadership in many ministries and committees. Today under Fr. Frank Rocchi, the current parishioners of Immaculate Heart of Mary continue to live the Gospel message and witness to Jesus Christ.

St. Joseph, Maplewood

St. Joseph Parish began in 1914 in the Hilton area of Essex County, now part of Maplewood. Several residents successfully petitioned the Bishop of Newark and the Benedictines of Newark Abbey to help them found a parish to serve their rapidly growing neighborhood. The first Mass on Sunday, April 20, was offered in a private home on Hilton Avenue by Fr. Peter Petz, O.S.B., first pastor of St. Joseph. The parish soon occupied all but one house on its block, expanding from private home to small brick church to a modern large church. A school, still open, and a convent that now serves Archdiocesan and parish needs, were constructed. Since 1996, the parish has been served by Archdiocesan priests and a lay pastoral staff. A smaller but active faith community spearheads spiritual, social and outreach ministries, including Habitat for Humanity, the Interfaith Hospitality Network and Food Pantry services. The parish maintains a close association with the Benedictine parish of St. Mary, Newark.

Immaculate Conception, Montclair

Immaculate Conception Parish, Montclair, was established by Bishop James Roosevelt Bayley in 1856 as a mission of St. Peter, Belleville, and erected as a parish in 1864. The parish facilities were located at their present site in 1892 when the cornerstone of the church was laid. In 1881 Fr. Joseph Mendl invited the Sisters of Charity to open Immaculate Conception Elementary School (closed in 1997), and in 1925 Msgr. Edward Farrell started Immaculate Conception High school, which continues in the tradition of Catholic education, sending 95 percent of its graduates to college annually. A parish Pre-school, Tegakwitha Academy, was begun in 1997 for 3- and 4-year olds A Mausoleum built in the 1980s complements Immaculate Conception Cemetery, which was dedicated at its present location in Upper Montclair in 1895. Today Immaculate Conception serves 1100 families from Montclair and surrounding communities, maintaining a wide variety of ministries of worship, formation and charity.

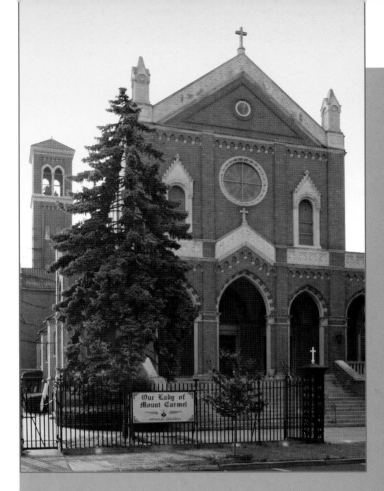

Our Lady of Mount Carmel, Montclair

Our Lady of Mount Carmel Parish was established in 1907 to serve the needs of newly arrived immigrants from Italy. A wooden structure served for worship until 1937, when the imposing church that now dominates this section of Montclair was built. Both the current rectory and the church were constructed during a suffocating depression, and yet the people and their pastor were determined to overcome all obstacles to see the fulfillment of their dream. This same spirit has possessed successive generations in the parish.

Over the years many of the children of the original immigrants themselves migrated to other communities. Today Mount Carmel is experiencing a renaissance. It, like the Montclair community, is now a diverse parish, serving people of a variety of ethnic origins. And like their forebears, today's members form a warm and welcoming congregation who reach out to their neighbors. The "Montclair Connection," a conjoining of two railroads that takes one directly into New York in about 15 minutes, augurs well for the parish's future. With God's help, Mount Carmel will continue to serve future generations with the same Christian zeal and warmth as it did those of the past.

St. Peter Claver, Montclair

St. Peter Claver, Montclair, was founded as a mission in 1931 of Queen of Angels Parish, Newark. Sr. Peter Claver was in the formation of the parish. A Missionary Servant of the Most Blessed Trinity, a congregation founded to serve the dispossessed and poor, Sister helped to bring the matter of a black church to the attention of the Vicar General of the Diocese. Thus, in 1931, the first meeting in the basement of Immaculate Conception Church was called. A little later the first converts of the Mission were baptized.

By 1934, St. Peter Claver mission had 205 members. Many of the converts were members of no church or were Episcopalians. Most of them

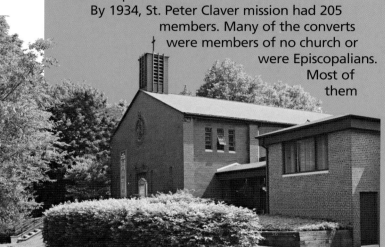

were immigrants or migrants looking for a community of believers who would welcome them. Dedication of St. Peter Claver as a mission took place on November 5, 1935 and ground was broken for a new church building the following year.

The cornerstone was laid in July 1939 and dedication took place in November. The African-American parishioners saw St. Peter Claver as their church. Materials from Africa were used in the huge teakwood crucifix and the ebony altar.

Officially the church remained a mission until 1973. The late Sixties and Seventies brought a new sense of African American identity as well as liturgical and theological changes stemming from Vatican II. Work on the Parish Council was an innovation in the post-Vatican II church that gave lay people greater authority in the operation of the parish.

More recently new immigrant groups have found a home in the parish and relive the patterns of previous generations of Catholic immigrants. Until they obtained their own church, a Korean community celebrated their own Mass. The parish now includes a large group of Haitian Catholics and the parish embraces some of the innovations of the charismatic movement. Today a large portion of the congregation is white and the parish defines itself as a community of diversity committed to spiritual growth.

Notre Dame, North Caldwell

In the 1960s, many young couples left urban Newark to house their growing families. They headed to West Essex, and Notre Dame was founded in North Caldwell in 1962. Fr. John E. Murphy, the founding pastor, had to find land and funds for a new church, a rectory and a school. At first a home served as a rectory and a temporary site for the daily celebration of the Eucharist. Sunday Masses were celebrated in the auditorium of West Essex High School.

Over the next two years, a building committee was formed and to the delight of all 450 families, the new church of Notre Dame with attached school was dedicated on May 25, 1965. A convent housing four Sisters of St. Joseph of Chestnut Hill followed. After 1980 a number of renovations brought the church into line with new liturgical guidelines. The parish community grew to 880 families.

In 2002 the rectory was sold and a new modular priests' residence was constructed on a knoll to the right of the church. The vacated school building was renovated and became the Note Dame Parish Center. The parish offices as well as a number of newly decorated meeting rooms provide needed space for an ever-growing parish community. The parish family now numbers almost 1350.

Ethnic peoples brought their customs and costumes.

New Religious Invited

For all of the controversies, Bishop Wigger's determination was often set on worthy goals and he was able to accomplish a very significant number of achievements during his service in Newark. To minister to the burgeoning population, new communities of religious women and men were invited into the diocese, almost doubling the number of sisters working in the diocese and more than doubling the number of brothers serving here. Considerable numbers of Catholic educational and charitable institutions were founded or augmented throughout the diocese by these religious during Wigger's time. Of particular note are the Sisters of Charity, who made up almost three-quarters of the 1100 women religious of the diocese, and were able to establish St. Elizabeth's College at Convent Station in 1899.

Controversies Brew

Indeed, Bishop Wigger was often to find himself in the midst of controversy. One of the most significant altercations in which he was to be involved was that of "Cahenslyism." All of the ethnic groups that were filling the diocese in the latter part of the nineteenth century brought with them their own significant and unique pastoral needs which the Church, on both sides of the Atlantic, attempted to address. In Germany, the Saint Raphael Society had been founded by Peter Paul Cahensly for the aid of Catholic emigrants. They published the Lucerne Memorial, which was taken by many in the United States as containing far too much German nationalistic sentiment. Thus, when the Sixth German Catholic Congress asked to meet in Newark in 1892, Bishop Wigger, though very proud of his own German heritage, asked that the Cahensly disputes be excluded from the proceedings. They were not and a number of bitter attacks against Wigger, including from some of his own priests, found their way into the newspapers.

Another important controversy Bishop Wigger was involved in was that of Catholic schooling. Many Catholics, especially among the clergy, felt that parochial schools were the only sure way to preserve and transmit the Faith, especially among recent immigrants. And yet a number of immigrants, in precarious financial condition, sent their children to public schools. Never one for half measures, Bishop Wigger instructed his priests that all Catholic parents were actually to be denied absolution in Confession if they sent their children to public schools.

Felician Sister aspirants. In the 20th century, vocations to religious life mushroomed.

Mother Mary Xavier Meehgan, foundress of the Sisters of Charity. Women of the 20th century responded creatively and generously to the needs of their times.

Another enduring project for the Church of Newark that was significantly advanced by Bishop Wigger was the Cathedral of the Sacred Heart. Though St. Patrick's in Newark had served the diocese since its inception as its cathedral, both Bishops Bayley and Corrigan desired that a more spacious and fitting cathedral church be constructed for the diocese. Following the Civil War, Bayley had purchased a lot on High Street on which he hoped to build. He dispatched Msgr. Doane and the noted architect Jeremiah O'Rourke to Europe to visit a number of cathedrals there and draw up plans for an appropriate church, but Bishop Bayley was transferred to Baltimore before any plans could be realized. Bishop Corrigan, struggling with the depression of the 1870's, chose to invest in parish support, new hospitals, and schools, although he was able to clear land for construction for the cathedral, now to be located in the highest part of Newark. It was Bishop Wigger who gave new life to the dormant cathedral plans, deciding in 1897 that construction should finally begin. The total cost of the cathedral was not to exceed $1,000,000, and it was to be completed in 10 years' time. To avoid debt, the cathedral was to be paid for by annual assessments on the clergy and churches as well as fund-raising among the laity. On June 11, 1899, Bishop Wigger laid the cornerstone before a crowd of 50,000. Alas, the Bishop was unable to see his new cathedral brought to completion or, indeed, even to see much progress

made, for eighteen months after the laying of the cornerstone, soon after Christmas 1900, Winand Michael Wigger contracted pneumonia and passed away just before midnight on January 5, 1901.

Motherhouse of the Sisters of Charity of St. Elizabeth.

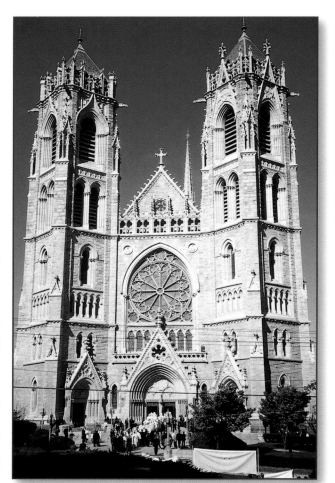

Fr. Winand Wigger purchased the land to erect a combination church / school, completed in 1872. St. Patrick Parish was incorporated in 1875.

Bishop Winand Wigger's decision to begin construction of the Cathedral in 1897 resulted in the magnificent edifice completed and dedicated in 1954.

Holy Family, Nutley

Holy Family Church, Nutley, is well known for its large membership of diverse cultures working together to proclaim the Word of God. Begun by a few Italian immigrant families in 1909, the parish has grown to more than 4300 families.

Upon entering the present church of contemporary design, one is greeted by a magnificent stucco and mosaic tiled wall depicting the Holy Family and the Choirs of Angels. A monumental, jewel-toned stained-glass window/wall reflects a rainbow of colors onto the majestic interior walls when the sunlight streams through.

The priests who serve the parish community are assisted by three dedicated religious communities of Sisters: the Religious Teachers Filippini, the Franciscan Sisters of St. Elizabeth and the Sisters of St. Joseph. A Senior Youth Group gathers teenagers in high school and a Junior Youth Group serves fifth to eighth graders. The parish boasts a magnificent choir, adult education groups and many other organizations.

Stewardship is not new to Holy Family since the faithful stewardship of past priests, sisters and laity founded the Mount Carmel Guild in the early 1950s. The members have done marvelous work over the past five decades.

The former church, erected in 1938 and located next to the rectory, is currently being renovated into a Parish Center as the growing family of Holy Family marches joyfully into the new millennium.

Our Lady of Mount Carmel, Nutley

Our Lady of Mount Carmel Parish, Nutley, is renowned for its warmth and inviting spirit. The parish was founded in 1925 to serve the needs of the small local Polish community. Today, the parish continues to celebrate its Polish heritage, while also embracing those of other ethnic backgrounds. The parish serves people from Nutley and from the surrounding communities of Belleville, Bloomfield and Clifton.

The present church, known as the "Little Church on the Hill" and built in 1949, replaced the first church originally on Franklin Street. On the sanctuary wall, the Church features a wooden relief of the parish patroness, Our Lady of Mount Carmel, who presents herself predominantly and graciously to all whom enter the church. The windows are traditional stained glass pictorial windows made by Heimer & Company whose family traces their origins to 19th century Munich.

The parish strongly encourages the role of the laity in ministry and worship. Although we are a small parish, many parishioners give generously of their time, talents and treasure for love of God and their parish.

In order to accommodate a congregation that grew over the years and to plan for future needs, renovations were completed refurbishing the church in 2002. Besides expansion to increase seating, there were many other improvements including making the church handicapped accessible and barrier free. But the most striking feature of the "Little Church on the Hill" continues to be its warmth, charm and welcoming intimacy. Whoever comes, immediately feels at home.

St. Mary, Nutley

St. Mary's Church, originally dedicated Our Lady of Grace, was built on land donated by William and Elizabeth Joyce, after she became concerned for the religious needs of the Irish and Italian quarrymen. She approached Father Hubert DeBurgh, pastor of St. Peter in Belleville, and he agreed to help establish a new church.

Though the Cornerstone was laid September 22, 1872, the first Mass was celebrated in an incomplete church on Christmas Day 1876. The church was incorporated the following year, with Fr. DeBurgh as pastor.

In 1921, St. Mary's opened the first parochial school in Nutley. Eighty-three students in seven grades were taught by three Sisters of Charity. The following year enrollment rose to 150 students, taught by four sisters.

In 1992, due to declining enrollment, St. Mary's School merged with Holy Family School to form Good Shepherd Academy, which is sponsored by all three parishes in Nutley. In 2001, the parish leased the school building to the Phoenix Center, a school for special needs children.

Our Lady of Mount Carmel, Orange

Our Lady of Mount Carmel was established in 1896 by Msgr. Ernest D'Aquila who saw a need for spiritual and religious guidance among the Italian parishioners of the area. A chapel was built on Matthew Street, which was to be superseded by a larger structure on South Center Street in April 1902. As the community grew, a plot of land on Hulburt (Capuchin Way) and South Center Street was acquired.

On December 14, 1926, the parish of Mount Carmel was entrusted to the Capuchin Friars. Bishop Walsh formally blessed the new Church of Our Lady of Mount Carmel on December 8, 1933. In 1959, an outdoor shrine to Our Lady of Lourdes was built. In 1963, a fountain with a statue of St. Francis was erected in front of the Friary. In 2003, after more than 75 years of service to the community, the Capuchin Friars reluctantly returned the parish to the care of Archdiocesan priests. Today, Our Lady of Mount

Carmel serves people from Central and South America, Northern Africa and the Caribbean nations as well as its Italian parishioners.

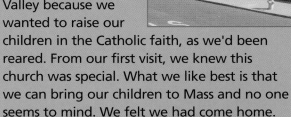

Our Lady of the Valley, Orange

Among statements submitted on "What Our Lady of the Valley Means to Me," the following was chosen as representative:

Our Lady of the Valley has drawn my husband and me firmly back to the Catholic Church. For the first time in quite a while, we go to church because we want to. We set our alarm every Sunday so that we can make the 9:00 A.M. Mass to see which props Fr. Steve will use to illustrate his funny, wise and compelling sermons, which lift our spirits all week long. We are enjoying getting to know the new pastor, Fr. George, with his kind and gentle manner. We look forward to special events like the pancake breakfast. The parishioners—and all the Salesians—have welcomed both of us and our two children with such warmth and enthusiasm that we feel we are surrounded by extended family. It is a parish unlike any that either of us has ever been part of.

Our feeling of belonging is remarkable because, like so many of our generation, we had become "lapsed" Catholics, attending church mainly on holidays. We began going to Our Lady of the Valley because we wanted to raise our children in the Catholic faith, as we'd been reared. From our first visit, we knew this church was special. What we like best is that we can bring our children to Mass and no one seems to mind. We felt we had come home.

When I asked my husband what Our Lady of the Valley means to him, he answered, "It means that our children will know God." Our youngest was recently baptized here and our little girl is learning to pray here. As for my husband and me, we are getting to know God all over again. We've been away for a long time. It feels good to be home.

St. John, Orange

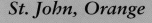

On October 8, 1851, about 150 people gathered to offer Mass in a small frame church erected at the corner of White and Chapel Streets in Orange. St. John the Evangelist was the new mission parish formed from St. John the Baptist, Newark. In 1862, Fr. John Murray, the first resident pastor, founded the present St. John School, staffed by the Sisters of Charity of Convent Station and enrolling 50 children.

By 1868 the present church was built, but soon after placed on the auction block. A collection saved the church. By 1888, besides a tower, a magnificent reredos carved by a Bavarian woodsmith for the sanctuary and a Hastings church organ were added. In 1892 St. John School named its auditorium Columbus Hall for the fourth centennial of America's discovery.

During her long history, St. John earned the title, Mother Church of the Oranges. for the seven daughter churches carved from her parochial territory. Between November 1968 and October 1991, the aging buildings of St. John Parish plant, Orange, were renovated. In 1997, the church interior, frescoes, art works and exquisite parquetry were painstakingly restored and a Parish Center erected. Rapidly changing demographics brought the parish a mix of English, Spanish, Creole and Filipino people who constitute the congregation today.

Our Lady of the Blessed Sacrament, Roseland

Our Lady of the Blessed Sacrament Parish in Roseland was founded in 1955 to serve the growing Catholic population of West Essex. Originally largely rural, the parish has grown into a thriving suburban community numbering some 1700 families in a colorful mosaic of various ethnic groups. The parish co-sponsors K to 8 Trinity Academy and is home to Trinity Academy Early Childhood Center with a combined enrollment of 500+. A large Religious Education Program holds classes for 800 students as well.

Along with a vibrant liturgical and sacramental life, the parish also offers traditional devotions, days and evenings of reflection and faith-sharing groups. Study programs and formal presentations help deepen the knowledge of the faith. The parish also boasts an active Social Ministry Outreach involving both the very young and adults.

In 2001, Blessed Sacrament was nationally recognized as a recipient of the Excellent Catholic Parish Award. "This study identified parishes that nurture the human spirit, draw people closer to God, bring them into loving service and exemplify what is best in local church throughout America."

St. Rose of Lima, Short Hills

St. Rose of Lima Parish was established in 1852 when the area was still part of the Archdiocese of New York. The first church was dedicated on December 16, 1852, on a site in Springfield. Fr, Bernard McQuaid, the first pastor, was subsequently named the first president of Seton Hall College, beginning a long relationship between the parish and Seton Hall. Fr. McQuaid became Bishop of Rochester, New York. When Seton Hall moved from Madison to South Orange, the priest community at the college assumed responsibility for the parish. In 1868 Fr. Louis Schneider, a professor at Seton Hall, became pastor.

Under his leadership, the first parish school was opened and land was purchased for a cemetery, a school, a convent, a rectory and a church. The original wooden church was moved to the new site in Short Hills in 1880 and replaced with a brick structure in 1909.

Several priests who served St. Rose have achieved prominence. In addition to Bishop McQuaid, the list includes Archbishop Michael Corrigan, Bishop of Newark and later Archbishop of New York; Bishop Winand Wigger, also a Bishop of Newark; and Fr. James Corrigan, president of Seton Hall and brother of the Archbishop.

Under Msgr. John Ryan's direction, which began in 1945, the church was remodeled and the school enlarged. In 1968 Bishop John Dougherty, president of Seton Hall University, was named pastor. A Council Father at Vatican Council II, Bishop Dougherty formed the parish in the conciliar spirit and added another chapter to the illustrious clergy who have served St. Rose of Lima.

Our Lady of the Lake, Verona

Our Lady of the Lake Parish was founded in 1924 to serve the communities of Verona and West Orange. A parish church and a parochial school were constructed with the view of serving the spiritual and Christian formational needs of the Catholic families in the area.

Our Lady of the Lake now has 2700 families. In response to community needs, it operates a K-8 school, in session since 1924, and offers an extensive program of before and after school care for 3- and 4-year-olds.

In accordance with the spirit of Vatican II, and under the guidance of Fr. Michael A. Hanly, Pastor, the parish has begun a renovation of the church. During the period of construction, liturgies are being conducted in the school auditorium. The parish completed the renovation of its liturgical space, dedicated by Auxiliary Bishop Arthur Serratelli.

St. Cassian, Upper Montclair

St. Cassian Church was founded in 1895 as a mission of Immaculate Conception, Montclair. The original church was built in Upper Montclair, opening its doors in September 1895. In November 1992, the church building was condemned and during the summer of 1994, the church and rectory were demolished. Groundbreaking for a new church, seating 350 people, took place on January 22, 1995, The Parish Life Center is on the lower level.

St. Cassian School opened in 1953. The school enjoys a rich history and continues to flourish today with an enrollment of about 220 students.

St. Cassian has had eight pastors and nine curates. Fr. John Judge was appointed pastor in August 1997 and continues to lead the parish of approximately 1350 families. With many young families, St. Cassian has implemented programs to further attract new families. It is a vibrant parish teeming with activity all week long, from the celebration of the Mass and the sacraments to meeting the educational and social needs of the community.

Our Lady of Sorrows, South Orange

Our Lady of Sorrows was organized in 1887. The present church was dedicated in June 1931 and restored in 1986. An exquisite work of 1920's Gothic Revival architecture is fit to continue Christian Worship into the twenty-first century. Among the restored sacred art and furnishings, the stained glass windows are a dominant feature. The west apse windows depicting the Annunciation and the Four Evangelists speak the title of the church and parish in artistic brilliance. Mary, the Virgin is Mother of the Church and Perfect Christian. The son she conceived is central to the Gospel and Christian Life. We identify with her in the "Sorrows" of human nature to rise up with her Son to restored human dignity and eternal life. Our Lady of Sorrows Church building is a reflection of the holiness of the lives of the Christians who are the Living Church of Our Lady of Sorrows. This is a Church of Worship, Service, Community Support, and Education. Currently, 2200 households support a school of 400 students, a religious education program and over 60 volunteer groups and ministries. Along with the Archdiocesan Clergy, the Sisters of Christian Charity coordinate and facilitate the apostolates of the parish.

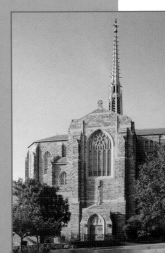

St. Joseph, West Orange

In 1931, the Saint Cloud area of West Orange was home to a number of Catholic families. Their hope for a church in the local area was realized when Mrs. Charles S. Schweinler donated a tract of land on which a church was built in memory of her late husband. Bishop Walsh formally established St. Joseph Parish on September 10, 1931, naming Fr. Thomas B. Glover as administrator. Fr. Glover celebrated the first Masses at St. Joseph on Christmas Day 1931, appropriately held in a former stable. The Schweinler family had converted their stable into a carriage house, which was then adapted for use as a chapel until the church could be built. Groundbreaking ceremonies were held in February 1932. Fr. Glover was made pastor in 1938.

The parish grew as the Saint Cloud area developed. In 1953 a wing, donated by the four children of Charles Schweinler, was added to the church. In 1956 St. Joseph School opened, staffed by five Caldwell Sisters of St. Dominic and four local women. The parish had grown from 65 families at the time of Fr. Glover's arrival to 550. St. Joseph School continues its commitment to the families of St. Joseph Parish.

Our Lady of Lourdes, West Orange

The people of God in West Orange were called by the Holy Spirit in 1914 to form Our Lady of Lourdes Parish, a community centered on Jesus Christ and its patroness, the Blessed Virgin Mary. Starting with the founding pastor, Msgr. Nicholas A. Marnell (1914-1942) and the priests who followed, the parish has been blessed with superior spiritual leadership as well as the selfless dedication of the Sisters of Charity who have taught and influenced the children since 1925. Our Lady of Lourdes is the home parish of the second Archbishop of Newark, Thomas A Boland (1953-1974), and of numerous other religious vocations.

The Holy Spirit remains with the parish as it continues its journey to God. Inspired by the Gospel of Jesus Christ and nourished by the Eucharist, parishioners are deeply responsive to their call to respect life and proclaim the Catholic faith.

The Quarter Century

Of all of the bishops and archbishops of Newark, John Joseph O'Connor, who succeeded Bishop Wigger, has served the longest, almost the first 26 years of the new century. A native son of the city of Newark, O'Connor was born of Irish immigrant parents on June 11, 1855. Evidently, John O'Connor had thought of entering the priesthood early on and his parents had him educated at Seton Hall College.

Procession entering St. Patrick Pro-Cathedral at Bishop John J. O'Connor's ordination as bishop. Left to right, Bishops O'Connor, McQuaid and Ludden

Graduation class of St. Joseph, Newark, 1906, where Bishop O'Connor was pastor.

There, Bishop Corrigan was impressed with the young man and sent him on for priestly studies at the North American College in Rome, where he was remembered fondly and noted in the first history of the College as an excellent student and consummate piano player. Completing his academic work there and being ordained a priest in Rome, Fr. John O'Connor then spent another year in Europe, studying at the American College in Louvain, Belgium, where he finished his doctorate in philosophy. He returned to the United States to join the faculty of Seton Hall College and the seminary, where he became professor of philosophy, theology, and plain chant at the age of twenty-three.

Though his class schedule and faculty duties kept him busy, his talent was recognized, and O'Connor found himself called upon to undertake an increasing number of diocesan responsibilities. In rapid succession, he was made a member of the College of Consultors, Vicar General of the diocese, rector of the seminary, and pastor of a sizeable parish – St. Joseph's – in the city of Newark.

Seminary Professor

As a college and seminary professor, O'Connor became a favorite among the seminarians, both for his ability in the classroom and his approachability outside of it. While he was quiet and noted as a firm disciplinarian, Fr. O'Connor was also considered a friend to many of the seminarians and would spend almost two decades in teaching and administration at the seminary. Indeed, O'Connor had a deep and lasting affection for both Immaculate Conception Seminary and Seton Hall College – he would bring the seminary to a greatly expanded home in Darlington, and, when he had become bishop, make his episcopal residence on the campus of Seton Hall College.

As Vicar General, John O'Connor found himself the administrator of the Diocese of Newark following the death of Bishop Wigger in January, 1901, and, under the direction of Archbishop Corrigan of New York, the consultors of the

Diocese Doubled

Crowd outside the unfinished Sacred Heart Cathedral, awaiting the installation of Bishop Thomas J. Walsh as fifth Bishop of Newark, May 1, 1928.

Diocese met to recommend to the Holy See a *terna*, or list of potential successors, to Bishop Wigger. Father O'Connor must have been somewhat surprised to discover that his fellow priests were recommending him as bishop and actually placed his name at the top of the list. Pope Leo XIII accepted the recommendation of the Newark consultors, and in late April John Joseph O'Connor was appointed the fourth bishop of Newark.

Bishop O'Connor's tenure in the Diocese of Newark would make him one of the longest-serving Catholic leaders in the state's history, and his years of service would witness dramatic social and technological transformations in the state. Bishop O'Connor's years would watch the exchange of horse and buggy for the automobile, the birth of flight, the entry of the United States into the struggle of a world war, as well as fresh waves of immigrants arriving at the shores of New Jersey. Throughout it all, O'Connor worked to provide for the pastoral care of his people and to help them cope with the profound changes in society. While, perhaps, the introverted Bishop O'Connor was neither as colorful as a number of Newark's bishops, nor did he approach his tasks with the same form of exuberance as some who have served the church of Newark, he did indeed labor – quietly but solidly – on behalf of his people.

Rococo Revival style basin and ewer presented to Bishop O'Connor from children of St. James, Newark, 1901.

In 1901, when O'Connor became bishop, 190 diocesan priests, aided by 75 religious priests, worked in 155 churches and missions, ministering to 290,000 Catholics. In 1927, the year of his death, the Diocese was served by 470 diocesan priests as well as 240 religious priests, working in 273 churches and missions, serving 683,000 Catholics. The school population of the diocese more than doubled to almost 90,000. Hospitals, religious houses, diocesan organizations, charitable institutions, and academies all swelled in similar proportions. A statewide Catholic newspaper, *The Monitor,* was founded. A new center of worship for the diocese, the Cathedral of the Sacred Heart, rose steadily, if slowly, in the city of Newark. Presiding over all this growth and expansion was Bishop O'Connor.

One of the most significant developments during the early 1900's in New Jersey was the renewed press of immigrants that arrived at her shores. While this influx would be largely halted with World War I and the passage of restrictive immigration laws in the 1920's, the first years of the new century saw fresh generations arrive in the New World, coming chiefly from Eastern and Southern Europe. Many of these immigrants passed through New Jersey on their way to other parts of the United States, while a number, particularly Italians, Poles, and Slovaks, chose to settle in the cities and towns of the Diocese of Newark.

A sketch of St. Michael Hospital, one of several that went into operation circa 1880

National Parishes

In order to provide pastoral care for them in their own language and according to their own customs, Bishop O'Connor continued and accelerated the establishment of "national" parishes to serve particular ethnic groups. Half of all the new parishes and missions established during O'Connor's episcopate were dedicated to the care of particular ethnic groups. Indeed, on average, he opened two new national parishes a year every year during his whole tenure. With the construction of church buildings, the recruitment of overseas clergy and religious to minister to these communities also became a priority. These parishes often became cultural centers for the communities they served and offered a number of language and educational opportunities for the émigrés.

Relationships, however, between national/ethnic parishes and regular – or as they were called, "Irish," – parishes were, by and large, strained. Often ethnic and "Irish" parishes existed in very close proximity and yet it was quite rare that they would share facilities. The established Catholics of the diocese, though frequently themselves children or grandchildren of immigrants, were eager to be considered "Americans," and were generally not overly hospitable to their co-religionists. The tensions between new and old arrivals were exacerbated by language barriers, differences in customs, and the challenges inherent to city life – in which the majority of immigrants found themselves – all of which contributed to the increased number of ethnic parishes. A significant number of the new immigrants in the early part of the 20th century in the Diocese of Newark discovered that while as accepted as they might be in their own churches, a full and general welcome to wider church life would have to wait for the future.

Like other immigrants who brought their customs and crafts to the New World, Ukrainians contributed their amazing egg decorating skills to the celebration of Easter.

Guardian Angel, Allendale

BERGEN COUNTY

In Allendale, the first stirrings of Catholicism were celebrated by visiting pastors from Ridgewood in 1903. In 1912 a mission was established out of St. Luke, Ho-Ho-Kus. In June 1954, Guardian Angel was incorporated as a new and separate parish in response to the growing Catholic population.

Since then a Church and auditorium have been built on its 11-acre site. The barn, the gatekeeper's house and the main house have all been used for catechetical purposes.

More than anything else, generosity characterizes the church family, especially in attention to youth and sensitivity to the needs of the poor and distressed.

For years the community has fed the homeless of St. John, Newark, every week, used the parish barn as an overflow shelter for the homeless of Bergen County, adopted a school in Paterson and collected food and personal items for the County Center for Food Action. In addition parishioners operate an AIDS ministry that serves several shelters in the Archdiocese.

St. John the Evangelist, Bergenfield

St. John the Evangelist Parish, Bergenfield, was established in 1905 by a small group of Irish residents. A school was soon to follow. Currently, the parish serves more than 3500 families and offers Masses and ministries in English, Spanish and Tagalog. St. John School educates some 350 students, and the Religious Education Program reaches more than 900 other children. St. John prides itself on welcoming liturgical celebrations with a diverse music ministry and an abiding commitment to the community through social outreach and interfaith cooperation. There are opportunities for everyone to share the love of Christ of which the Apostle John so eloquently spoke in his Letters and Gospel. St. John's was designated a pilgrimage church for the Great Jubilee 2000 and is now preparing to celebrate its centennial in 2005.

World War I

The Diocese of Newark was presented with a unique challenge by the entry of the United States into World War I. Unsuccessfully attempting to remain aloof from what was considered a European conflict, when war came in April of 1917, American armies went off enthusiastically to make the world "safe for democracy." Over 700,000 of them would depart for the trenches of France from ports located in the Diocese of Newark. Thus, in addition to the military chaplains that the Diocese had always provided for each conflict in which the United States found itself involved, the Church of Newark found herself straining mightily to supply some form of pastoral care for this great influx of troops during the brief windows of opportunity provided by shipping schedules and military necessity.

The capability of providing for the rising expectations of native Catholics, for the tens of thousands of new immigrants, for the hundreds of thousands of soldiers, all help to reveal the growing organization, sophistication, and professionalization of the Catholic community in northern New Jersey. While the very first Catholic social services in New Jersey (an orphanage in the city of Newark administered by the Sisters of Charity) actually predated the establishment of the diocese, social

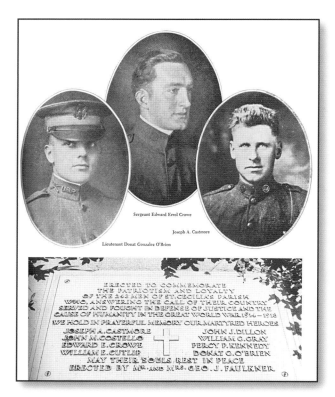

Soldiers from St. Cecilia, Englewood, were among many Catholics who gave their lives in World War I.

services, both diocesan and religious, experienced growing maturation and development in the early 1900's.

Parish Social Services

The most basic of all social services was provided on the parish level. Over two-thirds of all parishes in the Diocese of Newark had parochial grammar schools attached to them, with a combined enrollment of more than 82,000 pupils. More than 7,300 of these students went on to high school. Seton Hall College, conducted by priests of the Diocese, found both its student enrollment and number of priest instructors triple during the tenure of Bishop O'Connor. Many young people found educational advancement through the support and generosity of their parishes and, in particular, their pastors.

Amid the industrialization and urbanization of America, Catholic social conscience grew rapidly. The most basic of all parish charities, the St. Vincent de Paul Society, for the assistance of the poor and needy, was first organized in the Diocese in 1857. A few brief months after O'Connor's becoming bishop, the many parish societies were organized into a diocesan-wide "Central Council of St. Vincent de Paul Conferences," to better coordinate their efforts. Also, in 1902 the Diocese established the Catholic Children's Aid Association.

From early days, the sisters devoted themselves to the care and development of physically challenged children.

In addition to these organizations, fourteen orphanages, a protectory for boys, and home for girls helped to round out the diocese's efforts to offer practical assistance to the difficulties faced by numerous young people. Beyond serving the young people, the Church of Newark began a number of initiatives in the first decades of the twentieth century, building residences for working girls, homes for the elderly, schools for the blind, even (far ahead of its time) a treatment center for "alcohol and tobacco habits."

BERGEN COUNTY

St. Joseph, Bogota

St. Joseph Parish was founded in 1913 through the efforts of a tiny group of devout, but frustrated, Catholics, 64 all told, who lived in the Bogota-Teaneck area. In 1913 the nearest parishes were St. Francis, Ridgefield Park, and Holy Trinity, Hackensack. Each was a mile and a half in the opposite direction, and, given the poor roads of the era, neither was easy to reach, particularly in bad weather. On December 12, 1912, Mr. C.B. Ryan wrote to Bishop O'Connor regarding the "urgent need of a Catholic Church in Bogota." Bishop O'Connor's reply noted the insufficiency of available priests, but promised to ask the Carmelite Fathers for help.

After a meeting with the Carmelite Provincial in Borough Hall on April 24, 1913,

Fr. Basil Kahler, was appointed the first pastor of the newly formed parish. Sunday Masses were celebrated in the fire hall until the groundbreaking of the present church in 1927. A parochial elementary school was founded in 1925. The Franciscan Sisters of Peekskill, and now the Franciscan Sisters of Peace, have served in the parish school since the beginning. A long line of Carmelites have ministered as pastors and associate pastors since the parish's inception. The current pastor is Fr. Terrence Cyr, O.Carm.

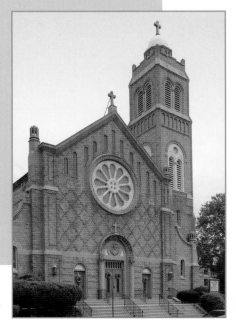

St. Michael Hospital, Newark

Catholic Hospitals

One of the most concrete ways in which the Church sought to serve her people was through striving to make available professional medical care. The first Catholic hospitals in the state were launched in 1868, when St. Michael's Hospital in

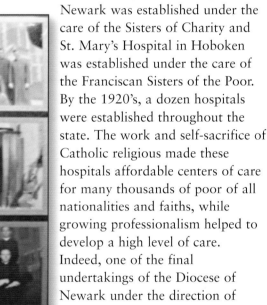

Newark was established under the care of the Sisters of Charity and St. Mary's Hospital in Hoboken was established under the care of the Franciscan Sisters of the Poor. By the 1920's, a dozen hospitals were established throughout the state. The work and self-sacrifice of Catholic religious made these hospitals affordable centers of care for many thousands of poor of all nationalities and faiths, while growing professionalism helped to develop a high level of care. Indeed, one of the final undertakings of the Diocese of Newark under the direction of

Priest graduates of Immaculate Conception Seminary, Darlington, when priestly vocations were abundant.

Immaculate Conception Seminary, Darlington

Nurses in training at St. Mary Hospital, Orange

Front entrance of Immaculate Conception Seminary, Darlington

Bishop O'Connor was the establishment of a medical and dental program for Seton Hall College.

Another of the most important educational expansions that took place during the final days of Bishop O'Connor's tenure was the transfer of the diocesan seminary from Seton Hall College in South Orange to Darlington in Mahwah, New Jersey. Staffed by the clergy of the diocese, Darlington eventually had room for some three hundred seminarians and, for more than half a century, would train priests to serve the people of Newark, the other dioceses of New Jersey, as well as many religious orders. Although he was able to preside at the dedication of the new seminary, Bishop O'Connor would not live to see the full fruition of his work, passing away quietly at his home on the campus of Seton Hall College at the age of seventy-one on May, 1927, the very day Charles A. Lindbergh made his successful solo flight to Paris.

Church of St. Mary, Closter

With the celebration of Mass in a private home on December 3, 1911, the Catholics of Closter became an official Mission of the Carmelite Fathers of Englewood. The Mission became a canonical parish on January 25, 1914, when Ft. Ferdinand van der Staay, O.Carm., was installed as pastor. The parish was to remain under the pastoral leadership of the Carmelite Fathers for the next 80 years.

In 1936 Fr. Dion Lickteig, O. Carm., purchased the property where the present church, school, convent and rectory now stand. In 1951, Fr. Kevin Cahill saw the completion of the school and convent in 1954 with the Felician Sisters of Lodi staffing the school. The present church building was completed in 1960, and the parish has grown from the original 11 families to more than 710 today. The school enrolls

approximately 150 students under the direction of the School Sisters of St. Francis of Bethlehem, Pennsylvania. When the Carmelite Fathers withdrew from pastoral leadership in 1995, the parish became the direct responsibility of the Archdiocese with the appointment of Fr. James T. McKenna as pastor.

Church of the Epiphany, Cliffside Park

Prior to January 6, 1915, Catholic residents of Cliffside Park were parishioners of St. John, Fairview. With the increase of Catholic worshipers in Cliffside Park, the Archbishop of Newark determined that an independent community and resident pastor were

required to minister to their spiritual needs. Appropriately, the name chosen for the new parish was The Epiphany, "manifestation." As in the past, the local Catholic community continues to manifest the presence of the everlasting Son and the knowledge of God the Father through the Holy Spirit.

Highlights of the Church of the Epiphany's growth and spiritual development:

- January 6, 1915   Property purchased
- May 1917   First Mass
- May 1921   Resident pastor
- 1929   Epiphany School built
- 1929   Rectory built
- 1930   School opened (4 grades)
- 1961   Cornerstone, new school addition
- 1968   Renovation of church interior
- 1991   Diamond Jubilee

St. Therese of Lisieux, Cresskill

In 1924 the 100 or so Catholic families of Cresskill petitioned to build a church. Previously they had attended Mt. Carmel Church in Tenafly. An enthusiastic core of lay people set out to raise the needed funds.

The new church was to be named for Blessed Therese of Lisiieux. The first Mass was celebrated in the nearly completed church. Six months later Blessed Therese was declared a saint and three weeks after that in June 1925, the church was dedicated to the new 20th century saint, making the Cresskill church perhaps the first to be named for her.

Like all Bergen County, Cresskill experienced an influx of new residents in the late 1940s and '50s. St. Therese grew to a large, active congregation. In 1956, a parish school was built and staffed by the Felician Sisters. Today the school is administered by the Missionary Franciscan Sisters of the Immaculate Conception. In 1970 a new church/parish center/rectory complex was completed.

From its inception, St. Therese of Lisieux has been served by the Carmelite Fathers of the province of the Most Pure Heart of Mary.

St. Joseph, Demarest

The first Catholic Mass was celebrated in Demarest in 1894 at a building owned by a Mr. Palumbo, who wished to establish a place of religious training for his children. Following his departure from Demarest, Catholic services were discontinued until 1910 when the old schoolhouse at Hardenburgh and Brookside Avenues was purchased and used as the first established Catholic Church in town under the leadership of Carmelite pastors supplied through Englewood and Tenafly parishes.

This building served the local Catholic population until 1953 when the new church at Old County Road was constructed. The rectory was the brownstone Westervelt homestead on the west side of County Road, which was built in 1723. The parochial school on Piermont Road was added in 1956; a gymnasium and two new classrooms, in 2002.

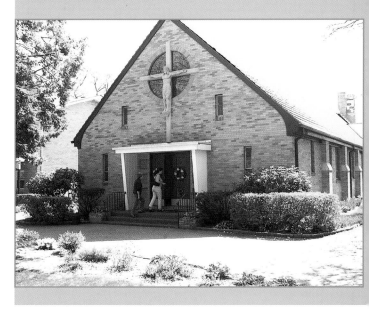

St. Joseph Korean Catholic Parish, Demarest

St. Joseph Korean Catholic Church started in 1989 as a mission church at St. Joseph Church of Demarest, N.J. It celebrated its inaugural mass on March 26th, 1989 with 300 parishioners.

Today, the community has grown to over 1900 parishioners and it continues to grow each year. In a remarkably short time, the status of the community has been raised from a mission church from Korea, to a parish of the Archdiocese of Newark. Bishop Boniface Choi (Diocese of Inchon, Korea) started the mission 14 years ago and the community continues to grow in the Catholic faith and in the great Korean heritage.

Fr. Yongjae Kim, the current pastor, is pictured in front of the house at 274 County Road that serves as the Korean Community's convent for four sisters, and as a place for parish meetings.

St. Mary, Dumont

On October 5, 1913, the first Mass in Dumont was celebrated in the Old Town Hall. The attendance was so encouraging that plans for a church to be known as St. Mary were launched. The first Mass was offered in the original St. Mary Church the following year, and on May 21, 1915, the church was dedicated. The cornerstone for the present church was laid in 1961.

During World War I, parishioners prepared and served a Thanksgiving dinner in 1917 to more than 250 servicemen in St. Mary Hall. After the building of the rectory, a school with eight classrooms and an auditorium was planned, but the Depression years prevented progress in that endeavor. A new school was added in 1950.

St. Mary can be proud of its organizations, which include, the Altar and Rosary Society and participation in a diocesan CYO movement, the Boy Scouts, the Knights of Columbus and the Catholic Daughters of America. For years the Sisters of Charity of St. Elizabeth taught Sunday School and prepared the youth for the sacraments.

The Sisters of St. Joseph of Peace also served in St. Mary's School.

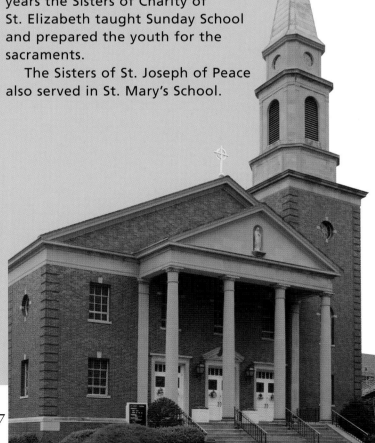

St. Joseph, East Rutherford

The history of St. Joseph Parish goes back to 1872, when Catholic residents of Carlstadt / East Rutherford, mainly German, came together to make plans for the building of a church to serve their spiritual needs. By summer of 1873 the new church was completed. Dedication took place in May 1874.

Next on the agenda was a parish school--three classrooms in the church basement. The next year, five Benedictine sisters assumed teaching responsibilities. A nearby building was converted to a convent and rectory. A site for a cemetery was purchased in nearby Lyndhurst.

The Franciscans took over the administration of the parish in 1913 and still serve the community's 2800 families. Through the ministry of the Dominican Sisters, the Allegany Franciscan Sisters and the Sisters of St. Joseph of Peace, the parish school has provided an excellent education for children pre-K through grade 8. The old school, church and convent have long since been replaced.

The parish is proud of its vibrant and caring community and its dedication to worship, witness and service. It looks to the future with hope and trust that it will continue to be a positive force in the community.

Holy Rosary, Edgewater

"We the members of the Holy Rosary parish family are the living sign of Christ's presence, reconciling life, light, hopefulness and healing within our community. Through the power of the Holy Spirit, we seek to realize the full potential of our creative energies—to be about the work of God in our commitment to the Lord, each other, the Church and our world. We are a community sharing responsibility and celebration."

These words from the parish mission statement are more meaningful than ever at the close of Holy Rosary's 95th Anniversary celebration in November 2002. For nine and a half decades, the mysteries of the Rosary have been reflected in the joyful, sorrowful, glorious and enlightened history of the church. Countless parishioners, sisters, deacons and priests have come together as one, sharing the Word, the Eucharist and the Spirit as precious gifts from God.

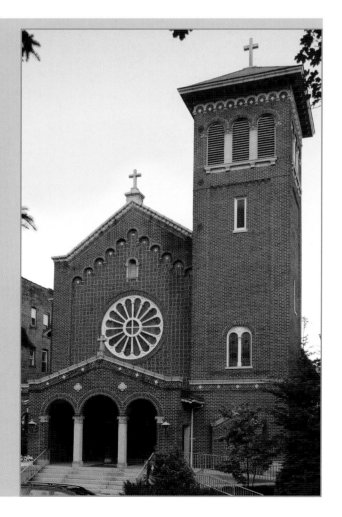

St. Leo, Elmwood Park

St. Leo Church was founded in mid-June 1909, when Fr. Francis Koch, O.F.M., decided to build a chapel for the people of "Dundee Lake," now known as Elmwood Park. Fr. Francis knew he would name the new chapel St. Leo, in remembrance of Fr. Leo Henrichs, O.F.M., who was assassinated at the altar on February 23, 1908, in Denver while giving Communion.

The first Mass was celebrated on October 24, 1909, in a hotel on the side of the Old Horse Race Track. A planning meeting for the new mission chapel followed the Mass. On November 24, 1910, Fr. Francis celebrated the first Mass in the new St. Leo's Chapel.

St. Leo's Parochial School opened its doors in the fall 1912 under the supervision of the Franciscan Sisters from Peekskill, NY. In 1943, Fr. Finbar Carroll, O.F.M., saw the need to expand both the school and the parish; a new church was dedicated in 1950, followed by the new school building in 1959.

In 1983, St. Leo's Church went through a complete and thorough renovation. Under the guidance of the Franciscan Friars, the parish community at St. Leo's continues to flourish.

St. Leo Parochial School

Our Lady of the Assumption, Emerson

The latter part of the 19th century saw a great influx of Italian immigrants who settled on the Lower East Side of Manhatan. All were seeking jobs. The advent of the railroad brought them to Kinderkamack, as Emerson was then a part of a larger township. A handful of Italian Americans held the first meeting of the Catholic Society, which raised funds for a church. After 20 years as a mission parish, Assumption welcomed its first resident pastor in 1925.

After the death of the pastor in 1934, Emerson could not support a resident pastor, but in 1943 the little parish was re-founded with the ordination and arrival of an energetic, enthusiastic priest from Jersey City who took up residence in 1947. By 1951 there were 300 families in the parish. Two years later the parish had 600 families and Assumption was the smallest parish in the Archdiocese to receive permission to build a school, which was staffed by the Capuchin Sisters of the Infant Jesus of Ringwood. In August 1959 the Brothers of the Poor of St. Francis arrived to teach in the school.

With the growth of church membership and school enrollment, it was decided to turn the school auditorium and, eventually, the cafeteria into a temporary church on Sundays. From 1953 the parish received a weekend assistant priest and in 1965, a new parish was built that carried out the directives of Vatican Council II.

Under Dominican Sr. Ann Therese, in 1991 Assumption School, which opened in 1988, was accredited by the Middle States Association of Colleges and Schools. In 1995 a year-long celebration marked the 70th anniversary of the parish.

Building the Archdiocese

At the time of the death of Bishop O'Connor, the Catholics of northern New Jersey were preparing to celebrate the Diamond Jubilee of the Diocese of Newark. Vast changes had overtaken the world, the state, and the Church during this time.

St. Margaret of Cortona's First Communion class, circa 1913, represents the growth of the Church in the first half of the 20th century.

The First Communion class, St. Francis Xavier, was so large that the Mass had to be held outdoors.

The next 20 years would see equally vast changes come about. Many older Catholics today have vivid memories of the Church at this time. Churches were erected in record numbers. Schools, filled to bursting with children, were run by efficient nuns, brothers, and priests.

Catholic intellectual life awakened on a national and international scale, with prominent converts such as Raisa and Jacques Maritain, G.K. Chesterton, and Ronald Knox leading the way. A young monsignor named Fulton Sheen began to use the new medium called the radio. Pastors became increasingly concerned with building parking lots for their churches. The humming, bustling, prospering, expanding, increasingly diverse communities of Catholics across the state looked very different from the little, beleaguered, hopeful group that had gathered around Bishop Bayley 75 years before. Deep roots had grown, ongoing institutions had been formed, and a vital life had developed. Indeed, the Church of Newark had passed out of its childhood and youth and was ready to take an important step on its journey to maturity. The man with the exuberance, energy, and vision to lead the diocese during this time was Thomas Joseph Walsh.

A Holy Name Society Communion Breakfast, May 9, 1937, reflects the vibrant life of the church.

Classrooms at Our Lady of the Assumption School bulge during Bishop Walsh's tenure.

Bishop Walsh

The first non-native son to become bishop of the Diocese of Newark since Bishop Bayley, he was born in northwestern Pennsylvania, in the little town of Parkers Landing. Thomas Walsh was the eldest son of Thomas and Helen Curtin Walsh. Soon after his birth, the Walsh family, which was to grow to four sons, moved to western New York State, where young Thomas attended public grammar and high school, until he confided to his pastor that he was considering the priesthood. He finished his high school at Immaculate Conception High School in Wellsville, New York, and then went on to St. Bonaventure's College to study for the priesthood for the Diocese of Buffalo.

Ordained in January of 1900, Walsh was assigned to St. Joseph's Cathedral in Buffalo, and later that year named Secretary to the Bishop and Chancellor of the Diocese.

In 1907, Thomas Walsh was sent to Rome for further studies. There he demonstrated an enormous capacity for work, earning a doctorate in Canon Law in just seven months and then a doctorate in theology after another seven. Returning to Buffalo, he resumed his work as Secretary and Chancellor, and would become pastor of St. Joseph's in 1915. Working ceaselessly in his parish, on diocesan finances, and on the organization of the Mount Carmel Guild in Buffalo, Walsh's ability was recognized and Pope Benedict XV appointed him the third bishop of the Diocese of Trenton, New Jersey, on May 10, 1918.

Bishop of Trenton

Covering the lower half of the state of New Jersey, the Diocese of Trenton in the summer of 1918 was considerably smaller in size, both numerically and geographically, than the Diocese of Buffalo. It was served by 191 diocesan priests, 35 religious priests, and over 500 religious sisters. They worked in 133 parishes, 55 missions, 49 grammar schools and 5 high schools, as well hospitals, orphanages, and homes for the aged, serving a Catholic population of about 186,000 people. Two thousand people, led by Frederick W. Donnelly, the mayor of Trenton, waited in pouring rain to welcome the chartered train that brought Walsh to Trenton on July 30th. The new Bishop, formally installed the next day in St. Mary's Cathedral, took up his duties

Bishop Thomas J. Walsh's diploma from the Pontifical Seminary granting his S.T.D., June 1908

St. Mary's Cadets at their Grand Military Drill, May 19, 1902. In the background is old Newark Academy.

Archbishop Thomas J. Walsh at the time of his ordination to the episcopacy.

St. Cecilia, Englewood

In 1863, the Catholic parish in Fort Lee was divided and the Rev. Patrick Corrigan was assigned to care for the Catholic community in the new Englewood mission, where he secured use of the local police station for religious services. His successor, Rt. Rev. Dr. Henry A Brann, wasted no time in getting the parish community to build its own church.

In 1866, enough money was collected to purchase a plot, which was dedicated on November 11, 1866 by Bishop Bayley. In the years that followed, the church grew and a school was opened in 1874.

The parish has responded to the many needs of the new faces in the parish community: a Spanish Mass is celebrated each Sunday; La Association Hispana de Englewood reaches out to those who have recently arrived from Latin American countries; the Office of Concerns offers social services to the homebound, elderly and poor; and the emergency family shelter provides temporary shelter to the county's homeless.

For 137 years, St. Cecelia parish has proclaimed the good news of God's loving kindness, and continues to do so.

rapidly, with an intense schedule of work and events in his new Diocese. Indeed, Bishop Walsh would add a total of 21 new parishes to the Diocese of Trenton during his time there, but the field of Catholic education was a particular center for his efforts – a trait that would continue when he came to the Diocese of Newark. Bishop Walsh would declare over and over again, pointedly and characteristically, that he would rather "lay a cornerstone for ten Catholic schools than for one Catholic church." He would lay 40 grammar school cornerstones, 15 high school cornerstones, and encourage the Sisters of Mercy to expand their Mount Saint Mary's College by moving it from North Plainfield to Lakewood. Georgian Court College thus became the first Catholic institution of higher learning in the southern part of New Jersey.

Archbishop Walsh presiding at a visit to one of the parishes in the archdiocese.

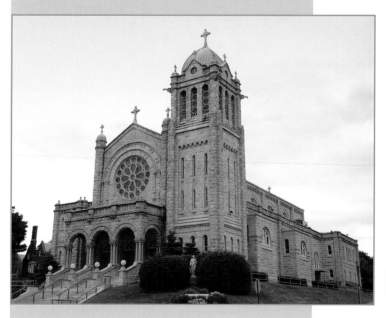

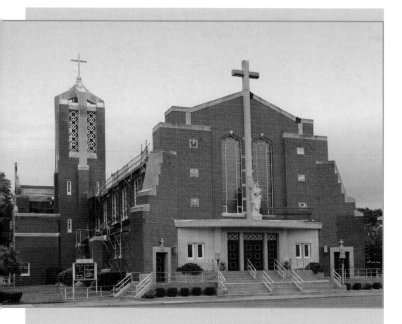

St. Anne, Fair Lawn

Catholics living in Warren Point at the turn of the 20ᵗʰ Century had hopes of having their own parish. Foremost among them were Angeline and Juan Ramirez, who were devoted to St. Anne. Shortly after his wife's death, Juan Ramirez donated a small home for use as a chapel dedicated to St. Anne. Fr. Peter Kramer, O.Carm., celebrated the first Mass there on Christmas 1909. In 1910, Fr. Hyacinth Rueberg, OFM, became the first in a long line of Franciscan pastors extending to the present.

In 1926 the community laid the foundation for a new church. Parish life continued to grow as did the population and activities for youth. Tremendous population growth during the 1950s and 1960's created the need and resources to build a school (1949), a second school building (1952), a convent (1953), a new church (1957) and a rectory office complex (1966). By the early 1960s, school enrollment of more that 1600 and parish registrations of 5000+ families made St. Anne the largest parish in the Archdiocese.

Demographic changes have somewhat depleted the school and parish, but with more than 3000 families, St. Anne continues as one of the largest and most active parishes in the Archdiocese.

Our Lady of Grace, Fairview

In the early 1900's, the Italian Catholics of the Fairview area longed for their own church where they could hear the Gospel in their native tongue. Our Lady of Grace Church, first known as La Madonna delle Grazie, became a reality on November 17, 1913, in a small structure, originally a meeting hall on Anderson Avenue.

Initially under the leadership of diocesan clergy, the church's administration passed to the Society of Catholic Apostolate (S.A.C.) in 1924. The rapid growth of the parish resulted in 1934 in the present beautiful church of Our Lady of Grace. Through the years, many Pallottine Priests, Brothers and Sisters have dedicated themselves to the mission of the teachings of Christ under the inspiration of St. Vincent Pallotti.

Now Our Lady of Grace School excels educationally. The CCD programs, run for more than 40 years by dedicated laity, have nurtured the spiritual life of the children. The parish youth group programs have kept the young people close to their church. And the 45+ organizations for adults of the parish have molded the "family of the church." This family helps the priests, brothers and sisters in carrying out God's plan of strengthening the faith and reaching those in need.

St. John the Baptist, Fairview

St. John the Baptist was established as a mission in 1873 in the Shadyside area near the river. Its first location in Fairview was a basement with a roof that also housed the convent and the rectory until 1922, when another basement church was built at the present location.

It was not until 1935 that the current church was built above that of the basement. The children attended school in the former basement church. A building fund campaign saw to the opening of St. John School in 1961.

This multi-ethnic parish has always been home to needy ethnic groups. The '50s saw displaced Hungarians. The '70s and '80s welcomed Croations and, from the '90s to the present, St. John is home to Guatemalans, Colombians and many other Hispanic groups. It continues to be a multicultural parish with Masses in three languages.

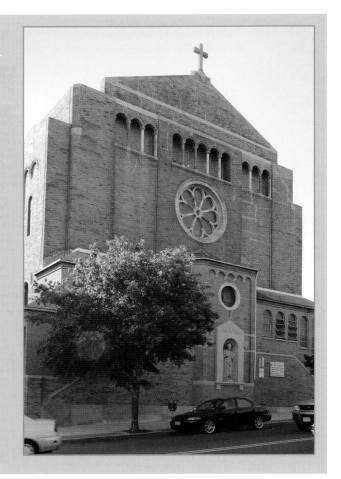

Holy Trinity, Fort Lee

The history of Holy Trinity, Fort Lee, begins in April 1905, when the residents of Coytesville formed a committee to establish a church. With permission, Rambo Hall was rented for church services. The First Mass with 200 present was celebrated on Trinity Sunday.

With Fr. Robert E. Freeman as the first pastor, the cornerstone was laid on June 30, 1907, and the rectory and church were ready for occupancy later that year. By April 1959 the school and convent were completed. With a decline in enrollment in the '80s, the school merged with the schools of Madonna, Fort Lee and Holy Rosary, Edgewater, under the name, Christ The Teacher Interparochial School.

Holy Trinity has since undergone extensive renovation and has guided and presented two vocations for ordination to the priesthood. The spiritual growth of Holy Trinity continues today as with confidence in God's providence, the parish continues to grow as a family.

Emphasis on Education

This emphasis on Catholic education would be brought by Bishop Walsh to the Diocese of Newark, as well as another cause that the Bishop was deeply concerned about: Catholic charities. The "Mount Carmel Guild," which had been so successfully organized by Walsh in Buffalo, was reproduced in the Diocese of Trenton. Assistance to the poor, war relief, "Americanization" for new immigrants, catechetical instruction, and employment assistance all were undertaken by thousands of Guild volunteers as well as many religious women and men, brought into the Diocese by Bishop Walsh to assist in caring for the growing needs of the community.

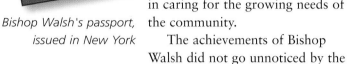

Bishop Walsh's passport, issued in New York

The achievements of Bishop Walsh did not go unnoticed by the wider Church. Soon after celebrating the twenty-fifth anniversary of his priestly ordination and shortly before the tenth anniversary of his episcopal ordination, Thomas Walsh was selected by Pope Pius XI to become the next Bishop of Newark.

Archbishop Walsh on visit to Mt. Carmel, Bayonne, in 1929 where 1640 were confirmed in one day.

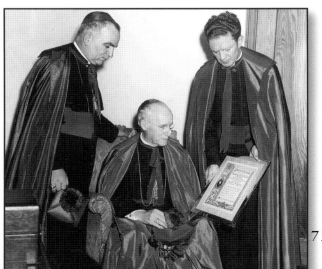

A gathering of Catholics at the 4th Annual Demonstration of Liturgical Music under the patronage of Bishop Walsh, 1937

"Roaring" Northern New Jersey

The year 1928 found the city of Newark and much of the northern part of New Jersey riding high on the crest of the "Roaring Twenties." Population, industry, commerce, and manufacturing were all expanding very rapidly. Indeed, at the time, Four Corners in Newark was declared to be the "busiest intersection in the world." As Bishop O'Connor's health had declined, however, the local Church in Newark had, in contrast, entered a state of relative quiescence. Even the Diamond Jubilee of the Diocese, planned in the final months before O'Connor's passing, was to be rather low-key. Bishop Walsh, arriving on May 1 of that year, had very different ideas, and immediately set out to reenergize his flock.

Education, which had been one of Bishop Walsh's primary concerns in the Diocese of Trenton, received some of his initial attentions upon arriving in Newark. During his very first month in the Diocese,

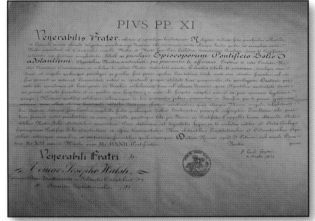

Papal Bull from Pope Pius XI appointing Bishop Walsh as an assistant of the Pontifical Throne, 1922

Archbishop Walsh at his Silver Jubilee with Bishop Boland and Msgr. Kelly in 1927

Silver crosier that adorned Archbishop Walsh's ceremonial staff

he would visit Seton Hall College, the College of St. Elizabeth, the Seminary of the Immaculate Conception, and two high schools. The Bishop would receive three groups of students and two groups of teaching sisters, and begin correspondence with the Jesuits to reopen St. Peter's College, which had been closed during the Great War. The Bishop also encouraged greatly the establishment of Juniorates for religious orders, to help provide improved training for young women considering the sisterhood. During the initial decade of Bishop Walsh's direction of the Diocese, he would open nine new grammar schools and two new high schools, as well as improve greatly the quality of Seton Hall and physical plant of the new seminary. Bishop Walsh, however, was unable to replicate entirely the numbers that had been possible in the Diocese of Trenton. A year and a half after his arriving in Newark, the Great Depression cast a heavy gloom over the Catholics of the Diocese of Newark and all Americans.

Archbishop Walsh leading a procession in one of the parishes of his jurisdiction

Mount Carmel Guild

At the regular Quarterly Conference of Clergy, held on September 25, 1929, Bishop Walsh announced his intention to establish in the Diocese the Mount Carmel Guild, dedicated to the work of Christian charity and education, which had played such a large role in Buffalo and Trenton. Just

The Depression years brought great hardship, but also offered opportunity for the Church to minister to needy people. The Church maintains that commitment today, as society offers new challenges to those in need.

before the initial organizational meetings, the stock market crashed and the Catholics of New Jersey found themselves faced with economic calamity, that made work of the Mount Carmel Guild all the more urgent. In the winter months of 1930, tens of thousands of Catholics gathered to help organize a wide system of physical relief, that would be open to all citizens, regardless of race, ethnicity, or religious affiliation. Thirty-five thousand volunteers in twenty-six centers throughout northern New Jersey, many struggling themselves, assisted thousands of families and individuals, providing food, emergency shelter, clothing, rent payments, and job opportunities.

While the Mount Carmel Guild worked on a diocesan level and St. Vincent DePaul Societies endeavored to help on parochial levels, many pastors also labored to provide their parishioners with both immediate relief and the chance to work. Building projects in the diocese, rather than being uniformly curtailed or suspended, were, when possible, extended and expanded for the jobs they provided. Sixteen new parishes were established and over a hundred and twenty-five churches, schools, convents, and other buildings were erected during the Depression years, at a final cost of over twenty million dollars.

Most Blessed Sacrament, Franklin Lakes

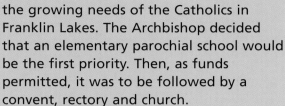

Most Blessed Sacrament Church was established in July 1961. The first pastor, Fr. Francis F. Boland, led 455 parishioners. Because there was not yet a church structure, Masses were held in the cafeteria of the Ramapo Regional High School. The collections yielded slightly more than a dollar per person.

In early 1962, Fr. Boland was directed by the Archbishop to proceed as rapidly as possible with a building program to meet the growing needs of the Catholics in Franklin Lakes. The Archbishop decided that an elementary parochial school would be the first priority. Then, as funds permitted, it was to be followed by a convent, rectory and church.

In June 1980, under the direction of its new pastor, Fr. Carl Hinrichsen, ground-breaking began for the new church. By mid-summer all the brickwork was completed and the off-white botticino marble altar, pulpit and baptismal font arrived from Italy. Installation of the pipe organ soon followed. At noon on November 21, 1981, the first Mass was celebrated. Today the parish numbers 1600 parishioners under the leadership of Msgr. Thomas J. McDade.

Madonna, Fort Lee

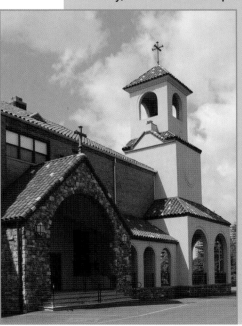

Overlooking the Hackensack Meadowlands from the highest geographical point in Bergen County, Madonna Chapel is also the county's oldest Catholic church. For 130 years this beautiful chapel has been watching over the lowlands of North Jersey.

The land upon which it now stands was part of one of the first grants bordering the Palisades. Given to Samuel Moor by British Army Major John Berry in 1726, it was purchased by Jacob Riley who started construction on the chapel, which was completed in 1854. The design of Madonna Church is a blend of classic styles typical of early 19th century American architecture. It is Gothic Revival with elements of Romanesque, Italian Baroque and English Colonial. The bell tower, more than 85 feet high, was inspired by the great Gothic cathedrals of Europe. The original bronze bell, weighing 300+ pounds, still hangs in the belfry, though no longer in use. The marble altar, now moved forward to concur with modern liturgical requirements, dates from 1903.

For a century parishioners have worshiped under a painting of the contented gaze of a Mother and Child reminiscent of Raphael's Seated Madonna. Restorations in 1939 and 1972 have kept this rural Gothic church a haven of prayer and worship for generations.

Most Holy Name, Garfield

Most Holy Name Church was established in 1911 and placed in the care of the Order of Friars Minor of the New York Province. The first Mass was celebrated on July 9 of that year. On August 27, Fr. Dominic Sonnabend, OFM, was named the first pastor. Property was purchased at the present church site. A school was opened in 1951. The present church edifice and friary were constructed in 1958. Subsequently, the school was consolidated with neighboring parishes, presently known as Garfield Catholic Academy.

The church, known for its dominant tower and gold cross, can be seen from four surrounding towns. Its stained-glass windows depict the life of Christ and the Blessed Mother from infancy to exaltation in glory. The Holy Name Cadets drum and bugle corps gained national prominence for the parish. Fr. Richard Ehrenberg became the first diocesan priest pastor when the Franciscans gave up the parish in 1991.

Garfield has always been a haven for immigrants. The Polish, Italian and German communities are served by the four Catholic churches in the city. The arrival of the Spanish-speaking community at the end of the 20th century allows Most Holy Name to be the welcoming community for its newest parishioners.

Our Lady of Mt. Virgin, Garfield

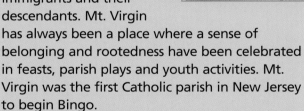

Like the sanctuary high on a mountain overlooking Avellino, Italy, Our Lady of Mt. Virgin Church stands on a high hill overlooking Garfield and Lodi. The theme of its centennial year was, "A Beacon of Hope for 100 Years." A beautiful nativity stained-glass window is dedicated to the memory of Louis Marrone, in whose barn the first Mass in Garfield was celebrated in 1901 for Italian immigrants. From that humble beginning, the Mission became a parish with a resident pastor. The Mother Church of Garfield, Our Lady of Mount Virgin is also the Mother Church of Italian parishes in Lodi, Passaic, Clifton and Hackensack.

For 101 years, the parish has served Italian immigrants and their descendants. Mt. Virgin has always been a place where a sense of belonging and rootedness have been celebrated in feasts, parish plays and youth activities. Mt. Virgin was the first Catholic parish in New Jersey to begin Bingo.

At one time the parish numbered 3000 families, welcoming immigrants mainly from Sicily. Today it registers 1450 households. Mass and devotions in Itialian, processions and a Feast, together with a school co-sponsored with other Garfield parishes continue to nourish the faith. While valuing its traditions, the parish has updated its liturgies, developed its ministries and initiated Cursillo, young adult and youth ministries, stewardship and involvement in interfaith food pantry. Along with its predominantly Italian culture, Our Lady of Mt. Virgin welcomes Peruvians, Ecuadorians, Albanians and Filipinos. That Spirit of Mission, born in Louis Marrone's barn in 1901, continues to flourish in the parish today.

Our Lady of Sorrows, Garfield

Our Lady of Sorrows, Garfield, was established as a mission of Mt. Virgin Parish in 1916. The following year the first permanent church was erected on Jewell and Market Streets, though the mission did not become a parish until 1930. A quarter of a century later, on October 7, 1956, ground was broken for a new church and school, which were dedicated the following year. A year after that a new convent was dedicated for the Sisters of St. Dominic who managed the school. In 1976, the rectory was remodeled and expanded and two years later, at the rededication of the parish, the mortgage was burned on May 6. Consolidation of Garfield Catholic schools took place under a new name, Garfield Catholic Academy. In 1977, under the pastorate of Fr. John K. Gurski, the church was renovated. A series of improvements in church, the school buildings and the rectory followed.

The members of Our Lady of Sorrows Parish are committed to being a dynamic faith community in the spirit of the Second Vatican Council as they strive to become a warm, loving and hospitable community.

St. Stanislaus Kostka, Garfield

During the late 19th century a large number of immigrants came from Eastern and Southern Europe. Many of the Polish immigrants settled in the small northern New Jersey borough, Garfield. In 1900 the Polish congregation of Garfield was designated a mission parish under title of St. Stanislaus Kostka. In June 1914 a new wooden church was dedicated. Now the Polish people of Garfield had their own place to worship and educate their children. Four Felician Sisters from Lodi came each weekday to teach in the parish school, but the parish, now established, was still technically a mission. The parish was not incorporated until 1917.

The parish family continued to grow and soon needed more room. A three-story structure containing the church, school and parish hall was completed and dedicated in 1929.

During World War II, St. Stanislaus parishioners collected $1,000 to purchase an ambulance for the Polish Army. The Fifties were years of growth for the nation and the parish community. The parish received a third priest. During the next decades St. Stanislaus entered a period of transition adapting to the revised liturgy and increased participation of lay people in the life of the Church. Vocations to both the priesthood and religious life flourished at the parish golden jubilee in 1968. Parishioners had much to be proud of. The small mission church had become a large flourishing faith community. Lay people were taking a more active role in parish life. The faith of the early pioneers continues to be transmitted to the present generation.

St. Catharine, Glen Rock

The Church of St. Catharine, Virgin and Martyr, Glen Rock, was begun as a mission in 1948 at the request of the people of Glen Rock, who were then parishioners of Our Lady of Mount Carmel, Ridgewood. When permission was granted for the formation of a mission church, the people immediately began the organization of societies and committees necessary to create a vibrant parish community. By the close of 1952, northern Fair Lawn was added to the mission, land had been purchased, and Fr. Albert Mooney, later to become the first pastor, had arrived to supervise the building and organization of the parish. On January 28, 1953, Archbishop Thomas A. Boland announced the official formation of the new parish.

Throughout its history, St. Catharine Parish has depended on the outstanding energy and talents of its lay people, with the guidance of its staff, to achieve a balance of what is both tradition and contemporary in Catholic life.

Holy Trinity, Hackensack

Mass has been offered in Hackensack since 1857. After a priest was assigned to Bergen County, the generous people of the area built a church, completed in 1861. Approved by Bishop James Roosevelt Bayley, it was named St. Lawrence because it was built on Lawrence Street. In 1866 property was purchased on Maple Avenue, the site of the present church, and a new church, dedicated on April 19, 1868, was dedicated and named Holy Trinity. In January 1869 a two-classroom school was attached to the church to replace the school begun in the old St. Lawrence Church. It had been the first Catholic School in Bergen County. The Sisters of Charity of St. Elizabeth arrived in 1885 and have remained in some capacity until today.

In 1908 a new school and parish center were built and in 1916, a new rectory was added. The present magnificent Romanesque Byzantine-style church was completed and dedicated by then Bishop Thomas Walsh in 1929. Archbishop Boland approved a new elementary school in 1954 and soon afterward closed Holy Trinity's Brownson High School, as enrollment was lured away by Catholic Regional High Schools.

Over the years, Holy Trinity parish has lost many of its parishioners to suburbia. However, it now numbers immigrants from Latin America, especially Columbia, among its parishioners.

Immaculate Conception (St. Mary), Hackensack

Immaculate Conception Parish came into being on August 21, 1890 with a purchase of land in the southern section of Hackensack. The first resident pastor, Fr. John Hennes, officially incorporated the parish on June 5, 1891. The church, built at a cost of $8,900, was dedicated on November 8, 1891. Fr. John Lambert was appointed pastor a year later, establishing the school in 1904. He was succeeded by Fr. Joseph Dolan, who installed the replica of the grotto of Our Lady of Lourdes in 1915.

Immaculate Conception has undergone many changes over the years. The construction of Route 80 cut the parish in half, taking the old school. A new one was built in 1961, closing 38 years later in 1999. Extensive improvements were made to the church and rectory during Fr. Thomas Lynch's tenure.

Today the community remains strong with 486 families under the guidance of Fr. Gerard Graziano.

Throughout the last century, the Church of the Immaculate Conception has done much to lift spirits and gladden the hearts of those nearby. It continues its proud tradition of serving the community, the nation and God.

St. Francis of Assisi, Hackensack

In 1917 Hackensack was a small rural community of 25,000 population. Approximately 4000 were Italian immigrants who took advantage of their skills and love of work, devoting themselves to agriculture and horticulture. Then they worked in the local silk, paper, chemical and slipper factories. Others began building homes and highways for the local citizenry. As they sank their roots deeper in the community, they felt a need to have their own church and a priest able to speak their language. Bishop John O'Connor sent them one.

In August 1917, the foundations of an old structure on Holt and Lodi Streets were removed to make room for a small, wooden church. Its construction took only four months and it was dedicated December 9 the same year, with the Capuchin Franciscan Friars in administration. Two goals of 1931 were to build a new church and to obtain Sisters to instruct the children. At first the Capuchin Sisters of Ringwood served, but in 1931 the Religious Teachers Filippini took over, endearing themselves through their ministries of music, dramatic presentations, day nursery and staffing of the elementary school when it opened in 1967. Lay staff replaced the sisters when they withdrew in 1984.

The parish has seen an influx of Hispanics who now call St. Francis home. A number of Filipinos have also joined the church. Of late, the Italian community has once again become active. Binding all together is the American community--the second and third generation of those who laid the foundation.

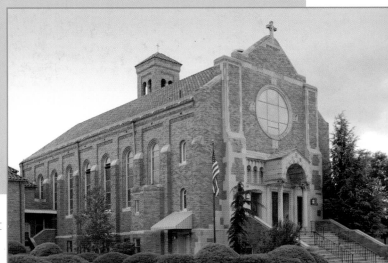

Our Lady of Victories, Harrington Park

In 1904, when the borough of Harrington Park was incorporated, Catholic residents demonstrated their hardiness by hiking four to six miles to the nearest Catholic churches. After six years, the walkers applied the same zeal that carried them through the snow, sleet and wind each week to building a church of their own. Forty-six people attended a meeting on October 2, 1910, to become charter members of the Catholic Church Building Fund Association.

Fr. James T. Delehanty celebrated the first Mass in a private residence on November 6, 1910 with 85 persons in attendance. Land was donated for the construction of the church, completed in September 1912. The first pastor traveled six miles by horse and buggy to hear confessions and to celebrate Mass.

The mission phase of Our Lady of Victories ended in June 1948 when parish status was bestowed and the first resident pastor appointed. In the 92 years since that first Mass, farms have given way to development, Our Lady of Victories has grown to more than 2500 members. A school was built in 1959 that served the parish until 1991 when it merged with Immaculate Conception, Norwood. With the little mission-style church still in use, the parish has moved into 2003 with people of strong faith willing to assist in the many ministries that developed over the years and with the same zeal as the early founders in continuing the mission of Christ.

St. Joseph, Hackensack

In 1895, about 20 Polish families in the Hackensack area attended Mass in at the nearby Immaculate Conception Church to receive preaching they could not understand. As the Polish population in Hackensack grew, they decided to found their own parish. In 1907 they received permission and the church was completed and consecrated in 1909. In 1945 the church was enlarged and renovated. In 1954 the Felician Sisters came to teach English language religion classes. By 1960 the parish had grown to 228 families, 80 percent of whom were of Polish descent. After 1963 the interior of the church was redecorated, a carillon was installed and the mortgage was paid off. From 1970 to 1990 the many beautiful religious traditions and customs of the Polish people were continued.

Corpus Christi, Hasbrouck Heights

In 1896 Mrs. Mary A. Murtha raised $2,700 for a church, and the faithful petitioned the Diocese of Newark for permission to build. Edward Anson donated a tract of land and the construction on Corpus Christi began that spring. By February 1919, the congregation had grown enough to establish an independent parish in Hasbrouck Heights. Fr. Andrew L. Clark was appointed the first resident pastor.

A school, which continues to this day, was opened in September 1928. Over the years, the parish expanded its building to accommodate the growing community, adding in 1957 a chapel that is actually larger than the main church. Church, chapel and school continue to build up Corpus Christi, the Body of Christ, in the 21st Century.

Sacred Heart, Haworth

The Catholic community of Sacred Heart Parish, Haworth, celebrated its first Mass on December 6, 1914. On April 26 of the following year, groundbreaking was held for the first church, affectionately known as "the little white church on the corner." Sacred Heart was a mission until 1950 when it became an independent parish with 80 families enrolled.

Today some 650 families make up Sacred Heart, and the "little white church" was replaced with the current structure in 1963. Recently Mass attendance and Religious Education enrollment have increased to an all-time high. Parish ministries and Service programs have expanded. In February 2001, construction

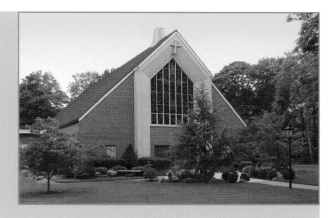

was completed on a new Parish Center, which now houses all Parish Offices and provides extensive meeting space for parish ministries and Religious Education programs.

The parish history is "a story of hopes and dreams, sacrifices and perseverance; a story of a church with a proud past and a hope-filled future."

St. John the Baptist, Hillsdale

On September 29, 2002, the Church of St. John the Baptist began the celebration of its 75th anniversary of foundation as a Catholic parish community with a year of opportunities to reflect on the theme: "Called to be Church." The newly established parish, originally a mission of St. Andrew's Church, Westwood, began with 28 registered families as the first parishioners in September of 1927.

By the year 1950, as the population of Hillsdale increased, parish enrollment numbered 1000 families. The pastor during this time, Msgr. Thomas Duffy, built an elementary school which opened in 1953. Following a fire in the original church in 1965, a new church was erected along with a new rectory.

The spirit of renewal called into being by the Second Vatican Council has resulted in a growing parish which today has more than 2100 families/single adults served by a pastoral staff including clergy, religious and lay people. It is a parish community which works to create a welcoming environment for its members and visitors.

The faith of our parishioners is most evident in the spirited liturgical celebrations in one of the largest houses of worship in Bergen County. There are approximately 60 ministries and parish organizations whose service is made possible by the sharing of time and talent of over 500 dedicated parishioners. Among the hallmark of our parishioners is the generosity to the parish and their compassion for those in need. The parish commitment to its young members is evident in its education of over 1000 children and youth in the Academy, the CCD program, and High School Youth Ministry. The spiritual and faith development of our adult members is also a priority. Numerous educational and spiritual programs are offered throughout the year in an attractive and accommodating new parish center conveniently connected to the church.

St. Luke, Hohokus

Prior to building the beautiful church on Main Street in Paterson, which now serves as the Cathedral for the Diocese of Paterson, the foundation for St. Luke Church, Ho-Ho-Kus, was blessed in 1864. Much has happened since.

In 1920 St. Luke, one of the oldest Catholic schools in Bergen County, opened. The original St. Luke Church burned down in 1948, and was replaced two years later by the present structure. In 1963 a rectory was added. Seven years after, the high school was closed. In the late '70s renovations were completed in the church to have it conform to Vatican II, and in 1989, the parish celebrated its 125th anniversary. The Church became handicapped accessible in 1998 and a renovation of the New Parish Center expanded it to accommodate 150 people in 1999.

In spite of its impressive buildings and well groomed property, the true beauty of St. Luke lies in the eagerness and generosity of its 1800 people in Worship, Word, Service and Community activities. St. Luke parishioners belong to more than 35 committees serving all age groups. Generations of Lucans are buried in the 140-year old cemetery on the church grounds.

St. John the Evangelist, Leonia

At the turn of the last century, Catholics in Leonia attended Mass in neighboring Ft. Lee. However, the long uphill walk was difficult for the elderly and sick. Community leader Frederick J. Sacks asked Bishop John J. O'Connor of Newark to assign Leonia a priest. Thus began Leonia's long and treasured association with the Carmelite friars in nearby Englewood.

Much has changed since the first Mass by Fr. Dion Best, O.Carm., on May 26, 1912 in a rented store. The growth of the young mission parish required a move to a former Methodist church. Renovations were quickly made and on New Year's Day 1914, St. John the Evangelist Church was dedicated. The small church was immediately and warmly embraced by local Catholics, giving St. John the feeling of family that characterizes it today.

During the Depression, Fr. Peter Karmer, O.Carm., built a new church, dedicated in January 1941. The following September St. John School opened under the direction of the School Sisters of Notre Dame.

Amid the many changes that ensued over the parish's 60 years, the constant factor has been the warm, faith-filled community. A strong sense of family and involvement in parish life has enabled St. John to keep growing.

St. Margaret of Cortona, Little Ferry/Moonachie

St. Margaret of Cortona was formed by a handful of people who, at the turn of the 20 century, met upstairs at Goodman's Dry Goods Store on Washington Avenue to worship. Today many of those family names are still an integral part of the parish roster. In every decade and every generation, there has been a core of people whose unshakable belief and trust in God has brought St. Margaret through good times and bad. There have been times of construction, times of loss, times of rebuilding, times of dissent and times of spiritual rebirth. Through every phase, the faithful have stayed strong and kept St. Margaret parish alive. The original church building, with its cornerstone dated 1912, still stands. Although no longer owned by St. Margaret, it is testimony to the perseverance, dedication and commitment of the parish's founders. What makes St. Margaret special can be summed up in the simple equation: parish = people.

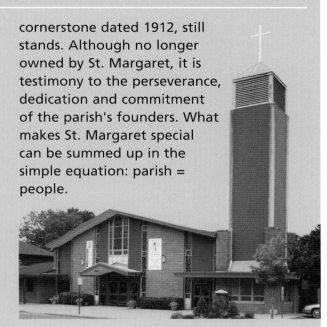

St. Francis de Sales, Lodi

On December 12, 1854, the Church of St. Francis de Sales in Lodi was completed and dedicated. Fr. Senez of St. John Church in Paterson was the first pastor. At the time, the parish served all of Bergen County and the city of Passaic. Earlier, Catholics had to travel to Paterson for Mass.

Over the nearly 150 years of the life of the parish, the people of Lodi and the surrounding communities have been well served by the priests, religious and lay faithful of the parish. To this day, a common sight is three generations of the same family worshiping together.

The parish has always strived to meet the changing needs of Lodi. For many years the parish served the Portuguese population of southern Bergen County and a flourishing Spanish ministry has just been inaugurated. With new outreaches to Single Parents, teens and other groups, the parish continues to minister to its parishioners. In the years ahead, the parish pledges itself to serve the Lord, the Church and the people of God gathered in Lodi.

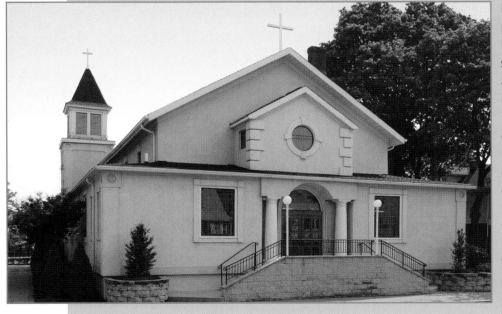

St. Joseph, Lodi

St. Joseph was established in 1917 as a national parish for Italian immigrants of the archdiocese. The parish began with the faith and vision of Italian immigrants who wanted a church of their own in honor of St. Joseph. From small beginnings, the parish has grown and for 83 years has served the Catholics of various nationalities in Lodi.

Past and present parisioners have devoted their time, talent and treasure to the growth of the parish. In doing so, they demonstrate the determination evinced by the founding members, adding a new elementary school in 1952, a new church in 1976 and a new rectory in 1989.

St. Joseph parish has the reputation of being a warm and friendly parish. Many who have raised their families here can bear witness to how well the parish has nurtured their faith and their family life.

Our Lady of Mount Carmel, Lyndhurst

Our Lady of Mount Carmel is a small church, but at one time it was even smaller. The parish origins are obscure. At the time, one family was in residence. The church building has been traced to 1849, but there the records stop. In 1882 the church was reconditioned into a Presbyterian church, which closed in 1901, allowing the Diocese of Newark to reopen the doors in 1909, bringing to birth the first Catholic church in Lyndhurst. The area still had no resident priest.

About 1914 a fire destroyed the sanctuary and forced the parishioners to worship at Sacred Heart. After the building was repaired and enlarged, it was officially designated as a Mission of Sacred Heart. Through the years, it became known as "the chapel." On July 23, 1966, Our Lady of Mount Carmel was designated a separate parish with Fr. Patrick Fitzpatrick as the first pastor. The little church holds fond memories for a great number of people and the stranger and the newcomer find in it a haven of peace to which they are welcomed with a friendly greeting that is a long tradition.

Sacred Heart, Lyndhurst

In the fall of 1901 the Catholics of the Township of Kingsland received permission to establish a parish and build a church. The community celebrated its First Mass at Herman Froelich's store in February in 1902.

The first church was completed by December. From 1907 through 1910, parish life flourished with the formation of various parish societies and the organization of religious education and sacramental programs and social gatherings.

On September 12, 1918 the first church was destroyed by fire and quickly replaced with a temporary structure until the new and current church was built and dedicated in 1925. With the '40s came the tragedy of war and the advent of the Dominican Sisters from Caldwell to staff the newly built Sacred Heart School in 1956.

In the '60s the parish incorporated the pastoral and liturgical changes of Vatican II and enjoyed a greatly increased involvement of the laity in the life and ministries of the parish. The '70s, '80s and '90s saw the spiritual life of the parish deepen through the establishment of the RCIA, Bible Study, Cursillo, Renew, various prayer groups and a complete liturgical renovation of the church interior.

Then in late 2000, serious damage was discovered to the floors and supporting structures of the church. The rebuilt and renovated church reopened for Christmas 2001 in time to mark the parish's Centennial Year.

With more than 2000 families, Sacred Heart stands ready and eager to proclaim the Gospel of Jesus and be a sign of Christ's presence for the community of Lyndhurst well into the next century.

First Auxiliary Bishop

The ever-growing Catholic population and institutions of the Diocese made additional help from the wider Church indispensable. The first auxiliary bishop of the diocese, Thomas McLaughlin, was consecrated on July 25, 1935. Vicar General of the Diocese, past president of Seton Hall, and serving as Rector of Immaculate Conception Seminary, McLaughlin would be the first of many auxiliaries who have provided important services for the Diocese. Bishop Walsh, who had been confirming over 21,000 people a year prior to the appointment of Bishop McLaughlin, was profoundly grateful not only for the sacramental and administrative assistance he was able to give, but for the friendship that they had shared for many years.

In 100 years the men and women of Catholic Community Services and its predecessor agencies have been the face of this local church of Newark to those in need.

Commemorative plaque given to Archbishop Walsh from Seton Hall College

Archdiocesan Status

The Diocese of Newark had undergone so much growth in the first part of the twentieth century that the Holy See decided it was time to raise it to the dignity of an Archdiocese, the chief diocese of the new ecclesiastical Province of Newark, which would also include the newly-created diocese of Paterson, as well as the dioceses of Trenton and Camden. The new Archdiocese of Newark itself would be geographically the smallest archdiocese in the nation, just 514 square miles, consisting of the counties of Union, Essex, Bergen, and Hudson. Thomas Walsh, the fifth bishop of Newark, was to become the first Archbishop of Newark. As a sign of his particular communion with the Holy Father and of his jurisdiction in the new Province, the new Archbishop received a *pallium*, a white lambswool stole, worn over his vestments at Mass, which was presented to the new Archbishop

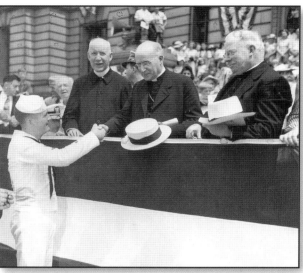

Archbishop Walsh congratulates Coast Guard Hero John Cullen in 1942 when the country was in the midst of war.

by Archbishop Amleto Cicognani, the Apostolic Delegate of the Holy Father in the United States, in a special ceremony held in the still-unfinished Sacred Heart Cathedral, on April 27, 1938.

Becoming an Archdiocese was indeed a recognition of the importance and maturity of the Catholic community in northern New Jersey and added a certain luster to the activities of the hundreds of parishes, schools, religious houses, and charitable institutions within the new Archdiocese as they struggled through the closing years of the Great Depression. Even greater challenges awaited the faithful as the next decade brought another world war to America.

Msgr. Mercolino speaks at a dinner given by the St. Anne Society to the U.S. Marine detachment stationed at the Bayonne Naval depot, 1942.

Portrait of Pope Pius XI believed to be signed by him. From Villa Walsh.

St. Michael the Archangel, Lyndhurst

The history of St. Michael the Archangel begins in 1912 in the small town of Kingsland, now Lyndhurst. While the early days of the parish saw an influx of Polish-speaking families, now peoples of many different nationalities are members of the parish family and present a rich and varied tapestry of Catholic life. But amazingly, the end product is the same--"maintaining the place of witness and service, a community of family and friendship."

In 1954 St. Michael Elementary School was added, enlarging the community of family and friendship. Seven years later, in continuing the expansion of St. Michael Parish, a beautiful new church was built and stands today. St. Michael Parish history is truly the story of the families of the community over the past 91 years.

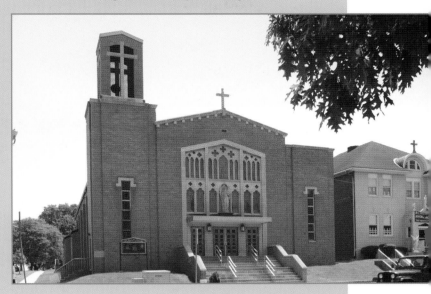

Immaculate Conception, Mahwah

Immaculate Conception, Darlington, in the northwestern corner of Bergen County, was founded in 1928 by Fr. Thomas J. Walsh. Msgr. Thomas H. McLaughlin was appointed first pastor. The parish's first Mass was celebrated in the seminary carpenter shop. Soon the church and school building was erected and dedicated in 1932.

The parish school opened in February 1929 with 17 students and served Mahwah and its environs until 1981. The Sisters of Charity of Convent Station staffed the school from its inception until 1978. Immaculate Conception received its first resident pastor, Fr. Gordon Byrne, in 1955, to be followed by Fr. Thomas Gillick, who added four more classrooms, a gym, a kitchen and offices. CYO was also very active during these years, winning many sports trophies and theater production awards.

The Religious Education program has grown rapidly and a Lenten Mission renews the parishioners spiritually each year. Pancake breakfasts, St. Patrick dances, theme dinners, picnics, carnivals and strawberry festivals make Immaculate Conception a parish family. Today it has an active Pastoral Council, a Finance Council, and a Buildings and Grounds Committee to serve the parish. Along with other services to the community, the parish has hosted a late summer program for homeless men and women, collected food for the Center for Food Action, prepared meals for AIDS patients, sponsored a holiday Giving Tree and supported a Kosovo family to U.S. citizenship. In 2005 the parish will celebrate its 75th anniversary.

Church of the Immaculate Heart of Mary, Mahwah

Immaculate Heart of Mary, Mahwah, was established in the fall of 1915 for Polish immigrants. The founding pastor, Fr. Thomas A. Patalong, SDB, was a member of the newly established Don Bosco High School, also founded in 1915 for Polish-speaking youth. The Mahwah parish became a haven for newly arrived immigrant families. The extraordinary care and concern of these families by the many Salesians who staffed the parish until 2002 accounts for the present-day demonstration of devout faith to Our Lord Jesus and the Immaculate Heart of Mary. The Polish traditions and adherence to Catholic doctrines and devotions remain a landmark of the parish community.

From the humble beginnings of a tiny church, a school, a convent and a rectory were added to the facilities. The last addition was the replacement of the original wooden church with a truly magnificent church that reflects the devotion, traditions and tremendous faith of the parish community. The influx of young Catholic families to the area throughout the years has changed the scope of the parish. Today, its composition is fast becoming multi-ethnic. Of the three weekday Masses and five weekend Masses, only one Sunday Mass is offered in Polish.

The magnificent spiritual and cultural traditions of the past are now melded with those of the present. The spiritual richness of the community continues to attract a flow of new parishioners. The motto, "To Jesus through Mary," is as vibrant today as it was to those who first heard it in the tiny Church in 1915.

Our Lady Queen of Peace, Maywood

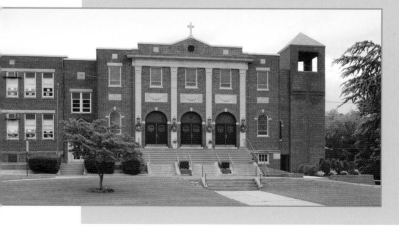

Fr. Thomas Burke, curate at Holy Trinity, Hackensack, announced that Archbishop Walsh had approved plans to split Holy Trinity by building a church, school and convent in Maywood. Groundbreaking for the $1 million building was September 1949. In June 1950, Fr. James Neafsey was appointed founding pastor of the new parish, Our Lady Queen of Peace. The following year the Religious Teachers Filippini moved into the convent to begin their long association with the parish school, which in its first year of operation enrolled 565 students. Five years later, enrollment reached an all-time high of 950 students.

During the 1960s the parish continued to grow, making the liturgical changes to the church called for by the Second Vatican Council. In 1992 the parish school was combined with St. Peter School, River Edge, to form a single, co-sponsored Academy of 260 students. In 1999, plans to celebrate the 50th anniversary of the parish the following year included much needed updating and repair on the church and school buildings. By 2000, through the generous gifts and sacrifices of the parishioners, the church renovation was completed and Our Lady Queen of Peace was rededicated by Archbishop Theodore McCarrick on December 16.

Nativity, Midland Park

Families who migrated from the city to the outlying suburbs of Bergen County worshiped at St. Luke, Ho-Ho-Kus, Our Lady of Mount Carmel, Ridgewood and St. Elizabeth, Wyckoff.

In May 1952 the Midland Park families were pulled together when the Archdiocese purchased the Klaas Bokma farm--15 acres of land with a house, barn, chicken coop, corn crib and other buildings for the Mission of the Holy Child. The buildings on the farm being inadequate for the celebration of Mass, Sunday worship was held in the public library.

At the farm, women transformed the farmhouse into a meeting hall and the barn into the first church. In January 1953, the Mission was designated a parish, assuming the title Church of the Nativity. In March of 1954, Fr. William Sheehan was named Pastor. On June 16, 1954, Archbishop Thomas Boland dedicated the new church. A bell specially cast in Loughborough, England, rang out from the newly built steeple to announce the first Sunday mass at Nativity Church. Soon plans for an attached church and school building emerged and construction started quickly. The Church-School opened in September 1958.

Today 1600 families worship in the parish. The school is now St. Thomas More Interparochial School, serving Nativity, St. Luke and Guardian Angel Parishes.

Ascension, New Milford

In 1952 St. Joseph, Oradell, was given permission to purchase land for a new parish and begin its construction.

Ascension was officially made a parish the following year.

In September 1953, the auditorium-church was dedicated, the First Mass was celebrated and Ascension School opened its doors under the direction of the Dominican Sister of Caldwell.

In March 1957, after a successful fundraising drive, groundbreaking took place for a church / rectory / convent complex to meet the expanding needs of the parish. The cornerstone laying and blessing of Ascension took place in September 1958.

During the past 50 years, Ascension has grown from the original 80 families to more than 1700 and is being led into the 21st Century by its sixth and current pastor, Fr. David Milliken.

Queen of Peace, North Arlington

Since its establishment in 1922 under the leadership of Msgr. Peter B. O'Connor, Queen of Peace Parish has served the people of North Arlington, Kearny and the surrounding area. With more than 3500 households, Queen of Peace is committed to making Jesus Christ known and loved in a community of faith that worships, prays, teaches and lives the Gospel, reaching out in service to those in need. Growth in faith and focus on family life have been its hallmarks.

The landmark Georgian colonial church whose steeple is visible for miles around is the anchor of an impressive complex of five buildings. Over the past few years, both the Parish Restoration Program and the Stewardship Way of Life have enabled the parish to renovate the physical facilities as well as provide material resources for its numerous parish organizations and programs, activities and service groups.

The parish commitment to Catholic education, carried out through the Sisters of Saint Joseph of Chestnut Hill, the Brothers of the Christian Schools and lay teachers and catechists, is nothing short of remarkable. Queen of Peace High School, enrolling more than 750 students and twice recognized as a Blue Ribbon National School of Excellence, has served the surrounding community since 1930. The parish elementary school, with more than 460 pupils, provides a solid Catholic education. The parish Catechetical Program brings the teachings of Christ and his Church to more than 450 youngsters who attend public schools.

Queen of Peace is a parish where the gifts and talents of clergy, religious and lay faithful blend to make the presence of Christ visible in the world.

St. Anthony, Northvale

St. Anthony, Northvale, was canonically established in 1890, but the recorded history of the area goes back to 1681 when the settlers of lower Manhattan purchased a large tract of land from the Tappan Indians. In 1859 the Erie Railroad came through Carieville, later Neuvy and now Northvale, with a line from Jersey City to Piermont, swelling the population. According to the best available information, however, St. Anthony was founded in 1890. The original parish church, built soon after the parish was created, was located on the present parish site.

Although the church burned down in May 1907, St. Anthony parish did not die in the embers. A new church replaced the old in 1919 and stood until 1963. The Sisters of St. Joseph traveled to Northvale from Englewood Cliffs on Sundays for nearly 40 years to teach catechism. In 1957 they moved into the parish to staff the school.

The expansion of the community and the return of veterans from World War II gave impetus to new growth, and the parish received an administrator. In January 1964 the last Mass was held in the church. The following year a new church, friary and convent were dedicated and Franciscan Brothers arrived to serve the parish. In 1976, CCD became an important function of the parish. After the mid-80s, lively liturgies have sparked the life of the parish.

92

Immaculate Conception, Norwood

Immaculate Conception, Norwood, was born in 1921 through the efforts of several local Catholic families. The first Mass in Norwood was celebrated in the Norwood Firehouse on June 24, 1921, the original name being St. John the Baptist. Later in 1921, the parish patron was changed to the Immaculate Conception. The story has it that the Carmelite Fathers agreed to take over the care of the parish only if it was dedicated to the Blessed Mother. The first Mass in the present church building (the old Borough Club) was at midnight on Christmas Eve in 1921. The Carmelite Fathers led the parish from 1921 to the end of 1994 when they withdrew. Beginning in January 1995, Fr. Charles B. Urnick took up duties as the first Archdiocesan pastor of the parish.

Our Lady of Perpetual Help, Oakland

In May 1960 Archbishop Thomas A. Boland announced the creation of a new parish to minister to the Catholics of Oakland. Until that time, Oakland had been served by St. Elizabeth, Wyckoff. The new parish was named Our Lady of Perpetual Help, a title unique in the Archdiocese.

Initially Mass was celebrated in the American Legion Hall and Religious Education classes were taught in the basement of the hall, the Sisters of Charity of Convent Station from Immaculate Conception School serving as teachers. The first Mass celebrating the First Communion of 150 children took place on June 16, 1962. The Church was dedicated the following September. The school opened that fall with the Chestnut Hill Sisters of St. Joseph moving into the convent. The school closed in 1991. The children had the option of attending either Most Blessed Sacrament School (Franklin Lakes) or St. Elizabeth (Wychoff). As the borough of Oakland has grown, so has the parish. Our Lady of Perpetual Help is now home to 1261 registered families.

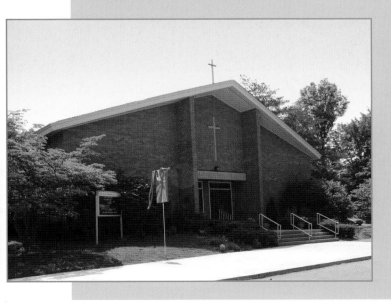

St. Pius X, Old Tappan

St. Pius X in Old Tappan is currently preparing to celebrate 50 years of service to its community. The parish was dedicated to Mary on September 21, 1952, under the title, "The First Mission of Our Lady of Refuge." Effective July 3, 1954, the church was officially named St. Pius X. The growth of the parish led to the purchase of a brick building in 1955.

Today St. Pius has a new Church and Parish Center, dedicated in March 1999. Fr. Patrick Mulewski, the current pastor, works together with a supportive staff: Deacon Dick Hodges, Religious Education Director, Angelina Rispoli, Youth Ministry Leaders, Ron and Jeanine Binaghi, Music Director, Rose Marie Maccaro, Liturgy Coordinator Jan Daly and others. St. Pius X ,

a strong, faith-filled community with Christ as its center, joyfully celebrates 50 years of a glorious tradition of living out St. Pius X's call "To Renew all things in Christ."

St. Joseph, Oradell/New Milford

St. Joseph Parish began in 1903 in Delford (now New Milford and Oradell) as a mission church of Holy Trinity, Hackensack. It has grown from a few devout members to one of the largest parishes in the Archdiocese with more than 2400 families and a campus with seven buildings. Although the cornerstone of the first church was set in 1903, Mass was celebrated in the basement until 1908, when the brown-shingled church was finally completed.

In 1939 the first Catholic school in the area was built with a convent and a rectory following shortly thereafter. In 1937 the little country church burned to the ground. Four years later, a new church was built, which in 1949 also burned down. The third church was completed in 1951. In 1957 a second school was built, which today houses 230 pre-K to grade 4 students while the original building is now occupied by 210 students in Grades 5-8. When in 1962 Brothers came to teach the boys, a special residence was built for them.

In 1972 St. Joseph was chosen for the experimental concept of "Team Ministry." Over the years, St. Joseph has been served by many dedicated priests, all of whom have helped the parish to flourish. The laity have introduced many special programs to enrich the lives of the parishioners. Today, with an award-winning school and a religious education program that serves more than 800 public school students, the people of St. Joseph greet their centennial with great faith in Our Lord and the future of their parish.

St. Michael, Palisades Park

In 1912, newly assigned Fr. John Carey inaugurated plans for construction of St. Michael Church and rectory. The first Mass was at midnight on Christmas 1912, the worshippers kneeling on newspapers, since the pews had not yet been constructed. To accommodate the growth of the community, by 1924 Fr. Carey made plans to erect the present church, the cornerstone for which was laid on August 10, 1924.

Fr. Thomas Padian came to St. Michael in June 1949, remaining seven years during which he renovated the church and purchased an additional lot and house on First Street for the present Father Carey Hall. In 1956 Fr. Thomas F. Duffy was appointed pastor. Keenly aware of the importance of Catholic education for the young, he initiated a Woman Teachers Organization, had classes on moral guidance offered after school in the public school and made plans for the renovation of the house at First Street to become the first St. Michael School, opened on September 8, 1958, for 112 children with three Chestnut Hill Sisters as teachers. Work was started on the new school building,

known today as Notre Dame Interparochial School, in February 1969.

In 1975 Fr. Anthony A Bryce, the newly appointed pastor, followed the directives of Vatican II by establishing the first Parish Council. The next pastor, Fr. Vincent J. Quinn, was beloved for establishing a feeling in the parish of family, kindness, stability and love of the Lord. He is remembered for his outreach to the poor and lonely. Fr. Quinn left behind a flourishing church for Fr. James F. Reilly, the pastor who came to St. Michael in May 1997. The parish history has formed a beautiful Rosary of years and there is more to come.

St. Nicholas, Palisades Park

Approximately 100 years ago, small Italian and Polish groups settled atop a hill in Palisades Park. Their zeal and determination provided them with a spiritual and physical strength that resulted in the purchase of the first site of St. Nicholas Church. On March 12, 1923, the parish was canonically established and named St. Nicholas. Four years later the Oblates of Mary Immaculate assumed the duties of the small parish.

The Filippini Sisters arrived in 1948 to teach in St. Nicholas School. They remained until 1982. The following year the Vocationist Fathers were assigned to continue shepherding the parish. St. Nicholas School merged with St. Matthew, Ridgefield and St. Michael, Palisades Park, to form Notre Dame Interparochial School in 1991. The Early Learning Center is now housed in the original school building. St. Nicholas celebrated its 75th anniversary in 1998.

The rise of totalitarianism during the 1930's had brought repeated condemnations from the Holy See, and particularly Pope Pius XI, who, in a series of encyclical letters, critiqued successively the excesses of Fascism *(Non abbiamo bisogno)*, Nazism *(Mit brenneder Sorge)*, and Communism *(Divini Redemptoris)*, all to no avail. War came to Europe on September 1, 1939 and while the United States was spared for the next two years, the horizon grew increasingly dark. On December 5, 1941, Archbishop Walsh wrote to his priests, asking them to volunteer to serve as chaplains in the armed forces. Two days later, the U.S. naval base at Pearl Harbor was attacked.

Catholics in the Service

The Catholics of the Archdiocese of Newark, many of them of German or Italian descent, went to war with the same patriotism and resolve as the rest of the nation. Conservation, Victory Bond drives, recycling, and victory gardens all took their places in Catholic parish life, along with novenas for peace and for the protection of those serving in the armed forces. Building and expansion plans were shelved throughout the Archdiocese. Seventy-nine priests – nearly fifteen percent of the presbyterate – responded to the call of Archbishop Walsh and volunteered for service during the war. Many would be wounded, one was killed, and one became a prisoner of war. As in the First World War, the Archdiocese

Rev. John P. Washington

became a major shipping point for troops going overseas, and many priests, not young enough for overseas duty, served as auxiliary chaplains in Bayonne, offering Mass and hearing confessions for both American soldiers who were shipping out of the Bayonne Naval Base as well as for Italian prisoners of war, who were incarcerated in another part of the city. One Newark priest, Fr. John P. Washington, would become famous for his heroic sacrifice during the war.

While the necessities of the war imposed many limitations on the expansion and progress

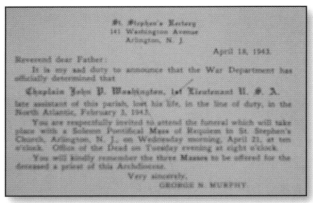

Death notice of Fr. John P. Washington, who died a casualty of World War II.

of the Archdiocese, Archbishop Walsh continued with planning throughout the conflict. One apostolate that would receive his particular attention was one of the oldest in the archdiocese, Seton Hall College. The College had seen many changes under Archbishop Walsh. The seminary had moved from its South Orange home to new facilities in Mahwah. The College was accredited by the Middle States Association of Colleges and Secondary Schools in 1932. New buildings rose on campus during the 1930's. An Urban Division and Summer Session of the College were started. Schools of Nursing, Medicine, Business, and Education were all opened. A full course of studies was continued throughout the war. And, perhaps most important of all, plans were made to raise the college to the rank of a university – an achievement that would be completed in 1950.

Original map of the Madison (Morris) County with sketch and map of Seton Hall College

Aerial view of Manor and Seminary at Immaculate Conception Seminary, Darlington

GI Bill

The immediate post-war years would bring ongoing changes for the Archdiocese of Newark and for the Catholics of northern New Jersey. For Seton Hall, these years would bring a surge of new students enrolled under the GI Bill. For Immaculate Conception Seminary, these years would bring a large number of young veterans who began studies for the priesthood and the religious life. For the institutions of the Archdiocese, these years would bring unprecedented expansion. The United States, almost alone among the major combatants of World War II, found her land untouched by the ravages of war, and enjoyed ever-increasing prosperity in the post-war years. This prosperity, combined with the generosity of so many Catholics of the archdiocese helped transform the enormous backlog of construction projects which had built up during the war to a boom in parish and school constructions in the diocese during Archbishop Walsh's final years, including a great press to finish the Cathedral of the Sacred Heart in Newark.

The Archbishop celebrated his golden jubilee of priestly ordination in 1950 by calling on the faithful of Newark to help in the completion of Sacred Heart Cathedral. He was justly proud of the many accomplishments of the Catholics of the Archdiocese of Newark and the Catholics of the

Immaculate Conception Seminary, Darlington, Class of 1950

Immaculate Conception Seminary, Darlington, Class of 1947

Archdiocese were equally proud (and fond) of their Archbishop. Many would mourn his passing and thousands would personally attend his funeral when Newark's first Archbishop passed away, after a very brief illness, on June 6, 1952.

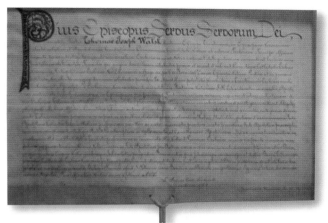

Papal Bull from Pope Pius XI appointing Bishop Walsh Bishop of Newark, 1928

Silver gilt monstrance designed in Rome for Bishop Walsh's 50th anniversary, 1950

BERGEN COUNTY

Annunciation, Paramus

More than 100 years ago, the Sisters of Charity purchased property at the corner of Midland Avenue and Route 17 to establish The House of Divine Providence for the Incurably Il. By 1925 they had 200 acres and 187 patients in their care. However, the House burnt down that year. They had also just finished construction of Mount St. Andrew Villa. When economic conditions blocked the rebuilding of Divine Providence, the sisters began to sell off the property, which the Archdiocese bought in 1952, constructing on it the Church of the Annunciation. The parish was established the next year.

In 1998 a capital campaign was launched to renovate the church while still maintaining its Gothic architecture, original stained-glass windows and Stations of the Cross. An addition was to create an environment suitable for the renewed liturgy that had been celebrated for more than 30 years.

The 50th anniversary, observed in 2002, marked the church's ability to change as the community grew into a vibrant parish of more than 1300 families.

Our Lady of the Visitation, Paramus

Our Lady of the Visitation was founded in the 1950s by families of faith in the newly developing suburb of Paramus. After celebrating the Eucharist in the Spring Valley firehouse for two years, the parish moved into the basement of its new, but unfinished, church on Christmas Eve 1951. Over subsequent years, parochial life was centered on the Eucharist and other sacraments. Holy hours, retreats, novenas and devotions characterized parish life and formed children in the faith. In clubs and organizations parishioners shared their common belief. As a vibrant and caring community, they finished their church, built a school and, later, its large extension.

Reflecting the Vatican II vision of Church as the people of God, OLV called forth and formed lay leaders and ministers. Liturgical, educational and other ministries flourished. Pastoral and Finance Councils assist in leadership of the parish which encourages all to take personal responsibility for parish life.

Today the same Spirit that motivated previous generations is moving the people to renewal in the form of stewardship. Faith based on habit is being called to become a faith of personal choice, "to become examples of Christ's love in the world by caring for one another through communal sharing and service; to celebrate the joy of understanding and caring through sacraments and prayer."

Our Lady of Mercy, Park Ridge

In 1902 a new parish was established at the northen end of the Pascack Valley. The next year construction of a new church in Park Ridge and St. Mary Parish began to serve the Catholics of Montvale, Park Ridge, River Vale and Woodcliff Lake. The population grew slowly until after World War II. In 1950 a much larger property was purchased for a parochial school that opened in 1953 with the Religious Teachers Filippini guiding the tremendous increase in students that led to the construction of three buildings in rapid succession.

In 1951 a new church, dedicated to Our Lady of Mercy, was built, and with young priests in the lead, meaningful programs were initiated that created vitality in the parish. In 2002 the Parish celebrated its centennial. A master plan was developed to adapt the church for today's liturgical needs, upgrade lighting and repair for the school, redo the parking and campus for safety and convenience and build a new Parish Center. Our Lady of Mercy Parish with its committed parishioners looks forward to its second century as it enters the Third Millennium.

St. Paul, Ramsey

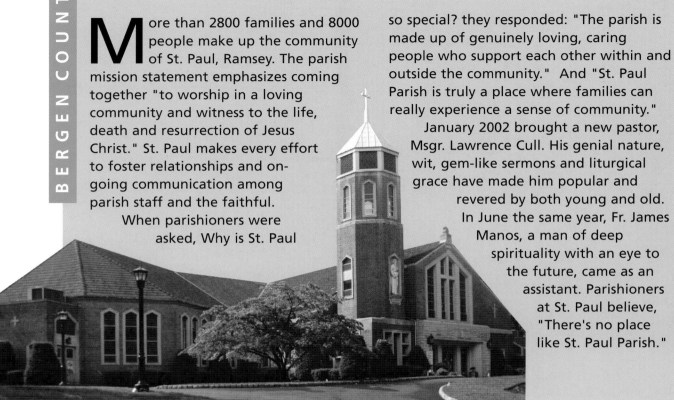

More than 2800 families and 8000 people make up the community of St. Paul, Ramsey. The parish mission statement emphasizes coming together "to worship in a loving community and witness to the life, death and resurrection of Jesus Christ." St. Paul makes every effort to foster relationships and on-going communication among parish staff and the faithful.

When parishioners were asked, Why is St. Paul so special? they responded: "The parish is made up of genuinely loving, caring people who support each other within and outside the community." And "St. Paul Parish is truly a place where families can really experience a sense of community."

January 2002 brought a new pastor, Msgr. Lawrence Cull. His genial nature, wit, gem-like sermons and liturgical grace have made him popular and revered by both young and old. In June the same year, Fr. James Manos, a man of deep spirituality with an eye to the future, came as an assistant. Parishioners at St. Paul believe, "There's no place like St. Paul Parish."

St. Matthew, Ridgefield

St. Matthew Church was incorporated on August 17, 1899, to serve about 50 families in Ridgefield and Palisades Park. Its first frame building was dedicated in December that year.

Until June 1924, St. Matthew was a Mission of Ridgefield Park. The following year the parish had 400 members. Three years later, the parish had a rectory, a convent and a school with 120 students. By 1933, eight classrooms and an auditorium were built. Three years later the school auditorium was transformed into a church, which was replaced in 1951 by the present stately structure. An eight-classroom school, the Clark Annex, was blessed in 1959. Three years later the rectory was occupied and the convent completed the following year in 1963.

In September 1991, St. Matthew School joined with two parishes, St. Michael and

St. Nicholas, Palisades Park, to create Notre Dame Interparochial School, which serves a multicultural Catholic and non-Catholic population.

St. Francis of Assisi, Ridgefield Park

A small group of lay people in Ridgefield Park convinced Bishop Winand Wigger that they could support a parish. The first Mass was celebrated in a newly built structure of wood and brick in July 1890.

Fr. James Flannagan was appointed resident pastor in 1900. Far ahead of his time, Fr. Flannagan involved the laity in church decisions and set an ecumenical tone for his Catholic community, encouraging cooperation with other denominations of the area.

The parish founded a school in 1890. In 1912 a new church / school was built to accommodate parish growth. In 1915 the Sisters of Charity came to teach in a newly created elementary school. By 1926 a new church building was needed. Under the parish's fourth pastor, Fr. Coyle, who served from 1954, the parish grew tremendously with more than 1000 students in the school and another 1000 in the religious education program. Associate pastors were added. A new convent and rectory went up and an addition was built on the school.

In the '70s, renovation of the church to meet the directives of Vatican II was complemented by expansion of lay involvement. A deacon and a pastoral associate were also added to the parish staff. Ongoing repairs and improvements to the physical plant followed, even as the spiritual life of the parish was enhanced by spiritual programs and a pastoral council. Given the tradition of St. Francis of warmth and generosity, the parish will try to continue to reflect the spirit of its founders and its patron.

Our Lady of Mount Carmel, Ridgewood

With a history of more than 110 years, Our Lady of Mount Carmel, Ridgewood, is vibrantly alive. By 1888 there were enough Catholics in Ridgewood to warrant establishing a congregation. Mass had been offered at a private home on Union Street. As the Catholic population increased, Fr. Michael Nevins was appointed to establish Our Lady of Mount Carmel. A house deeded to the parish served as church and rectory.

In 1890 the cornerstone of a new western Byzantine-style church seating 250 was laid. Mission churches beginning in Wyckoff and Ramsey caused the church to be called "the Mother Catholic Church of West Bergen County."

A new Gothic church went up in 1914 and the old church was razed. Trustees bought new property in 1920 and pew rent was discontinued two years later. The Sisters of Charity opened the parish school in 1923, replaced in 1930 by 10 classrooms, creating the largest school in the diocese. It was added to in 1952 and 1956.

The cornerstone of the present church was laid October 29, 1960, with Our Lady Chapel behind the sanctuary. The parish renovated the church in accord with Vatican Council directives and engaged in ecumenical activities after the Council. In 1976, an after-school program was initiated and a Blessed Sacrament chapel created. Many organizations make the parish spiritually alive. The 100th anniversary in 1989 commemorates a history of labors of love and remembrance as a legacy.

St. Peter the Apostle, River Edge

A close-knit, stable community in central Bergen County boasting three generations of parishioners as well as many new young families and ethnic groups, St. Peter the Apostle parish actively seeks to live out is new Mission Statement: "In faithful stewardship to the mission of Jesus Christ, St. Peter the Apostle Parish commits itself to proclaiming the Gospel, celebrating the liturgy of joy and thanksgiving, building a welcoming community, serving the needs of our neighbors, with special care for the poor and marginalized, and reaching out, inviting all to share this journey with us."

A vibrant, active parish with a welcoming spirit noted by parishioners and visitors alike, St. Peter offers more than 40 different ministries and programs, including social outreach and 30 small Christian communities, as well as a weekly children's Mass and choir. Committed to lifelong faith development and a collaborative approach to ministry,

St. Peter's encourages people to learn and grow and to share faith and friendship. Then it challenges them to live out their faith in the world.

Church of the Sacred Heart, Rochelle Park

The Franciscan Friars have served the Church of the Sacred Heart since 1916 when the parish was founded. The first church, dedicated in 1917, preceded the present church, dedicated in 1959.

But the great contribution of the Friars has been to lay a solid foundation of Catholic faith and morals in the hearts of their flock. Upon their base of sacramental spirituality, the succeeding generations built a lively and apostolic Catholicism for their children and grandchildren.

Among the outstanding features of the parish church are its beautiful stained-glass windows and its striking statue of the Sacred Heart.

St. Mary, Rutherford

At the heart of the success of St. Mary, Rutherford, is the long tradition of strong, vibrant pastoral leadership and a committed, caring congregation. In 1908 St. Mary

was established to meet the needs of the fledgling Catholic community of Rutherford. In a small, but beautiful, field stone building, the first church took root with Fr. William F. Grady as its pastor.

Over the next 20 years, growth of the young parish prompted the pastor to invite the Sisters of St. Dominic of Caldwell to open an elementary and a high school. Presently, nearly 1400 students experience the teachings of Jesus in an excellent Religious Education Program and in religion classes of both schools.

As it approaches its 100th birthday, the parish consists of 2800 families who are supported by many and varied ministries, including RCIA, Spiritual Life, Social Concerns and a Lazarus Group. Under the outstanding guidance of its present pastor, Fr. Michael J. Kreder, St. Mary continues to be both dynamic and progressive and gracious and welcoming to the People of God.

St. Philip the Apostle Church, Saddle Brook

In the years immediately after World War II, the community then known as Saddle River Township experienced tremendous change. Farms were transformed into tracts of new homes, ready to welcome hundreds of young families moving to the suburbs. To meet the needs of these many young families, a new Catholic parish was formed in 1953.

The school was built first, and the church came later in 1956. Father Thomas J. Kenny, the founding pastor, gathered the new residents and the "old timers" into a parish community. Later pastors, Monsignor Paul Lang, Father Raymond Doll, and Monsignor Charles Stengel built on the foundation laid by Father Kenny, and helped form a vibrant community of faith dedicated to passing on the faith to future generations through support for the parish school and parish religious education programs.

The parish celebrates its spirit of community in many different ways. Today the parish sponsors activities for children, young adults, adults and senior citizens. Every summer, St. Philip's Festival is a great event, giving everyone in the parish and in the wider community of Saddle Brook an opportunity to build up the ties of friendship that bind us together.

In 2003, Saint Philip the Apostle parish is celebrating its 50th anniversary as a vibrant community of faith. May the Lord bless us and help us to continue to be a beacon of faith in our part of the world.

Church of the Korean Martyrs, Saddle Brook

In May 1986, parishioners from St. Andrew Kim Church established the Korean Catholic Community at the Church of Madonna, Fort Lee. In the beginning, Fr. Augustine Park led the community of approximately 100 members from 50 families. Since there was a growing

Korean population in the Fort Lee region, the community also decided to open a Korean school that teaches Korean and other subjects to young Korean children of the area. Currently the school is located at St. Cecilia School in Englewood.

As the community grew, the members organized a committee to prepare for the establishment of a Korean Catholic Church. On November 29, 1983, Fr. Jacob Song arrived from Korea to serve as the first pastor. In April 1996, the Church Council decided to change the name to Church of the Korean Martyrs and established a committee to develop a new church facility. The Church then moved to the current facility .

Currently the Church of the Korean Martyrs has 752 families with 2486 members and continues to grow.

St. Gabriel the Archangel, Saddle River

St. Gabriel the Archangel Parish serves 1050 families from within its boundaries, which include the town of Saddle River and parts of the towns of Waldwick, Hohokus and Ridgewood. Originally built for an evangelical Protestant congregation, the church was known as Zion Tabernacle in the 1940s. This group ceased to function and the building lay empty until purchased for $1 by the Archdiocese in 1952. At first a mission church of St. Luke Parish in Hohokus, St. Gabriel was incorporated as a parish in 1953, the centennial year of the Archdiocese of Newark. The name St. Gabriel the Archangel is unique in the Archdiocese. Bright and inviting and built in the colonial style, the church building is considered one of the most beautiful in New Jersey. For the most part professionally successful and living in the comfort of northern Bergen County, St. Gabriel's parishioners demonstrate a remarkable generosity to those in need. The parish sponsors multiple projects for the poor, both in the Archdiocese and in the foreign and home missions.

Immaculate Conception, Secaucus

Immaculate Conception Church was established as a Catholic Mission on May 10, 1908. The first church was completed on March 7, 1909 with Fr. Charles F. Marshall as its first Pastor. As the parish grew, a new church and school were constructed and completed in August 1949 during the pastorate of Msgr. Patrick Reilly. A new school building was erected and opened in September 1961. Fr. Jeremiah Long died in October 1996, ending a 20-year pastorate in which he initiated and witnessed many changes in the parish. He was succeeded by Msgr. Donald E. Guenther who launched a major renovation of the church in 1998 and the following year, modernized the rectory. Today the parish consists of 2500 families of

diverse cultural backgrounds. The school continues to thrive with more than 220 students. Under the leadership of Msgr. Guenther, improvements continued to be made to parish ministries, including the introduction of stewardship as a way of life. A variety of religious services and social activities keep parish life at Immaculate Conception thriving.

Our Lady of Mount Carmel, Tenafly

In 1873 a group of Irish immigrant construction workers organized to form Our Lady of Mount Carmel, Tenafly, celebrating liturgies in a humble wooden chapel. In 1878 the Bishop entrusted the parish to the Carmelite Fathers of Englewood who have served ever since.

In 1879 Mount Carmel school opened with 30 students taught by the Sisters of Charity who stayed for 99 years, leaving in 1978. Newly arrived Italian families joined the original Irish Catholics in the 1890s. The little wooden church was moved from an obscure side street to its present prominent site.

In the 1920s the Catholic presence in Tenafly greatly increased. The Society of African Missions bought an estate in Tenafly and began the first interracial seminary in the States. Over the years, the Mission House has become a headquarters for the SMA Fathers who have added a profound depth to the character and spirituality of Mount Carmel Parish. Camp Merritt operated within the parish boundaries between 1917 and 1928, Mount Carmel boasted the largest Catholic congregation in the United States.

In the Fifties, the East Hill of the borough

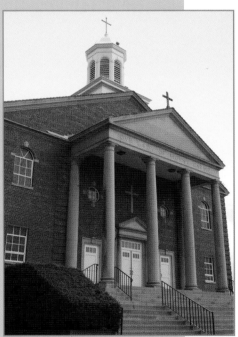

was developed with large and beautiful houses, bringing Catholic professionals from New York, Union and Jersey City. The current church and school were built, followed in the next decade by the rectory, convent and new school wing. Changes were made in the church interior to accord with directives of Vatican Council II. In 1977 the Franciscan Sisters replaced the Charity Sisters, supplemented by the School Sisters of Notre Dame and the Sisters of St. Joseph who took on various ministries. Today a lay principal heads the school.

Mount Carmel presently has 1400 registered families of varied backgrounds and cultures. It is an active and progressive parish involved in many ministries.

St. Anastasia, Teaneck

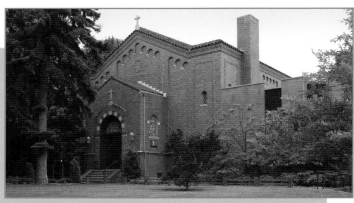

St. Anastasia Church, Teaneck, is a parish of 1600 families. The magnificent diversity of God's people is manifest in every aspect of the worshiping community. The Filipino American Society of Teaneck and the Black Catholics Committee of Bergen County are integral parts of parish life. St. Anastasia is a founding member of the Lutheran Anglican Roman Catholic Covenant in Teaneck. It is also an active participant in the interfaith activities of the community and has sustained a ministry to the Bowery every Saturday for more than 23 years. The parish has been staffed from its beginning by the Carmelites of the province of the Most Pure Heart of Mary. The Sisters of St. Joseph of Chestnut Hill also reside in the parish and serve as religious education directors. St. Anastasia is a co-sponsor of St. Cecilia's Interparochial School in Englewood.

Church of the Presentation, Upper Saddle River

The spiritual charism of Presentation Parish lies in the commitment of its parishioners to share their gifts and talents, both within the parish and in the world. More than 55 ministries engage the time, talent and treasures of hundreds of active parishioners. The parish has 4400 registered households.

The parish is structured around the cate-chumenal model, that is, ministries supporting the five different movements within the conversion process.

Evangelization ministries include the RCIA, Re-Membering Church, outreach to divorced and separated, the widowed and the Elizabeth ministry. Welcoming dinners for new parishioners are held twice yearly. Funerals provide liturgy-planning assistance, a post-service meal and a comforting bereavement series. The 12-page weekly parish Bulletin and a magazine published twice a year help spread the invitation.

Catechetical ministries include educational support for the more than 100 Religious Education catechists who each share community and learning with a small group of children. Adult parishioners learn through the Christian Foundations for Ministry courses and special training for Small Christian Community facilitators and other parish leaders.

Through the Worship Ministries, many parishioners join a particular Mass team and minister through hospitality, serving as lectors and Eucharistic ministers, choir and catechists. Teams lovingly prepare families for Baptism, couples for Marriage and parishioners for First Communion and Penance.

Spiritual Renewal is facilitated by many who work within the retreat ministries: Cornerstone and the follow-up Journey retreat for adults, several youth retreats, numerous days of reflection and ongoing monthly meetings of more than 80 Small Christian Communities.

Ministry Development provides opportunities for service, including weekly food preparation and delivery to inner-city soup kitchens, parishioners traveling annually to parish-sponsored missions in Haiti and Mexico, weekly educational supports to inner city schools and many others.

Most Sacred Heart of Jesus, Wallington

In June 1942 a handful of families gathered in a borrowed room and celebrated the first Mass of a new parish in Wallington. Sixty years later, the parish is a faith-filled community of more than 2000 families. The church's community traditions are based largely on the Polish heritage of the parish founders. Its liturgies and services have a rich ethnic flavor, from Wigilia and Koleda during Christmas, to the singing of Gorzkie Zale during Lent. Most Sacred Heart is known for its many outdoor processions-- true public manifestations of the deep faith of the community. It is no accident that the geographic outline of the parish is in the shape of a heart. The parish family strives to live the Gospel in everything. With many third and fourth generation members, the Church is blessed to be able to work hard, play hard and, most importantly, pray hard-- together--as the parish family of Most Sacred heart of Jesus.

Our Lady of Good Counsel, Washington Township

Our Lady of Good Counsel Parish was incorporated on July 29, 1959. Fr. Eugene F. X. Sullivan immediately began the care of the 450 Catholic families of Washington Township. The Diocese had purchased a six-acre tract on Ridgewood Road, where an old farm house and a broken down dairy barn existed. The shell of this dairy barn served as inspiration to Fr. Sullivan, who felt that the parishioners could lend their skills to the rebuilding of the structure into their own church. While a larger worship space, called the Marian Center, has been beautifully arranged from the all-purpose room of the CCD Center, the original church is still used for daily Mass, weddings, funerals and some weekend liturgies. Although the congregation now numbers 1400 families, the spirit of the original builders continues to live on and one of the most common remarks to be heard when someone dies is, "My father built this church."

St. Andrew, Westwood

From its humble beginnings as a mission church dedicated on June 17, 1888, St. Andrew Church, Westwood, has grown to serve more than 1600 families in Westwood, River Vale and other towns. The present church was dedicated in 1964 and renovated in 1988.

The Parish and Education Center, the site of the former St. Andrew School building, which was gutted by fire in 1998, serves as a meeting place for the many ministries that make up the vibrant church community. It also houses a religious education program for more than 600 students and a Youth Ministry program serving 200 teens. Summer Scene, a Vacation Bible School program, is open to young parishioners from 3 to 10 years old. A parish-based Scripture program is offered in the spring and fall. Parish children in grades 3 to 8 participate in basketball and cheerleading programs. Senior citizens are kept busy with recreational dance lessons and participate in an outreach entertainment program for local community groups. The ongoing activities of the Human Concerns Committee span a variety of efforts such as a Food Pantry and a clothing collection to help local people in need, as well as nationally and overseas. An annual holiday Giving Tree allows parishioners to donate gifts to the needy. There is a small, but growing, ministry to the Hispanic community in the area, which includes parishioner-taught ESL classes.

Our Lady Mother of the Church, Woodcliff Lake

Our Lady Mother of the Church began 25 years after the start of World War II. From its very birth, OLMC was faced with the challenge of facing a new world of suburbs and commuters and families who live far from parents and work far from home. The parish was no longer the center of life for its people. Then Vatican Council II seemed to create a "new Church," which opened the door to new roles for the laity.

It was during these times that the parish was formally incorporated in 1968. In the mid-'80s, the church grounds were beautified by the planting of stately Bradford Pear trees and a Biblical Garden. Plans for a new church included a semicircular arrangement of seats to focus on the people as church and the inclusion of only one statue--that of Mary, to center on Christ. The first permanent deacon was ordained in 1988 and participation of the laity in church decisions and ministries such as liturgical planning, parish prayer gatherings, pastoral councils and finance committees, social action, prison visitation and music increased. OLMC enters the Third Millennium a vibrant and growing parish.

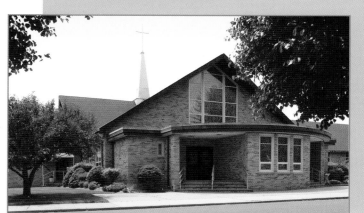

Assumption of Our Blessed Lady, Wood-Ridge

The Church of the Assumption of Our Blessed Lady, Wood Ridge, was founded in 1926 at Main Avenue and 1st Street by the Franciscans of the Holy Name Province. At present more than 2000 families are served by three Friars and a deacon. The parish school, accredited by Middle States, offers Catholic education from Pre-K-3, Pre-K-4, Kindergarten through Grade 8. In 2001 the Assumption marked its 75th anniversary with yearlong celebrations. The parish is deeply rooted in its Franciscan heritage and at the same time committed and proud to serve in the Archdiocese of Newark. Stewardship as a way of life has been embraced as a goal to continue the parish tradition of success.

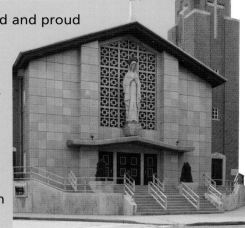

St. Elizabeth, Wyckoff

In November 2002, Saint Elizabeth of Hungary celebrated 100 years of pastoral service to the community of Wyckoff and surrounding areas. Saint Elizabeth was carved out of Mount Carmel Parish, Ridgewood, to serve a small Catholic community living among farmers with a Dutch Reformed background. The early Catholics included former Paterson residents and Irish Catholic servants who worked in area resorts of Franklin Lakes, Oakland and Midland Park. In 1903 the first church was built. The Franciscan Friars of Holy Name Province took over the pastoral care of the parish in 1909. Thus began the long connection between the Friars and the parish.

After the 1950s vast development took place throughout Bergen County. While the territory served by Saint Elizabeth continued to shrink because of the establishment of three adjacent parishes, the Catholic population of Wyckoff increased rapidly. Beginning in 1954, a massive building project was launched and a church/auditorium and a school facility were built with the Sisters of Saint Joseph of Peace staffing the new school. Some years later the building and the property of the first church were sold and the 1903 building was demolished.

In 1982 Holy Name Province of the Franciscan Friars made the decision that they could no longer staff the parish. Archbishop Gerety then assigned three priests of the Archdiocese to continue the pastoral service provided so faithfully by the Franciscans since 1909. The ongoing development of the area once again raised the question of expansion as the parish had increased in membership to 1900 families. In 1991, ground was broken in 1991 for the third building to serve as the church, as well as extra classrooms and parish meeting rooms. With the opening of the new church in September 1992, the 1954 church became the Parish Hall. The parish of 2003 has 2800 families registered, a parish school enrollment of 300 children, and an additional 1200 children who attend public school and who are enrolled in Religious Education offered by the parish. In addition, during the past ten years, through a retreat program for adults, over 900 men and women have experienced this opportunity for growth in community and have been brought closer to their faith. The parish in 1986 formed a "sister parish" relationship with Sacred Heart Parish, Jersey City, and since that time parishioners of Saint Elizabeth have assisted this inner city parish in their Saint Martin's Soup Kitchen, and in providing volunteers for school projects and financial aid for the further educational development of Sacred Heart School. All the prospects for the second century in the life of Saint Elizabeth Parish are bright and filled with new opportunities for ministry and service to and for the People of God.

Two Worlds

THOMAS WALSH, THE FIRST ARCHBISHOP OF NEWARK, WAS, ABOVE ALL,
A DOER. HE WAS KNOWN FOR HIS DRIVE, HIS OUTSPOKENNESS, AND HIS
DIRECTNESS IN SERVING THE PEOPLE OF THE ARCHDIOCESE OF NEWARK.
THOMAS BOLAND, THE SECOND ARCHBISHOP OF NEWARK, HAD A VERY
DIFFERENT SORT OF PERSONALITY. HE WAS A THINKER; A KIND, CALM,
QUIET SCHOLAR, WITH LUMINOUS BLUE EYES MAGNIFIED BY HIS SUBSTANTIAL
EYEGLASSES THAT BELIED A VAST PERSONAL CAPACITY FOR HARD WORK.

He would shepherd the people of the
Archdiocese through years of increase in the
1950's and early 60's, when Catholic identity
and self-understanding were reliably and
dependably solid and into the years of the late
1960's and early 1970's, when the Church and
the nation, seemed to face a brand-new world.

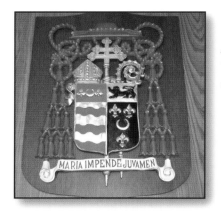

*Archbishop
Thomas A. Boland's
coat of arms*

Thomas Boland

Thomas Aloysius Boland was
born in the Archdiocese of
Newark, in the town of Orange
on February 17, 1896. His father,
John Peter Boland, was a
contractor in the town, while his
mother took care of Thomas, his
two brothers and his three sisters.
He went to public grammar
school, followed by studying
briefly with the Christian Brothers
at St. John's. When he completed
grammar school, being the eldest
son, he went to work (at the age
of 13) to help support his family,
starting out as a mill worker and
then a clerk in the town's power
house, while taking classes at
night to try to continue his
schooling. In the midst of his
work and study, the teenager felt
the call to the priesthood, and was

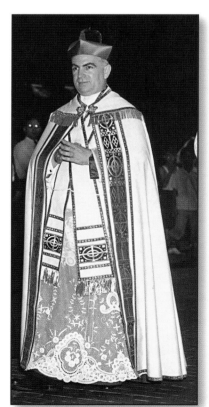

*Ordination of
Thomas A. Boland
as Auxiliary Bishop, 1940*

encouraged by one of his parish
priests, Fr. Nicholas Marnell.
After several years of working,
Boland was able to begin high
school, attending St. Francis
Xavier High School, a military
academy in New York.
Impressed by his Jesuit
instructors, Boland nevertheless
decided to pursue the diocesan
priesthood and entered Seton
Hall College, while continuing
to work part-time in Orange
to support his family until
residency requirements for

philosophy students at the College finally compelled him to stop.

His tireless capacity for work made a strong impression on Msgr. James Mooney, the president of the College. Mooney recommended in 1919 to Bishop O'Connor that the young man be sent to study at the North American College in Rome, which was reopening its doors following the end of the First World War. While happenings in the city of Rome over the next several years were tumultuous – Benito Mussolini took control of the city and the nation only two months before his priestly ordination – Boland applied himself to his studies, and earned successively a bachelor's, master's, and then licentiate in theology.

Returning to the United States, he spent the summer at St. Catherine's Church in Hillside, and then went on to Seton Hall, where he began teaching at Seton Hall Prep. Latin, Greek, English, history, religion, algebra: Fr. Boland was willing and able to teach wherever he was needed. After three years at the Prep, he went on to teach at the College and seminary, where he would prove to be popular with both clerical and lay students as a very gifted professor. Even

Rome's architecture and statuary near where priests from all over the world study for the priesthood

after the seminary moved from its South Orange home to Mahwah, Boland continued teaching at both institutions, as well as lecturing to religious and doing weekend duty at the parish of St. Mary's in Nutley. Boland's capability to handle many different assignments at once was used to full advantage by Bishop Walsh.

Archbishop Boland laying the cornerstone of Bergen Catholic High School at a time when Catholic schools were flourishing

Arriving in the diocese in 1928, he sought to expand the ministries of the diocese, and again and again the Bishop asked Fr. Boland to help organize and put the diocesan house in order. Not one to say no, Fr. Boland rapidly found himself simultaneously a seminary professor, university professor, spiritual director, member of the commissions for parish and convent visitation, diocesan consultor, vice-officialis, parish administrator, synod examiner, clerical examiner, moderator of the Guild of Catholic Doctors, moderator of the Catholic Forum, vistator general for the religious, moderator of diocesan conferences, chairman of the sites and building commission, diocesan director of the "National Organization for Decent Literature and Moving Pictures," while also assisting as a theological consultant with the revision of the Baltimore Catechism.

First annual priests retreat, 1939

The number and wide-ranging character of all these assignments highlight precisely how much Bishop and then Archbishop Walsh relied on the talents of Fr. Boland. Rather than request that the priest be made a monsignor, Archbishop Walsh took the opportunity presented in 1940 by the transfer of his auxiliary bishop, William Griffin, to the Diocese of Trenton, to have Boland named as his new auxiliary bishop.

Bishop Boland

So it was that Thomas Aloysius Boland was consecrated a bishop on July 25, 1940 by Archbishop Walsh. On the same day, he was named Rector of the seminary. The new bishop found that his duties simply increased. In addition to the numerous offices that he already held, Walsh asked Boland to help plan the first Archdiocesan

Synod, a gathering of priests to revise and reformulate rules for priestly life and conduct in the Archdiocese, last done under Bishop Wigger. Ill health on the part of Bishop Griffin of Trenton and Bishop McLaughlin of Paterson also pressed Boland into service in administering the Sacrament of Confirmation around the state. Indeed, the death of Bishop McLaughlin in 1947 led to the naming of Bishop Boland as the Ordinary of that diocese.

While Bishop Boland may have been a new name and face to the lay faithful of Paterson, he was well-remembered and welcomed by the clergy of the diocese, most of whom had had Boland as their instructor during their seminary formation. While Boland was the ordinary of Paterson for only a relatively brief period of time – five years – he was able fruitfully to apply his great administrative

Archbishop Boland at St. Joseph, Maplewood

experience to his new flock. The Diocese of Paterson, like the rest of New Jersey, and the country, was experiencing an extraordinary postwar growth in population. In the five short years of Boland's tenure, the Catholic population of the diocese would grow by almost a quarter, while the

Archbishop Boland's vestments made of Chinese silk

Archbishop Boland's miter

Sr. Mary Joseph Concepta, Lab Supervisor at St. Mary Hospital, Orange, 1954. Through the Sister Formation Movement, sisters of the mid-century joined the ranks of the most well educated women in the nation.

number of infant baptisms grew by 165 percent. What was in later years to be called the "Baby Boom" had begun. Church vocations and institutions also grew rapidly. The Bishop of Paterson, on average, opened one new parish, two new schools, and two new convents in each of his years of service. Bishop Boland was unable to remain long in his new diocese however. The death of Archbishop Walsh in June of 1952 was soon followed by an announcement that Thomas Boland would be returning to his home diocese as archbishop.

Catholic schools continued to burst their seams in the '50s. Holy Family, Nutley

Our Lady of the Assumption, Bayonne

Our Lady of the Assumption Parish was founded in 1902 when a small group of Italian immigrants petitioned the Bishop of Newark to establish a parish where they could celebrate Mass in their native language. With Fr. Michael Mercolino's arrival began the life of the parish.

In the 100 years since its founding, Our Lady of the Assumption has gone through various transitions. The present church building was erected in 1976, after the church that had served the parish for 65 years was demolished to accommodate growth. The school was opened in 1939, when the Filippini Sisters arrived to teach, and closed in 1998 because of declining enrollment. The Filippini sisters left the parish in 2002 as a result of new transitions in the parish.

The Hispanic community was welcomed in 1962 by the pastor, Fr. Dominic Del Monte. Because the number of Spanish-speaking residents in Bayonne has grown to 15 percent of the population of 60,000, an outreach program to the new immigrants has been initiated, including a bilingual Director of Religious Education. Liturgy each weekend is celebrated in English, Italian and Spanish and all major parish celebrations are trilingual. Our Lady of the Assumption is the only trilingual parish in Bayonne, serving the needs of the Italian-, English- and Spanish-speaking residents. Having just concluded its centennial year, parishioners look forward to continued growth and service to the people of Bayonne, Hudson County and the Archdiocese of Newark.

Catholics in Majority

The intimate knowledge of the Archdiocese which Boland had gained through the many responsibilities and years he had worked in Newark gave the new Archbishop a clear picture of the strengths and challenges with which the Catholic people of northern New Jersey were faced in 1952 and beyond. No longer a tolerated minority, Catholic New Jerseyans now found themselves the largest religious body in the state. No longer were priests taking care of multiple churches Virtually all pastors had at least one assistant, while many rectories had three, four or five priests. Indeed, beyond the parishes 150 priests were dedicated to fulltime teaching or chaplaincy. No longer did Catholic school children receive mixed messages about their faith as in the public schools of a bygone era. Rather, fifty Catholic high schools and more than 200 Catholic grammar schools were staffed by almost 3,500 dedicated and generous religious women and men. [Indeed, the Archbishop would undertake a tremendous commitment of resources for education in planning to build 13 new regional high schools

Archbishop Boland at the dedication of St. Joseph Convent, Maplewood, 1955.

HUDSON COUNTY

Our Lady of Mount Carmel, Bayonne

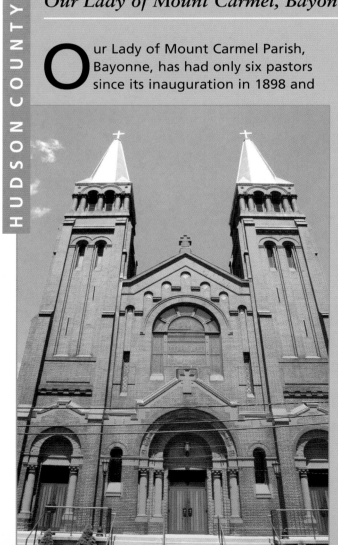

Our Lady of Mount Carmel Parish, Bayonne, has had only six pastors since its inauguration in 1898 and dedication on Christmas 1899. Two years later, when the demand for larger quarters for the growing parish continued, Msgr. Swider built the second brick church and the first rectory. With the completion of the second church in 1903, the original wooden structure was converted to a parish school. Finally in 1910, the present church was erected and the second church became the second school with the Felician Sisters making their quarters there. Bishop John J. O'Connor, Bishop of Newark, dedicated the third building October 16, 1917. A complete restoration took place in 1958.

In subsequent years, a parking lot, a parish center and a garage were added. After 1983, the school was reconstructed to accommodate safety regulations. In the late 1990s, under Fr. Anthony J. Kulig, the church was repaired for the parish centennial in 1998, and in 2000, Our Lady of Mount Carmel was named a pilgrimage parish of the jubilee year.

St. Andrew, Bayonne

In 1891 St. Henry was built for the growing Irish Catholic population in uptown Bayonne. By 1913, when the cornerstone of St. Andrew Chapel and school was laid, more than 10,000 parishioners attended, most of them working in the burgeoning oil industries of "Corktown." The parish was established the following year. The school opened a year later. Nine years hence, a new church was dedicated and in 1932, a new convent was in place. In 1950 properties adjacent to the convent were bought for a new school, dedicated in 1955.

The Sixties saw St. Andrew youth gather to pray for the success of Vatican Council II and lay Eucharistic ministers participated in a mandating ceremony. The Diamond Jubilee of the parish was celebrated in 1988.

for the Archdiocese.] The Confraternity of Christian Doctrine ensured that those children who were unable to attend Catholic school knew their catechism well.

Fr. Bernard stands by proudly as Archbishop Boland dedicates the new convent at St. Joseph.

Catholic higher education blossomed in the mid-1950s. The Dominican Sisters erected and operated Caldwell College for Women.

Catholic Higher Education

Seton Hall University, the College of St. Elizabeth, Caldwell College, and St. Peter's College all provided opportunities for Catholic higher education. Sacred Heart Cathedral, a symbol for the whole Archdiocese, was finally

St. Henry, Bayonne

St. Henry Church, Bayonne, has served the Roman Catholic faithful of the area for more than 100 years. At the beginning of the 21st Century, the future growth of the St. Henry faith family is well assured because of the strong spiritual leadership of its clergy and its partnership with the many talents of its parishioners who make a difference in the lives of young and old in the Bayonne community.

St. Henry was established in 1889 with 50 families of Bavarian descent. The parish currently serves 1800

families. The church, of modified English Gothic design, began construction in 1912 and was completed in 1915. In keeping with Vatican II, St. Henry has made the necessary interior renovations, while the ornate exterior of the nearly 100-year old structure has been meticulously repaired and restored in recent years.

St. Henry's Religious Education Program is acknowledged as one of the best in the city and boasts a larger enrollment than any other Bayonne religious program with more than 425 students. The program also serves high school students through its Youth Ministry.

Through a large variety of parish ministries touching all ages, interests and talents, St. Henry continues to meet the many spiritual, emotional and social needs of its faith family and warmly welcomes new parishioners with a friendly and loving invitation each day.

completed. Young men and women filled the seminaries and novitiates of the Archdiocese and religious orders. Catholic hospitals took care of the Catholic sick. Catholic orphanages, homes for the elderly, residences for the blind, and the Mount Carmel Guild gave witness to Catholic charity. Catholic magazines, Catholic book clubs, Catholic television shows filled Catholic homes. Catholic fraternal organizations such as the Knights of Columbus, the National Councils of Catholic Women and Men, Rosary Confraternities, and the Holy Name Society joined dozens of parochial groups to provide a complete Catholic social system for many of the faithful.

For all of the graces which the Catholic people of the Archdiocese of Newark enjoyed in the 1950's, there were also some significant areas which needed care and attention. Previous immigrant communities in the Archdiocese had usually brought their own clergy with them as they arrived in New Jersey. The growing number of Hispanic Catholics in the Archdiocese often did not have this advantage. Likewise thousands of African-Americans had come north during and after World War II. Their presence and pastoral care presented a significant challenge to a Church hitherto of overwhelmingly European heritage. New ethnic groups, new ways of thinking, and new ways of life had to be grappled with. "How most effectively to engage the modern world, so different from past ages, with the message of the Gospel?" This was a question that, not just the Archdiocese of Newark, but the universal Church was asking at the conclusion of the 1950's. The answer, the inspiration of Blessed Pope John XXIII, was for an ecumenical Council to be held at the Vatican – not solemnly to define dogma or to address threats to the Faith – but for the Church to take stock of herself and the modern world and to try to formulate ways to speak the truth of the Faith so that contemporary men and women might hear and respond.

St. Elizabeth Hospital dedicates its new polio unit in 1947, run by the Sisters of Charity.

Religious vocations flourished in the middle of the century.

The Knights of Columbus, generous contributors of time, talent and monetary contribution, also added color, style and dignity to religious celebrations.

St. Joseph, Bayonne

Founded in 1888, St. Joseph Parish, Bayonne, is the oldest Slovak Roman Catholic parish in New Jersey.

When Slovaks began to settle in the Constable Hook section of Bayonne during the 1880s, permission was given to establish a church for the new Slovak immigrants. By 1906 the parish had grown to more than 500 families. A new and larger church was erected.

In 1906 St. Joseph Parochial School opened under the direction of the Dominican Sisters of Newburgh, New York, and 15 years later, a new school, auditorium and rectory were built. In 1973, after 64 years of service, the Dominicans were replaced by the Sisters of SS. Cyril and Methodius of Danville, Pennsylvania. The school closed in 1991.

The parish continues to flourish with its strong societies that contribute to the vibrancy of its life. The parish also participates in the citywide Highways Food Pantry. St. Joseph continues to be the home of several Slovak-American religious, cultural and fraternal organizations.

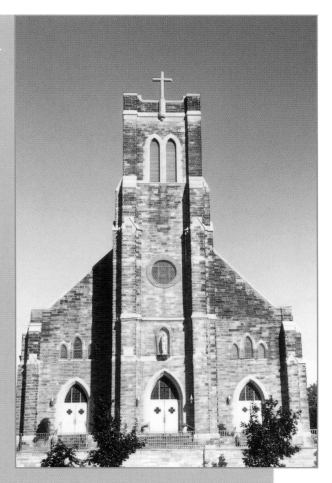

Women's societies contributed in many ways to the growth and vibrancy of their parishes.

Priestly vocations at the century's midpoint were numerous.

Vatican Council II

To this worldwide gathering of bishops went Archbishop Thomas Boland as well as the auxiliary bishops of Newark, Martin Stanton, John Dougherty, and Joseph Costello. The Archbishop would miss none of the sessions of the Council, which were held from 1962 – 1965. Indeed, he couldn't. Archbishop Boland was unanimously elected by the American bishops to head the Bishops' Study Committee, which was responsible for both summarizing and synthesizing the daily work of the Council, as well as translating this work, which was done in Latin, for those American bishops who found themselves out of practice in the ancient language of the Church. With his usual quiet efficiency, Archbishop Boland set about the tasks

St. Mary, Star of the Sea, Bayonne

With a proud history of 141 years as the Mother Church of Bayonne, St. Mary, Star of the Sea has served the Bayonne community since 1861. The small, humble church, located on Evergreen Street, was founded to serve the spiritual needs of Irish and German Catholic immigrants. The corner-stone of the beautiful Gothic church, brought from St. Clement in Rome, was laid on May 22, 1880. The church was blessed on November 8, 1881.

St. Mary has enjoyed the continuous presence of the Sisters of St. Joseph of Chestnut Hill since 1879,

when the parish school was opened. The school continues to thrive with a student body of more than 280 and a rich heritage of academic excellence, enriching the lives of the youngsters from pre-school through grade 8.

St. Mary has a long history of deep spiritually, great generosity and a warm welcoming atmosphere. Many vocations to the priesthood and religious life have been nourished by its parish life. This great church—a parish, a people and a tradition—stands ready, firm and eager to carry out the mission of Christ into the third millennium.

of the Council as well as providing for the pastoral care of the Archdiocese of Newark while he was in Rome, entrusting much of the day-to-day running of the Archdiocese to Msgr. James Hughes, V.G., the pastor of St. Aloysius Church in Jersey City.

The Council, from the time of its announcement, had engendered significant interest on the part of the Catholics of the Archdiocese of Newark. Prayers to the Holy Spirit for the success of the Council became a part of daily parish life. Newspaper reports kept the faithful and clergy apprised of the Council's progress, while the Archbishop himself, home for months between sessions, endeavored to translate the Council, not from just from Latin to English, but from Roman documents to New Jersey practices. This undertaking would be formidable.

Impact of the Council

While the achievements of the Second Vatican Council are many and varied, the impact of the Council on the Catholics of the Archdiocese was felt in two main areas. The first and chief place was in the liturgy. The Tridentine, or Latin, Mass was translated into English while the church altars were turned around so that priest and people faced each other. That part of a Catholic's personal relationship with God which was nourished by communal worship was deeply touched by these changes. Indeed, each of the Sacraments was revised, often changing parish life dramatically. A whole new style of architecture and vesture, a whole new hymnody, a whole new sense of understanding the Church were created.

The second area of transformation took place among the priests and religious of the Archdiocese. The theological training which they had received, for so long clear and supremely self-assured, was now fragmented as Immaculate Conception Seminary and the novitiates of the Archdiocese attempted to sift the genuine reforms of the Council from other, more speculative, ideas. Pastors and religious superiors, accustomed to deference, found many new ideas among the younger generation. Religious communities took the opportunity to change the habits, or distinctive garb, which they wore and to rethink the apostolates in which they were engaged. In some cases, there were Catholics in the Archdiocese – priests, religious, and lay – who thought that the Church did not go far enough with the reforms of the Second Vatican Council – too little seemed to have been accomplished. On the other hand, some Catholics thought that perhaps the Church went too far, or too fast, in

One of the innovations of Vatican Council II was to bring the people closer to the altar table. the circular seating arrangement adopted in many churches focused on the Church's new emphasis on the people as the Church.

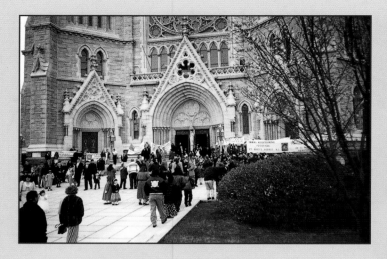

Since Vatican II, renewal of emphasis on Scripture initiated the rite of carrying the Gospel book in procession with candles and incense to show its dignity and value as the Word of God.

In the revival of the Rite of Christian Initiation of Adults, new catechumens from all the parishes of the Archdiocese join at the Cathedral in a ceremony of commitment and strengthening of resolve on their journey toward Baptism.

Many musical instruments were added to the traditional organ for liturgies after the Council.

Girls are admitted to the role of acolyte.

Since the 1950s, candlelight is used to symbolize Resurrection in the Easter Vigil service.

Laity now proclaim the Word from the sanctuary.

implementing the reforms of the Council, for it seemed that everything Catholic had become "up for grabs."

The atmosphere of change and uncertainty grew as a number of priests and religious chose to give up the active ministry. The long lines for the confessional, a common experience of parishes

in the 1940's and 1950's, evaporated. Mass schedules in parishes were scaled back as a number of Catholics gave up the practice of their faith. The daunting task laid before Archbishop Boland in the years

The traditional habit covered a sister from head to foot.

following Vatican II was to authentically and fully implement the directives of the Council without seeming to overwhelm the faith life and history of Catholics in the Archdiocese of Newark, to form a bridge between the two worlds of the pre- and post-Conciliar Church.

After Vatican II, habits were modified to accord more with modern culture and good health, leaving the laity to understand that all are called to holiness.

The sisters continued to minister wherever the need arose.

St. Michael, Bayonne

In December 1898, Lithuanian Catholics in Bayonne organized the Society of SS. Peter and Paul to share their language, customs and traditions. After several years of travel to other cities to worship, parishioners were joyful in 1907 that the Parish of St. Michael the Archangel Lithuanian Church was incorporated with Masses celebrated in the Italian parish of Our Lady of the Assumption.

In 1908 a property and church building were purchased and the people had their own church. Over the years the Parish flourished and in 1941 the Perpetual Novena in honor of the Miraculous Medal was begun. It continues to be a vital part of parish life.

In 1974 a new rectory was completed, and in 1977 a new church, on the site of the original church, and later, a new parish hall. At present the parish has 550 families and an average Sunday Mass attendance of 700. The parish is popular with people from all over Bayonne for novena services and adoration of the Eucharist. Its location near the shopping center of Bayonne makes the church popular for mid-day drop-in visits. The parish looks forward to continuing the sharing of the life and love of God.

St. Vincent de Paul, Bayonne

St. Vincent De Paul Parish was established more than 100 years ago and has stood as a beacon and tower of hope for all, especially immigrants from Europe. Established in 1894, its cornerstone was laid in 1905. After years of construction on the church, the first Mass was celebrated on the new altar of Algerian golden onyx. The church, of Romanesque style, has three main entrances and its tower, 44 feet high, is visible from afar.

Currently the church is undergoing major repairs and renovations. As in days past, St. Vincent De Paul Church is still today a place of beauty, peace, love and welcome.

St. Anthony, East Newark

On April 7, 1901 Bishop O'Connor established St. Anthony Parish in a vacant store on Third Street in Harrison for the Italian-speaking people of the area. Subsequently, the first pastor, Fr. Catalano, purchased a small Protestant church on Second Street in East Newark, which was converted and dedicated on June 24, 1901. In 1908 St. Anthony Rosary and Holy Name Societies were formed and are still active today.

Fr. John J. Rongetti's appointment as pastor in 1915 brought growth. Major renovations to the church and rectory were carried out. On January 20, 1935, a devastating fire destroyed the church and adjacent rectory. Worship services were held at Our Lady of Sorrows in Harrison and subsequently in the Clark Thread Mill's auditorium. The first Mass in the newly constructed church was offered on June 13, 1936.

Fr. Rongetti served as pastor for 31 years until 1947, when Fr. David J. Casazza became administrator, working hard for the spiritual well being of the parish. During his administration, the mortgage on the church was repaid. After serving as assistant for eight years, Fr. Michael Calabrese, appointed administrator in 1950, opened the parish school. The present pastor since 1976, Fr. Anthony F. Granato, renovated the church after its 75th anniversary. He also formed the Parish Council and expanded the Religious Education program.

St. John Nepomucene, Guttenberg

St. John Nepomucene Church was established on November 13, 1910 at a general meeting held with Fr. J. R. Vrana in its newly acquired church. Diocesan approval came about because of the determination of the area's Slovak people to have their own parish. Fr. Vrana was succeeded by Fr. William Biskorovenyi, the first permanent pastor. Fr. William A. Hornak was appointed second pastor in 1952. With the permission of Archbishop Thomas A Boland, he built the present parish school in 1955 on Polk and 72nd Streets, North Bergen. Assistant Fr. Thomas W. Onacilla became the pastor when Fr. Hornak died in 1971. Frs. John F. Renard and Eugene P. Heyndricks served as pastors until 2002 when Fr. Richard D. Carlson was appointed administrator. Originally formed for the Slovak Catholics of Guttenberg and vicinity, today the parish is composed of people of many nationalities.

Holy Cross, Harrison

Fr. Bernard J. McQuaid built St. Pius, the first church in Harrison. It was located on the corner of Jersey and Third Streets. Between 1873 to 1886, priests from St. Patrick Cathedral served the church and the Sisters of Charity taught in the school.

The first resident pastor, Rev. James J. McGahan, purchased lots on Harrison Avenue and Jersey Street, allowing Fr. Maurice P. O'Connor to lay a new foundation for the church, now known as the Church of the Holy Cross. On August 15, 1886, the cornerstone was placed and the church was dedicated on February 16, 1890.

Fr. George L. Fitzpatrick built a new school for the parish in 1915. Fr. William A. Costelloe had a new convent constructed in 1948. Msgr. Harold Fitzpatrick (1964-1972), and Frs. Edwin Paulmenn (1972-1981) and Msgr. Hugh O'Donnell (1981-1993) preceded Msgr. John Gilchrist, the current pastor.

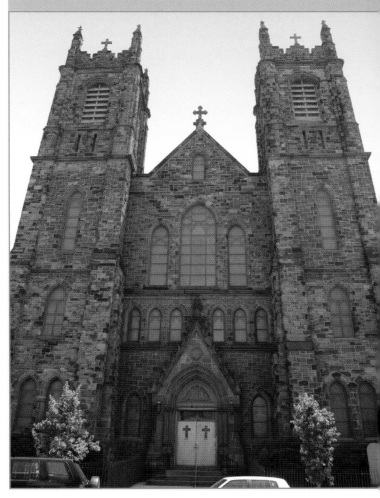

Our Lady of Czestochowa, Harrison

Our Lady of Czestochowa Parish was incorporated in Harrison on August 6, 1908, and the first Mass celebrated on August 21 in the Parish Hall of Holy Cross. Sunday Masses were held there until permission was obtained to erect a church on the corner of Cleveland Avenue and Second Street.

A small frame building was erected and the first Mass celebrated on January 1, 1910. The new church was dedicated on January 30 of the same year. A new school was also opened.

In 1916 the parish purchased the old St. Pius School on Third and Jersey Streets. The building was remodeled for use as a church and school, but on December 26, 1927, a suspicious fire destroyed the complex. Permission was granted in May 1928 to build a new church and school.

The new church and school were blessed and dedicated on May 26, 1928. Nowadays, the parish continues to serve the Polish American community and follow time honored polish traditions such as May devotion, Corpus Christi procession, Lenten devotion, and Blessing of Homes and Food. Recently the Divine Mercy Novena has been instituted.

Our Lady of Grace, Hoboken

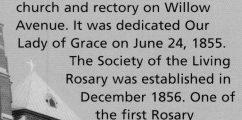

Founded in 1851, Our Lady of Grace is one of the oldest Catholic parishes in the United States. Although Hoboken had its first pastor in 1844, a small frame church, Our Lady of Mercy, in West Hoboken (later Union City) wasn't built until 1851. When it was completed, Fr. Cauvin moved to Hoboken to begin building a brick church and rectory on Willow Avenue. It was dedicated Our Lady of Grace on June 24, 1855.

The Society of the Living Rosary was established in December 1856. One of the first Rosary Societies in the country, it is still active. A small, select school operated with one teacher from 1859 until 1964. In 1864, when Our Lady of Grace was incorporated, the first Catholic Public School in Hoboken opened under the Sisters of Charity of Madison.

In August 1865, the Sisters of Charity started to build a hospital and asylum. St. Mary Hospital was blessed on May 6, 1866. By 1873 the parish owned the entire block along Church Square Park. After completion of the church and chapel came a new convent in 1915 for 30 Sisters of Charity running the school. In 1941 the interior of the church was renovated and in 1958 the school experienced a complete interior renovation. In 1968 the church interior was repainted. In 1994 the church in its present form began to take shape. After restoration, it was placed on the New Jersey List of Historic Places in 1996.

In 1998 the interior and exterior renovation of the church led to rededication on December 7, 1998. The following year the parish school merged with other Catholic schools in Hoboken to form Hoboken Catholic Academy, and Our Lady of Grace marched into the new millennium at its 150th Anniversary Mass on October 7, 2001.

Social Changes

At the same time as the impact of the Second Vatican Council began to be felt in the Church of the United States, the nation was also undergoing profound social changes. The civil rights movement, the women's rights movement, the debate over the conflict in Vietnam all touched the Catholics of the Archdiocese deeply. In the summer of 1967, riots swept through many American cities, including the city of Newark. Archbishop Boland visited the riot-torn area and determined to try to help solve one of the causes of the riots by establishing a special affordable housing program under the guidance of the Mount Carmel Guild. Yet, the nature of the cities of the Archdiocese had changed dramatically. Some city pastors found their parish populations drop by over half in just a few months time as many of the old-time residents fled to the suburbs. How could the vast parish plants of these urban churches now be maintained by such reduced congregations in these troubled times?

Catholic classrooms were still full as civil disturbances rocked the country.

How could Catholic inner-city schools be maintained in neighborhoods that had become overwhelmingly non-Catholic? Archbishop Boland was committed, however, to the poor and to the cities of the Archdiocese. Cajoling the pastors of financially stable parishes, the Archbishop undertook the ongoing subsidy (in both material resources and also personnel) of a great number of parishes, schools, and charitable works in Newark, Jersey City, Elizabeth and the other struggling cities of the Archdiocese.

Managing the waves of secular and ecclesial changes during these turbulent times called for great efforts by the Archbishop. He had to become aware of social justice issues in a way that had not been done before. Indeed, notwithstanding the work of the Mount Carmel Guild and other Catholic charities as well as the support Archbishop Boland gave to urban parishes in funds and assignment of priests,

The Civil Rights Movement, led by Dr. Martin Luther King, Jr., asked that the dignity of every individual be honored.

Inner cities were becoming more and more racially mixed as the 20th century progressed.

in 1969, he was accused by a group of priests of the Archdiocese of not combatting racism or promoting the civil rights movement. Wounded by these charges, which were contrary to everything he was attempting to do, Archbishop Boland met with the priests, "as a father to his sons," and established an interracial committee of priests and laypeople to meet regularly with the Archbishop to discuss community problems. Beyond civil rights, Boland had to listen closely to parishioners distraught by physical changes in their churches. He had to begin to change the nature of decision-making in many areas in the Archdiocese. He had to treat clergy who wanted to leave the active ministry with kindness and grace. Financial burdens grew and grew. Above all, Archbishop Boland had to continue to proclaim the Gospel with fidelity and charity.

After 21 years of challenging service, at the age of 78, Thomas Boland retired as Ordinary, and entrusted his flock to the third Archbishop of Newark, Peter L. Gerety.

Archbishop Boland (right) and Archbishop Gerety (left) the day after announcement of retirement and appointment, 1974

St. Ann, Hoboken

Since its establishment in May 1900, St. Ann, Hoboken, has grown with the times. Begun to serve the ever growing Italian community, St. Ann welcomes those of all ethnic backgrounds who bring their own heritage to enhance their faith and service. The Capuchin Franciscan Friars of the Province of the Sacred Stigmata of St. Francis have served the parish since 1920. Love and devotion to the patron of the parish have made St. Ann a place where many have experienced God's compassion for

them through the intercession of Good St. Ann. Thousands of people who have attended the Feast and Procession of St. Ann down through the years attest to an ever growing faith and devotion that go beyond the years and social changes. The Franciscan Capuchin charism has added the "little extra" to the spiritual and social life of the parish. The mission statement of St. Ann reads: "We the family of St. Ann Parish, a Catholic faith community, are called by God to love, forgive, unite, listen and share. We are further called to be an exciting spiritual community guided by the Gospel of Jesus Christ in the Capuchin Franciscan tradition of humility, simplicity and service to those most in need."

St. Francis, Hoboken

St. Francis Parish can be traced back more than 100 years to when mostly Genoese Italian-Americans of Hoboken worshipped at the old St. Joseph Church on Ferry Street (now Observer Highway). On May 5, 1888, as a result of a meeting to consider the building of a church, a new parish was formed and placed under the direction of the Conventual Franciscans who built the new structure, dedicating it on May 26, 1889, a little more than a year after the initial meeting The church in late Gothic design is substantially the same today as when it was built.

During the next 10 years, in addition to windows of St. Francis of Assisi and St. Dominic, other stained-glass windows were added. A two-story frame house on Adams Street was purchased on November 5, 1890, to be used as a Friary.

With the dreams of a church and a friary realized, the parish directed its attention to building a parish school. In the fall of 1902, the first floor of the building at 215 Jefferson Street was rented from the George Focht Estate. St. Francis Parochial School opened there on September 8, 1902, with 154 pupils. It was staffed by the Third Order Sisters of St. Francis of Syracuse, New York. The friary was moved to 303 Madison Street to free the ground adjacent to the church on Third Street for the new school in 1903. June 1906 saw the first graduation class of two, a small, but eloquent testimony to the devotion and sacrifices of the first parishioners and Franciscan friars and Sisters.

St. Joseph, Hoboken

In the beginning St. Joseph's was intended as a German parish. On October 22, 1871, Fr. Angelus Kemper began to offer Mass in a hall at Grand and Newark Streets known as "Kerrigan Flats." Seven days later the first Baptism was recorded.

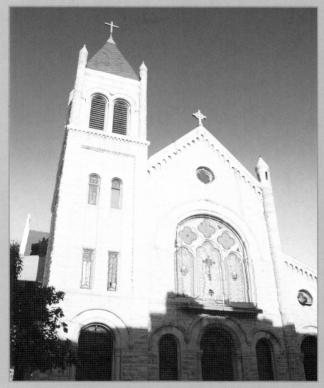

Soon after, a larger chapel opened on Meadow Street (now Park Avenue) to accommodate the increasing number of parishioners, yet there were more non-Germans than Germans. In 1872, a Franciscan friar, Fr. Alphonse Zoeller, was appointed to found a German parish. He immediately had St. Joseph incorporated. Property was purchased on Monroe Street and a church was built. At this time there was a great influx of Italian immigrants, so much so, that the Sunday sermons were preached in German, English and Italian. As a new German congregation was in process of being formed on Hudson Street, St. Joseph became a Territorial Parish to serve all people, regardless of their national origin. In the early 1960s, a very large influx of Spanish-speaking immigrants prompted St. Joseph to begin offering Masses in Spanish as well as English. The parish remains a bilingual parish today.

SS. Peter & Paul, Hoboken

SS. Peter & Paul Parish has been proclaiming the Good News of Jesus Christ in Hoboken since 1889. Through the years, the parish has provided for the spiritual, social and educational needs of countless people.

SS. Peter & Paul originated as a German parish. In 1889 the first Mass was celebrated in the parlor of the rectory on Hudson Street. Those present unanimously consented to name the parish after Saints Peter and Paul. A short time later, permission was given to start a school. By 1890 the first Church of SS. Peter & Paul was dedicated.

By 1929 people of a variety of ethnic origins were parishioners. Growth of the parish made it necessary to erect a larger building. The present church was dedicated on March 18, 1929. The parish continued to thrive and in 1965, the present school and convent were opened.

The parish has come a long way since its German roots. A multi-ethnic parish now, it ministers to a variety of people. There has been outreach not only to those who have been born and raised in Hoboken, but to the Hispanic community and to the young adults who call Hoboken their home. The parish has been an effective sign of the presence of Christ, because many have given of their time and talent to serve in the many ministries and organizations that make up the vibrant life of the parish.

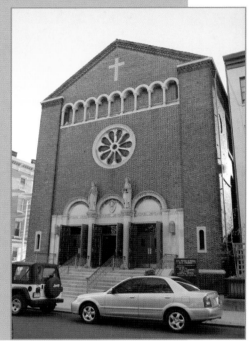

Assumption and All Saints, Jersey City

In 1896 All Saints Parish opened to serve Catholics in the Lafayette section of Jersey City. In 1906 Assumption Parish opened to meet the spiritual needs of the Slovak Catholics in the area. Because of demographic changes, the two parishes were merged in 1979 to form Assumption / All Saints Parish. Since the merger, the parish serves a diverse community. Mass is regularly celebrated in English and Spanish. An integral part of the parish is Assumption / All Saints School, which is staffed by the Sisters of Charity of St. Elizabeth and lay faculty.

Christ the King, Jersey City

In 1930 Mrs. Mary Ward approached Bishop Thomas Walsh about the needs of the African-American Catholics of Hudson County. Mrs. Ward

was convinced that if Black Catholics were to preserve and spread their faith, her people would need a church whose mission was serving the Black community. Bishop Walsh sympathized with Mrs. Ward's desire and appointed Fr. Joseph A. Shovlin to work with the Black Catholics in Hudson County. By June of that year, Mass was being celebrated in a house that served as a chapel and rectory. By August, land was purchased and construction begun on the corner of Ocean and Forrest in Jersey City. The Missionary Servants of the Most Holy Trinity sent sisters to support the ministry. These many years later, the efforts of a lay woman with the heart of an apostle has produced a church that takes seriously the invitation of Pope Paul VI: "Give to the Church the gift of your blackness."

Holy Rosary, Jersey City

Holy Rosary, the oldest Italian parish in New Jersey, was founded in 1885. Some families count seven generations of parishioners. The parish is preparing for its centennial, October 25, 2003. The church is one of the few in the country hallowed by association with a canonized saint, Mother Frances Cabrini having visited and worshiped within its walls.

The bronze plaque in the church vestibule since the church's consecration in 1934 marks in Latin that the church was built "with the offerings of Italian immigrants." Numerous societies were established to perpetuate the customs and devotions of the immigrants. The parish celebrates an annual Festa Italiana in August to honor St. Rocco and Our Lady of the Assumption.

Outstanding pastors include Msgr. Felix Di Persia (1913-1940) who established the parochial school, inviting the Teachers Filippini to conduct the educational program. Msgr. Gerard M. Santora (1946-1968) enlarged the school to accommodate the increased post-war generation and erected a new convent and rectory for the parish's 75th anniversary. Bishop of Wilmington, Deleware, Michael A. Satarellio, is a native of the parish and Bishop of Brooklyn, Nicholas DiMarzio, served as pastor from 1984 to 1985.

Msgr. Joseph Chiang, who had resided at Holy Rosary from 1972 to 1992 and returned in 1998 to become pastor, made Holy Rosary a center of the apostolate for Chinese-speaking Catholics. Today a Chinese Mass is celebrated every Sunday. With English, Italian and Latin Masses besides, Holy Rosary reflects something of the Church's universality and continues its ministry to immigrants.

The Work of Renewal

AT HIS INSTALLATION MASS, ARCHBISHOP PETER LEO GERETY RELATED THAT HE FOUND OUT ABOUT HIS APPOINTMENT AS THE NEW ARCHBISHOP OF NEWARK WHILE HE WAS RELAXING AT HIS RETREAT IN MAINE.

Archbishop Gerety officiates at Archbishop Boland's funeral

Unable to share the secret immediately with friends or the public, the Archbishop-designate spent the next two weeks talking about it with "the Lord and the whole heavenly court" and studying closely the statistics about the Archdiocese of Newark in the Official Catholic Directory. Prayer would certainly be fundamental to the ministry of Archbishop Gerety, and the statistics of the Official Catholic Directory revealed the vast work that had already been accomplished by the faithful of the Archdiocese of Newark, as well as much that still needed to be done.

Peter Gerety

Born in Shelton, Connecticut, Peter Gerety was the oldest son of Peter L. and Charlotte Daly Gerety. Both of his parents were natives of the Archdiocese of Newark – his father, an industrial engineer, was from Jersey City and his mother was from North Bergen. They had moved to Connecticut soon after their wedding and it was there that they raised their boys, for they would have a total of nine sons. As an engineer, Peter Gerety Sr. was able to provide well for his family during the 1920's and even during the Depression the family was sustained by his work and the labor of his sons, including Peter Leo, who worked hard at all available jobs, one of which would bring him to the city of Newark as a clerk.

During this time, young Peter, with the great encouragement of his family, also began to seriously explore the possibility of becoming a priest. He applied to the Diocese of Hartford and was asked to study abroad, at the Seminary of St. Sulpice in France. Equipped only with high school French to begin with, Gerety would spend much of the late 1930's at St. Supilce, where his love of history and a natural academic bent were

Archbishop Gerety before the welcoming doors of Sacred Heart Cathedral.

whom Gerety had reached out in the neighborhood of Dixwell Avenue in New Haven. Following the Second World War, the little community, shepherded by Gerety, was able to build first a church and then a school and finally became an official parish in 1956. The church also sponsored a parish credit union and even a cooperative housing project with the local Congregational church to help its struggling members. After nearly 24 years at St. Martin

DePorres (who had been canonized in 1962), Msgr. Gerety (who had been named a monsignor in 1963), was appointed by Pope Paul VI on March 4, 1966 to be the coadjutor bishop (that is, bishop with right of succession) of the Diocese of Portland, Maine.

given full reign. He was ordained a priest at the Cathedral of Notre Dame in Paris on June 29, 1939, barely two months before the outbreak of World War II. Only his mother and his aunt were able to be present at his ordination – his father was suffering from Parkinson's disease.

Unlike many of the previous bishops and archbishops of Newark, who, soon after their priestly ordinations found themselves teaching or caught up immediately in administrative work, Fr. Gerety had the great good fortune to spend most of the first 27 years of his priesthood in parish ministry – the longest of any of the bishops and archbishops of Newark. The future Archbishop would be able to draw upon this long experience throughout his service in Newark. The first parish Fr. Gerety was assigned to was St. John the Evangelist in New Haven, Connecticut. After just two years there, Gerety was asked by the bishop to help establish an inter-racial center to serve African-Americans in the inner city of New Haven. This would be his home for over two decades. The Blessed Martin DePorres Center, created in 1942 out of a former police station, served the poor and working class and began with just over a hundred families to

Archbishop Gerety, having served as a parish priest 24 years at St. Martin de Porres, made it a priority of his episcopacy to work for African Americans.

Bishop of Portland

The Diocese of Portland, which covers the whole state of Maine, had about 350 diocesan and religious priests, administering 134 parishes in 1966, while over a thousand sisters worked in 56 grammar schools, 14 high schools, as well as 9 hospitals, and many other diocesan institutions, serving 270,000 Catholics through-out the state.

Our Lady of Czestochowa, Jersey City

Our Lady of Czestochowa Church is part of the Paulus Hood Historic District of Jersey City. Originally the church building, parts of which date back to 1831, housed the congregation of St. Matthew Protestant Episcopal Church. In the early 1900s, as the area became more industrialized and populated by immigrants, the congregation of St. Matthew began to dwindle, its affluent members moving to the Heights section of Jersey City.

In 1905 the church building was sold to St. Anthony Church, which served the ever-increasing number of Polish immigrant Catholics of the waterfront. The name of the church was changed to Our Lady of Czestochowa. On August 26, 1911, the mission church was incorporated as an independent Catholic parish and Fr. Constantine Ferdyn was named its first pastor.

The parish continued to grow and soon included a rectory, a school, a convent, a social hall and an athletic field. The church building was expanded and a chapel was constructed below the church.

In 1995 the mission of the parish was altered to reflect the dramatic changes that had taken place in Paulus Hood and along the entire waterfront area of Jersey City, now increasingly called the "Gold Coast" or "Wall Street West."

A once industrialized, blue-collar neighborhood is now a thriving financial and commercial area populated in large part by a young, professional, highly educated class of people from across the country and around the world. The Parish now serves this very diverse community and strives to be a beacon of faith, hope and love on the Jersey City waterfront.

Over all this presided Bishop Daniel Feeney, who was not in the best of health and welcomed the assistance that Gerety would bring. Just as Bishop Gerety began to travel the state to learn his way around the far-flung diocese and to put his French from St. Sulpice to work among the many French-speakers of northern Maine, he found himself with far wider responsibilities when Bishop Feeney suffered a stroke. Bishop Gerety had to take over the full day-to-day administration of the diocese.

The Diocese of Portland, like the Archdiocese of Newark, and indeed the whole Catholic world, was coming to grips with both the full implications of the Second Vatican Council and the vast social changes that marked the 1960's. How to turn this ferment into creative energy? This was one of the most important challenges that lay before all post-Conciliar bishops. In Portland, Bishop Gerety sought to do this on many levels. Diocesan-wide goal setting was undertaken. The Bishop mandated that his pastors establish parish councils in each of the churches of the diocese. As a long-time city pastor, the poor of Maine would receive his special attention. His experience in working with African-American Catholics in New Haven was put to good use by his brother bishops who asked him to chair the bishops' liaison committee to the National Office of Black Catholics. Bishop Gerety also sought to reach out to Native Americans by sending teachers to work on three reservations and worked to mediate disputes as they arose between Anglophones and Francophones in the state. Change was slow but steady. Yet Gerety was acutely aware of the dangers of building a "program-driven" diocese, stating, "Undergirding all the planning and goal-setting and changing of structures and altering of ministries must be our own union with Jesus Christ..."

A Bigger Diocese

Unlike the many years he was able to be in New Haven, Bishop Gerety did not have the satisfaction of watching both the sowing and harvest of his ministry as bishop of Portland. On April 2, 1974, Pope Paul VI appointed Gerety as the third Archbishop of Newark.

His new archdiocese was considerably smaller in geography...but that was the only way it was smaller. Five times as many religious, four times as many Catholics, three times as many priests, twice as many parishes, a host of institutions, and a great diversity of peoples, all of whom offered much to their new Ordinary, but who also needed attention, prayer, and a guiding hand, awaited Peter Leo Gerety.

The Archbishop-designate knew that harnessing the gifts of the people of Newark and addressing the needs of his people was an undertaking far beyond the ability of one man. Even before he was installed on June 28, 1974,

Archbishop Gerety believed that all work for racial equality in his diocese must always be undergirded by "our union with Jesus Christ."

Gerety traveled several times to the Archdiocese to meet with officials in his chancery, members of the Priests' Senate, Religious Orders, and lay Catholics, introducng them to his own unique management style. To listen and to learn, to delegate and confidently entrust tasks, to identify

HUDSON COUNTY

Our Lady of Mercy, Jersey City

Our Lady of Mercy, Jersey City, is among the youngest parishes in the Archdiocese. Within its 40-year history, the parish has always focused on meeting the needs of the assembly. The parishioners reflect very strongly the changing face of Jersey City. Transitioning from the predominantly Italian-American identity of foundation days to the Filipino-American reality of today, the community remains welcoming to all who pass through its church doors. The parish continues the focus of evangelization to all people of all ages. Its foundation stone continues to be the Eucharistic Table. Its mission statement reads: *We, the faith community of Our Lady of Mercy Parish, joyfully and humbly seek to make Our Lord Jesus Christ ever more real in our lives and in the lives of others. We enliven our Mission by a commitment to Stewardship as a Way of Life. We strive to pursue our mission by being a welcoming community that provides a home for all and celebrates life, hope and reconciliation through WORD, WORSHIP and SERVICE.*

a wide array of capable people and to give them the desire, authority, and ongoing support to effect the changes which Gerety saw as necessary: all these would be prominent features of the new Archbishop's stewardship in Newark.

Archbishop Gerety worked with priests, seminarians, religious orders and lay Catholics to effect changes he saw as necessary.

Difficulties

Archbishop Boland had slowed down considerably because of age in his later years and was reluctant to create new initiatives that might not reflect the priorities of his successor. As a result, many Catholics felt a certain sense of excitement and of new possibilities with Archbishop Gerety. Yet, for all of the ideas and possibilities, there were also many concrete matters which demanded Archbishop Gerety's immediate concern. The ambitious program of building expansion which had been undertaken in the decade before, that was to include a number of new high schools, new homes for the elderly, and a philosophy house for Immaculate Conception Seminary, had fallen far short of its goal. Just as these projects were begun in earnest, the estimated costs for several – particularly the high schools – were discovered

Our Lady of Mount Carmel, Jersey City

Our Lady of Mount Carmel Parish was founded almost 100 years ago at the beginning of a new century. In April 1905, Fr. Ernest Monteleone purchased an obsolete Baptist Church on the corner of Broadway and Giles Avenue to serve the Catholic population in the Marion section of Jersey City. On July 16, 1905, he celebrated the first Mass under the title of Our Lady of Mount Carmel.

The parish served the needs of Italian immigrants.

Over the years, the parishioners created a parochial life centered on the Eucharist and a special devotion to the Blessed Virgin Mary. In 1910 the annual Feast of Our Lady of Mount Carmel was created in her honor and continues to this day. A school was built in 1954 to form and educate the children in the faith. Other organizations grew to meet the changing and growing needs of the parish.

Today at the beginning of another century and millennium, Our Lady of Mount Carmel stands in a unique position to once again minister to the needs of immigrants while maintaining its rich Italian heritage. Through its early experiences of leaving a familiar land and coming to a new country, the community was prepared by the Lord to welcome and help new immigrants of multi-ethnic backgrounds. The parish continues to offer the opportunity for all who come to experience a deeper life of faith through the Gospel's ongoing call of conversion.

to be woefully inadequate. The sudden drop in the number of practicing Catholics and the flight of many Catholics to the suburbs left many parishes so drastically reduced that dozens needed assistance from the Archdiocese, precisely at the time when the Archdiocese also wanted to begin a whole new series of social justice programs and programs to implement the reforms of the Second Vatican Council.

Moreover, the Archdiocese of Newark was still feeling the financial effects of a protracted court battle with the State of New Jersey. Seton Hall University had announced in 1954 its intention to form the first medical school in the history of New Jersey. Evidently, some in the state government at the time were not open to the idea of the sole medical school in New Jersey being administered under the auspices of the Catholic Church. Soon after Seton Hall's announcement, the state government announced that it was going to found the College of Medicine and Dentistry. Thus for years, the Archdiocese of Newark had had an extended and very expensive legal struggle with the state, which only concluded in the early 1960's.

The newly appointed auxiliary bishops of the Archdiocese with Archbishop Gerety: Bishops Robert F. Garner, Jerome A. Pechillo, Joseph A. Francis and Dominic Marconi (Advocate photo)

Our Lady of Sorrows, Jersey City

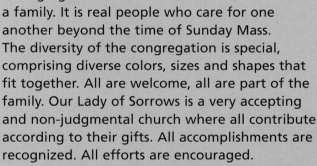

Guided by the conviction that church is the people of God, parishioners of Our Lady of Sorrows were asked what makes their parish special. The responses were woven into the following statement:

Our Lady of Sorrows is not just a congregation. It is a family. It is real people who care for one another beyond the time of Sunday Mass. The diversity of the congregation is special, comprising diverse colors, sizes and shapes that fit together. All are welcome, all are part of the family. Our Lady of Sorrows is a very accepting and non-judgmental church where all contribute according to their gifts. All accomplishments are recognized. All efforts are encouraged.

Our Lady of Sorrows reaches beyond itself into its community to serve the needs of the neediest. The parish mission statement is taken from Psalm 87: "The Lord loves his city, and so do we!"

All these factors combined to present Archbishop Gerety during the summer of 1974 with an Archdiocese operating at an annual deficit and an accumulated debt which had ballooned to some 30 million dollars – mostly in short term, variable rate notes.

All of this the Archbishop laid out in the Archdiocese's first financial statement, published in 1975. Once the entirety of the actual debts was identified through rigorous auditing, the Archbishop and the new Office of Planning and Research began to address it. Archdiocesan agencies found their budgets drastically trimmed or wholly eliminated.

Archbishop Gerety signs the Assumption-All Saints, Jersey City, merger document in 1979.

Salaries and hiring were frozen. Many schools were informed that their subsidies were being reduced. The Mount Carmel Guild and Associated Catholic Charities were combined into one new organization: Catholic Community Services. A fundraising drive, under the title of "Lifeline," was begun in 1975. Eventually, by asking the pastors of the Archdiocese to allow their parish accounts to be used for leverage, Archdiocesan financial officials were able to renegotiate the total debt and its terms into manageable limits.

Our Lady of Victories, Jersey City

Increase in the membership of St. Aloysius Parish, Jersey City, prompted the founding of a new mission church in 1916. A small factory was converted and the first Mass of Our Lady of Victories Parish was celebrated April 22, 1917. The church received its first pastor in 1919.

Ground was broken for a new church on May 7, 1922, and the cornerstone was set on September 24, 1922. On September 30, 1930, the Sisters of Charity opened Our Lady of Victories School. When the number of parishioners again increased, the church basement was renovated to provide additional Masses and a new convent was built. In 1970 the Sisters of Charity withdrew and were replaced by a staff of lay teachers. The years that followed brought many changes in the school. Today it continues to be an innovative, future-oriented institution proudly serving the parish and the community. As the parish celebrates its 85th anniversary, it remembers its past with gratitude and makes plans to secure its future.

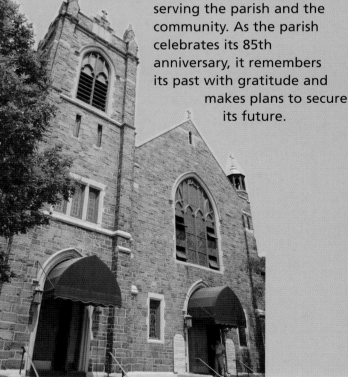

Parish of the Resurrection, Jersey City

The Churches of St. Boniface, St. Bridget, St. Mary, St. Michael and St. Peter

The Parish of the Resurrection came into being on July 1, 1997, a powerful sign of God's presence in downtown Jersey City. As a bold vision to unite five neighborhood churches into one new parish, the entire faith community was invited to participate in its planning. Their ideas, dreams and faith became the cornerstone of the parish. The result is a unique combination of five church communities, varied in ethnic, cultural and language backgrounds, but united in the love of God and the profound desire to share that love with others through:

- Dynamically rich and varied Catholic liturgy
- Religious education for children from Grade 1 through high school
- Catholic school for children Pre-K through high school
- Outreach to the poor and homeless and a parish nurse program
- Varied religious devotions, including perpetual adoration, Bible study, seminars and retreats
- A committed effort to capitalize on a 150+ year heritage of faith and facilities to meet the needs of a new and emerging community

The Parish of the Resurrection is a beautiful work-in-progress. There remains much work to accomplish in the Lord's name.

Parish of the Resurrection

St. Mary Church

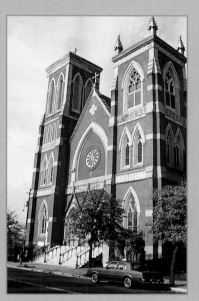

St. Bridget Church

St. Boniface Church

St. Michael Church

St. Peter Church

All of these measures rapidly eliminated the Archdiocesan deficit and made an important start at debt reduction. For the long term, Archbishop Gerety made sure that careful financial controls were institutionalized, as was the "Lifeline" program, which became the "Archbishop's Annual Appeal." Budgets were scrutinized. The Office of Development and Finance Council were created. A capital giving campaign was undertaken, and the construction of new mausoleums enabled the Archdiocesan cemeteries to make a substantial contribution to the financial stability of the Archdiocese.

Archbishop Gerety in St. Peter Square, Rome, October 16, 1978, the day Pope John Paul II was elected

Renewal Activities

While the Archdiocese was setting its financial house in order, Archbishop Gerety also began a series of renewals which would touch each aspect of Catholic life in the Archdiocese. Religious communities of women and men, often struggling themselves with how to live most

---

HUDSON COUNTY

Sacred Heart, Jersey City

The Church of the Sacred Heart had its beginning on February 14, 1905. Masses were held for three years in Fr. John MacErlain's Alcohol Sanitarium on Bayview Avenue. In 1908 the first church was dedicated. In 1910 the school began with Dominican Sisters. Classes were held on the top floor of the sanitarium. In 1912 the Sisters of Charity took over and a new school was built. With the advent of the Dominican Friars in 1919, the parish experienced new growth. In 1924 the present Spanish Gothic church, designed by Ralph Adams Cram and Wright Goodhue, was completed. Sacred Heart Parish became an important center in Jersey City. Since the 1960s the Irish, German and Italian families of the parish were replaced by African-American, Haitian and African families. In February 2005, Sacred Heart will celebrate 100 years of ministry and its rich heritage of many cultures.

faithfully the charism of their founders, were given a much higher profile in the work of the Archdiocese. Archbishop Gerety encouraged them to look beyond the traditional areas of teaching, hospital work, and care for the poor to new apostolates. He encouraged the creation of the "Sisters' Assembly" and asked many talented religious to start working in administrative posts in the Archdiocese formerly held exclusively by diocesan priests, including several important offices such as Personnel, the Tribunal, and so on.

Installation of Pope John Paul II in St. Peter's Square, Rome 1978

The restoration of the Permanent Diaconate had been called for by Pope Paul VI in 1972. Rather than continue preparation for the priesthood, these men would be ordained deacons on a permanent basis. They would have the ability to baptize, to preach, to bury, to witness marriages as well as assist in charitable works. The first two permanent deacons had been ordained shortly before Archbishop Gerety's arrival in Newark, while Gerety himself would ordain hundreds more for service throughout the Archdiocese.

As in Portland, Archbishop Gerety mandated that all churches in the Archdiocese set up parish councils, to better facilitate communication and cooperation between priests and their parishioners. The Archbishop also organized the parishes of the Archdiocese into "deaneries," administrative groupings in which the deans, elected by their fellow priests, would serve as sounding boards for the concerns of pastors and help explain and ensure the implementation of Archdiocesan-wide policies. Beyond the deaneries, the Archdiocese of Newark was divided into vicariates – one for each of the four counties of the archdiocese. The auxiliary bishops would serve as the vicars for the Archbishop in each county and assist him in the practical administration of the Archdiocese and help the new Personnel Board match priests and parishes.

Ordination of priests here shown was complemented by the ordination of permanent deacons. Today the Archdiocese has more than 250 permanent deacons who preach the Word, serve in charitable ministries and assist in some of the sacraments.

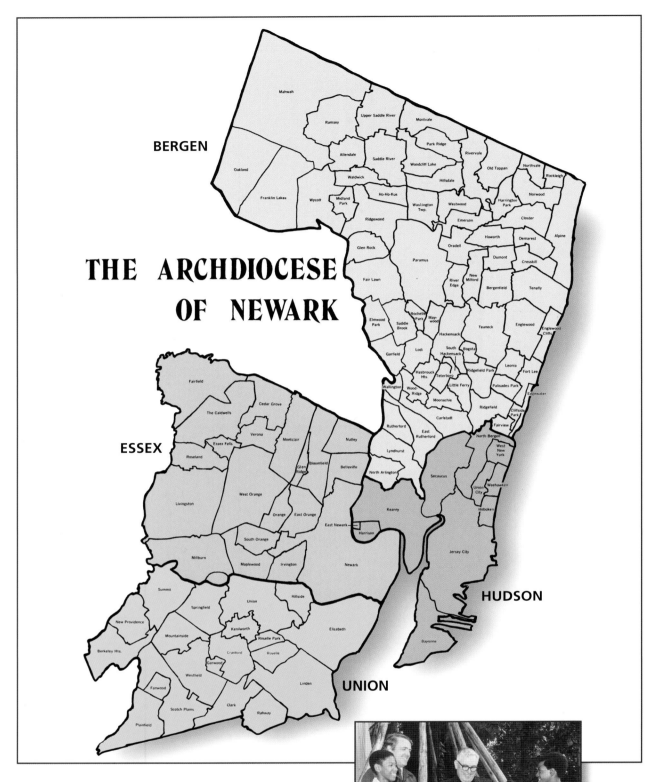

THE ARCHDIOCESE OF NEWARK

BERGEN

ESSEX

HUDSON

UNION

New Programs

Additional programs took shape as needs were discerned. The Office of Immigration helped organize the different sources of assistance for recently arrived immigrants. A Ministry to Divorced and Separated Catholics sought to provide for the pastoral care to a growing number of Catholics who were unable to remain in their marriages. The Worship Office continued

Archbishop Gerety at CYO camp, Lake Hopatcong in 1978

Communion after Vatican II could be taken under two species. In large celebrations, many cups are required.

Communion in the hand became the common method of receiving.

its work to catechize the Archdiocese about ongoing liturgical changes, including the possibility of receiving Communion in the hand and the popularization of "reconciliation rooms," or expanded confessionals that permitted face-to-face Confessions with ease. The Office of Pastoral Renewal, a reinvigorated Ecumenical Commission, the new Religious Education Office (which replaced the venerable Confraternity of Christian Doctrine) all had important contributions to make to the life of the Archdiocese. The importance of small faith-sharing communities was underlined as the popular scripturally based RENEW program, begun in the Archdiocese of Newark, became nation-wide and international in scope.

HUDSON COUNTY

St. Aedan, Jersey City

On June 23, 1912, St. Aedan Parish was established for Irish immigrants attracted to Jersey City's canal and railroad industry. They were followed by Italians, Hungarians and Poles, also attracted by jobs in Hudson County, the gateway from New York westward. Immediately the next year St. Aedan School opened and 13 years later, ground was broken for a convent, which was ready for occupancy in 1927. Four years later a new church was dedicated. A marvel of light and ornament in the Romanesque style, with semicircular arches, massive walls, enormous piers and small windows providing a sense of stability, permanence and security, it was completed at a cost of $1 million. An important feature of the main façade is the unique design of the rose window.

The mortgage was burned in January 1945. Two years later new bells were dedicated and in October 1981, the parish celebrated the 50th anniversary of its dedication. In 1985, the restored Bell Chime was rededicated. The following year Fr. Pierce D. Byrne was named pastor.

In the 60's and 70's many Irish families moved out and were replaced by Hispanics, African-Americans, and Asians-mainly Filipinos. Archbishop McCarrick, responding to this pastoral situation, appointed Msgr. Jeremias R Rebanal as the first Filipino pastor to work for the renewal of the parish life.

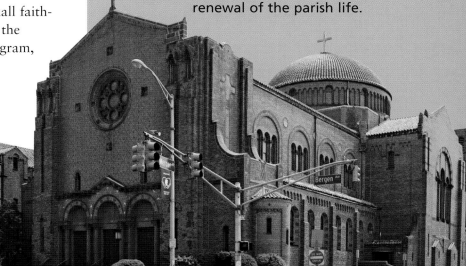

St. Aloysius, Jersey City

The first Mass remembered in Jersey City (Paulus Hook) was in 1829. The needs of the growing Catholic population there prompted approval of a new parish in West Bergen and another (All Saints) in the Lafayette Section. The area of St. Patrick, west of Hudson County Boulevard was detached to form the new parish of St. Aloysius, which was incorporated on May 12, 1897.

Parish interest in Catholic education is reflected in the first building, a combination church and school. The cornerstone was laid in 1897 in the presence of 5000. Work then began on a rectory, completed in 1899. The school began with a staff of four Sisters of Charity and 194 children with 225 in Catechism classes. The combination building was moved to its present location. Plans were drawn up for the present granite church in French Renaissance style. Church membership reached 4900 in 1912. In 1922 the cornerstone was laid for a new grade and high school, and three years later, a Social Center in the basement was opened. As school enrollment grew, renovations were made in 1929, 1938 and 1959. By 1940 the total school enrollment reached 1450, which led to plans for a new high school building.

A striking change in the complexion of the parish occurred with the erection of the A. Harry Moore Apartments as a low-income public housing project. The 664-dwelling units were occupied in 1953. Since then there has been a marked thrust in the direction of social action.

St. Aloysius implemented the reforms and changes of Vatican Council II, and modern technology was installed for smoother running of the parish plant. Spanish Masses and Masses for the elderly in the projects were added as a new Sacramental Program with accent on family life was begun. The parish continues alive and well and filled with hope as it enters the Third Millennium.

St. Ann, Jersey City

St. Ann Roman Catholic Parish (Parafia ´SW. Anny) was founded in 1911. The church was erected in 1946 to minister to the spiritual needs of Polish immigrants and to serve all Catholics in the neighborhood. Its pastor is Fr. Thaddeus Stasik, and Parochial Vicar, Fr. George Idzik. Trustees are Joseph Rakowski, Theresa F. Kotlowski, and Chester Sienkiewicz, Business Manager.

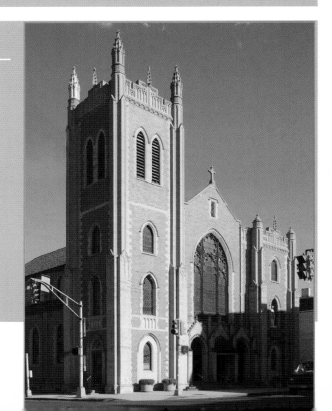

Archbishop Gerety strove to be open to any possibility that might deepen people's relationship with Christ. Many initiatives were well grounded and well received. Others became quite controversial and would eventually be discontinued. Beginning in the season of Advent 1977, the Archdiocese experienced "The Father's Embrace." "The Father's Embrace" was a series of reconciliation services – one held in each county and one for the Spanish-speaking community – at which the Archbishop presided. Instead of the service being concluded with the usual opportunity for individual confessions, Archbishop Gerety believed that the number of penitents at each gathering warranted the giving of general absolution. The intended effect of the

Archbishop Gerety presents a Caritas Award recipient with a medal, 1983.

Archbishop's generous action – an experience of grace and peace and growing closeness with God – was felt by many. The unintended effect – a deepening of the post-Conciliar confusion about the Sacrament of Penance – was also experienced by many.

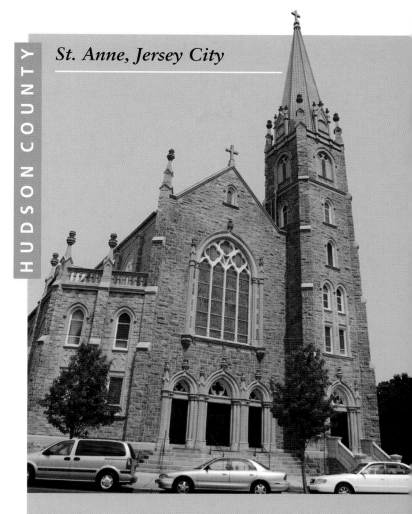

HUDSON COUNTY

St. Anne, Jersey City

B ack in 1887, parishioners in the "western slope" area of Jersey City worshiped at St. Paul of the Cross Church. In June 1904, St. Anne Church in Jersey City Heights became an incorporated parish. A farmhouse served as the priests', first rectory. It wasn't until February 1906 that property was purchased on Congress Street (presently St. Anne Convent) for a new rectory to accommodate the rapid growth of the parish. A new church was built and the old church converted to classrooms. Between 1945 and 1954 a number of facilities were added and the old rectory was moved onto the property with the new church. A convent was also erected.

Many changes and many years later, St. Anne Parish had grown to more than 1500 families. The early 1990's saw a restoration of both the exterior and interior of the church. As the Archdiocese of Newark celebrates its 150th Anniversary, St. Anne Church, as well, prepares to celebrate its centennial with an alive, active and vibrant community.

St. Anthony of Padua, Jersey City

In 1884 the hearts of the first Polish immigrants in New Jersey were gladdened at the formation of their own parish, St. Anthony of Padua, where the culture of their homeland could be preserved. During the next eight years, the number of St. Anthony parishioners grew from 500 to 10,000. When the small wooden church became too small, the cornerstone of the present, magnificent church was laid on June 13, 1892. A major fire in 1895 brought about the enlargement and refurbishing of the church. The only remnant untouched by the flames was a large crucifix. When the parish installed a marble, Gothic style main altar some years later, this cross was relocated to the vestibule, where it is still venerated by the faithful as they enter and leave the church.

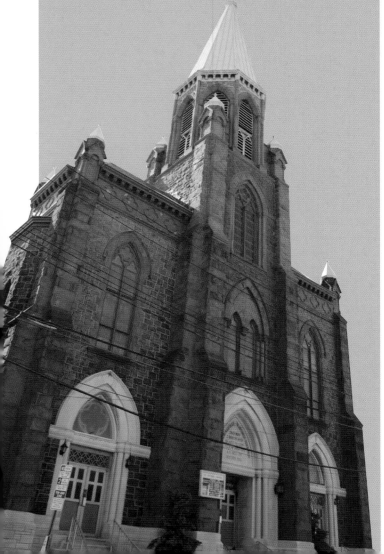

St. John the Baptist, Jersey City

On December 6, 1884 in a vacant room in the Marion Section of Jersey City, with 18 people present, the first Mass was offered in the newly established St. John the Baptist parish. By Christmas, a frame church had been erected and 900 people joined in worship.

In 1886 the Caldwell Dominicans opened an elementary school, which still functions. The present magnificent church's cornerstone was placed in 1892, dedication taking place in 1897. With the new century a permanent convent and school were completed. The stately church features the third largest display of mosaics in a church in the United States. The greater participation of the faithful laity, the fruit of the great Vatican Council II, became a reality at St. John's and continues today. A liturgically correct sanctuary was installed in 1997.

The original families of St. John were either immigrants or children of immigrants from Europe. They brought a lively faith and bestowed a living inheritance of Catholic life. Though substantially smaller now than in the past, St. John the Baptist is significantly blessed by recent arrivals from Asia, South and Central America and Africa. St. John is now truly catholic in its mosaic of God's people.

St. Joseph, Jersey City

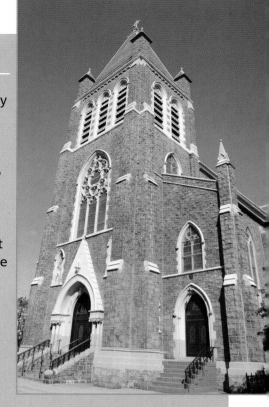

St. Joseph on the "Hilltop" of Jersey City was established as the second parish of Jersey City in 1856 with its first Mass on October 26. It was begun for Irish immigrants who were hewing out the "Palisades" for a railroad cut. For the 147 years of its Christian ministry, the parish has given witness to the faith commitment of European, Hispanic, Asian and Third World Catholics who have partnered with 12 pastors and countless priests and Sisters of Charity to live the Lord's command to love God and neighbor on the shores of the Hudson.

For many, Jersey City was and is a "first port of call" or a reunion with already settled family members who open their doors to arriving relatives. Rich in vibrant family traditions, the parish continues to promote Christian principles in a Catholic elementary school and pro-active religious education programs for young and old. All who come to the parish's sacramental fountain of faith are welcomed, initiated and nourished as they gather around the Table of Plenty. Though of many cultures, parishioners constitute one body in the Lord. "Politics," which is part of the life-blood of any city parish, prompts parish members to sit at the seat of County government aware of the social mission to feed the hungry and speak out for justice and peace for all. At the hub of Journal Square and trans-Hudson transit systems, the parish works to protect the environment and the neighborhood and acts as a vigorous neighborhood steward who effects change when civic planning is in its best interest. St. Joseph looks forward to the celebration of its 150th anniversary with a pledge to continue to be the people of God in the city of God, Jersey City.

St. Nicholas, Jersey City

St. Nicholas was founded in 1986 to serve the many German immigrants who had settled in the Heights section of Jersey City. The original church included the first parish school. In 1896 the parish built a new school that still stands. It is served by the Sisters of Christian Charity. In 1906 the present church was erected.

In 1986 the church was renovated to conform to the liturgical innovations of Vatican Council II. Three years later the aging buildings needed repairs. In 1999 the fifth pastor, Fr. Kevin Carter, brought Stewardship as a Way of Life to St. Nicholas. On September 11, the school, eyewitness to the destruction of that day, produced more than 1000 meals from its cafeteria to feed police, fire and rescue workers. In the spring of 2002, the parish embarked on a campaign named "Restoration of Love and Pride" to restore many of its structures.

Civil Rights Involvement

Another aspect of reconciliation and peace in which Archbishop Gerety felt it was important for the Catholics of the Archdiocese to be involved was in the subject of civil rights. His long experience at St. Martin DePorres attuned him to the needs of minority and urban communities and to the injustices which they suffered.

The Keoghs, advised to abort their quintuplets, opted otherwise and are blessed with five healthy children: Elizabeth, Brigid, Jacqueline, Meaghan and Patrick.

Archbishop Gerety was always singularly direct and forthright in expressing his opinions, whether about the "bloody horror" of abortion, legalized the year before he came to Newark, or

Archbishop Gerety was direct in his views about the horror of abortion and many joined him in demonstrating against it.

St. Patrick, Jersey City

HUDSON COUNTY

In 1869 the first pastor, Fr. Patrick Hennessey, had a vision of a magnificent Gothic church to serve the immigrant Irish population of Jersey City. Through the years, St. Patrick has seen transformation as the demographics of the city changed. Today the parish is truly multicultural and again serves immigrants new to the area. It is staffed by priests and sisters carrying out the mission of the Church in the inner city.

The parish school opened in 1909 with the Sisters of Charity of St. Elizabeth as faculty. Thousands of students have graduated from the school, many with fond memories of theatrical productions staged in the mini-Broadway theatre in the school building. The school, still staffed by the Sisters of Charity and lay faculty, educates 500 students in Christian values.

Archbishop Gerety devoted himself to the needs of minorities.

about the rights of the unemployed and underprivileged, the dignity of the aging and the terminally ill, and the just needs of racial and ethnic minorities.

The Archbishop was the principal speaker at the first northeast regional *Encuentro* of Hispanic Catholics. He worked hard to listen to and cooperate with African-American ministers' groups active in the city of Newark and in the state. Archbishop Gerety was able to call upon the gifts of many people as he grappled with justice issues, including the Archdiocese's first African-American bishop (fourth in the whole nation), Joseph Francis, SVD and Bishop Jerome Pechillo, TOR who brought a wealth of experience to the Archdiocese from his pastoral work in Paraguay.

Bishop Jerome Pechillo, at his episcopal ordination, 1966, brought a wealth of experience from his pastoral work in Paraguay.

St. Paul the Apostle, Jersey City

St. Paul the Apostle Parish is a community committed to celebrating and communicating the life and spirit of Jesus by word and action. Together with the Archbishop, it strives to build a living, caring and evangelizing church. The parishioners commit themselves to this mission by the sharing of their time, talent and treasure for the benefit of all in the community.

Since 1861 St. Paul, Greenville, has been served by generous and social-minded priests, Sisters and laity looking after the spiritual, academic and social care of the great Greenville community. The welcoming spirit embodied in its motto makes the community vital and vibrant to this day: "There are no strangers here, only friends yet to be met."

Seminarian Decline

Archbishop Gerety's work and his example certainly bore much fruit in the Archdiocese of Newark. However, one area in which the Archbishop was less than successful was that of vocations. In 1963, the Archdiocesan seminary (built for 300) was so full that students had to be housed elsewhere at Darlington. Beginning the next year however, the number of young men studying for the priesthood for service in the Archdiocese of Newark began to decline precipitously, a drop which was mirrored in the religious communities of the Archdiocese. Parish communities, which had become accustomed to being served by four and five priests, found themselves lucky to have two. Priests in the past had sometimes spent decades in one parish. Now, as gaps appeared and needs opened around the Archdiocese, they were moved with a frequency that was disconcerting to both the priests and their people. Ordination classes of five – which had not been seen in a century – were considered good. The vast seminary of the Immaculate Conception at Darlington, pride of Bishops O'Connor and Walsh, seemed as if it belonged to a vanished world. To operate so large a physical plant with such a decline in enrollment no longer seemed feasible.

While the Archdiocese was no longer in debt, its financial position was still uncertain, and Archbishop Gerety could not see his way clear to retaining the seminary campus. Darlington was sold and in 1984 the seminary returned to its original home at Seton Hall. Shortly thereafter, Archbishop Peter L. Gerety retired.

Bishop Walsh lays the cornerstone of the chapel at Immaculate Conception Seminary, Darlington, 1957. By 1984 the Campus had to be sold and the Seminary relocated to Seton Hall.

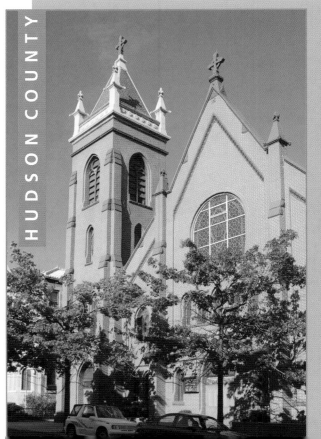

HUDSON COUNTY

St. Paul of the Cross, Jersey City

The Church of St. Paul of the Cross was incorporated in 1868 and the cornerstone laid on August 15, 1869. The parish, one of 16 parishes founded by the Passionist Order Missionaries in Hudson County, was named to honor Paul Francis Danei (Paul of the Cross), the founder of the Passionist Order.

The basement was completed that fall and fitted as a temporary chapel. The first Mass was celebrated on the following Christmas Day. The interior of the church was finished and ready for dedication in October 1870.

St. Paul of the Cross is made up of individuals from diverse backgrounds who have freely chosen to come together to form one community of faith in Jesus Christ. They are gifted people, created by God and guided by the Holy Spirit to be good stewards of all God's creation and called to a life of intimacy with God, love for one another and outreach to the poor, sick and forgotten.

Our Lady of Sorrows, Kearny

Like so many national parishes, Our Lady of Sorrows Parish had its birth in humble surroundings. It was created not only to fulfill religious needs, but also to satisfy emotional and social demands. The parish was formally established in 1915 and designed to serve the needs of approximately 700 Lithuanians in Harrison and 400 in Kearny.

The first place of worship was the hall of St. Cecilia Parish, Kearny. The Lithuanians yearned to worship in their native tongue and according to their national customs. The Blessed Mother had long been loved and venerated by their forefathers in Lithuania, and it seemed appropriate that the people of the newly erected parish choose Our Lady of Sorrows as their patroness.

The parish celebrated its first Mass in February 1915. During his 30-year tenure, the fourth pastor, Fr. Leo Voiciekauskas built a new church and rectory in Kearny, dedicated in 1954. In 1965, a school was purchased and a convent built. Today Our Lady of Sorrows is a thriving spiritual institution. Most of its parishioners come from Kearny, but as a national parish, it also draws worshipers from Harrison, North Arlington, Lyndhurst, Belleville and Nutley.

The parish is growing through an influx of non-Lithuanian people. Parishioners now include a good portion of highly skilled technicians, office, computer and manufacturing personnel and professional men and women. The laity have proven again and again that they are willing to undertake apostolic and other tasks for the good of the parish. Many of the parish societies and organizations are primarily spiritually oriented, though many also serve cultural and social functions.

In June 2002, the parish welcomed Father James J. Reilly as its Administrator.

St. Cecilia, Kearny

September 1, 1893, was one of the more monumental days in the history of Kearny as the Parish of St. Cecilia was born, an offshoot of Holy Cross Church, Harrison. At that time, Kearny's population comprised mainly Irish and Scottish immigrants. Shortly after, the first school, a two-story building that housed classrooms and an auditorium, was built. Subsequently, a brick elementary school opened in 1909, staffed by the Sisters of Charity well into the 1970s. St. Cecilia High School opened in September 1931, closing in 1983 when strapped with financial problems.

From 1956 on, the parish community saw its greatest changes, building a new rectory in 1968 and initiating a marvelous outreach program to the growing Spanish-speaking population of Kearny. To serve a growing Portuguese community, the first Portuguese language Mass was celebrated in 1978. After 1996, the parish experienced a growing unity of the three language communities of the parish. In 2002 the elementary school closed, however the parish continues to serve the spiritual needs of the English-Spanish and Portuguese speaking community.

St. Stephen, Kearny

"Like living stones, be yourselves built into a spiritual house." St. Peter's words find an echo in the church and parishioners of St. Stephen in Kearny's Arlington section. The magnificent church building, a great temple to God wherein the love of God and neighbor has grown strong throughout the years, is a visible reminder of the unseen bond of grace shared with the Holy Trinity and the Church universal. A parish is a mystery of faith that eludes neat, easy explanation. St. Stephen reflects both Kearny's deep roots and its adaptability. Just as the parish is basic to the life of the Church, so too is St. Stephen's integral to the town of Kearny. Gospel faith, divine worship and the sacraments produce the fruits of strong education, commitment, social justice, community involvement and youth formation. St. Stephen's people are stalwart, generous and faith filled. Like its proto-martyr patron, the parish continues to bear witness as it begins its second century next year.

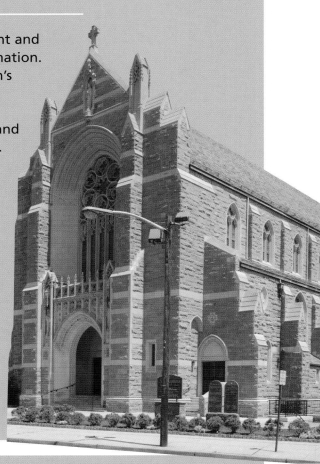

Our Lady of Fatima, North Bergen

Erected as a separate parish on June 29, 1963 by Archbishop Thomas A. Boland, Our Lady of Fatima had as its first pastor, Fr. (later Msgr.) George A. O'Gorman who worked tirelessly to rally the support necessary to build the modern structure that became the parish church, completed in 1965. Since its inception, the parish has been noted for its dedicated core of parishioners who have kept it alive and well. With only a church and a small rectory, it has managed to enhance the lives of several thousands of people. Having had only two other pastors since its founding, Msgr. John Gilchrist and Fr. John Korbelan, it is a relatively young parish in terms of years, but its parishioners are faithful and supportive, a vibrant mix of cultures that have come to make up its congregation in northern Hudson County. Its care for the poor and homeless is well known. The parish celebrates its 40th anniversary this year.

Sacred Heart, North Bergen

Often referred to as "the best kept secret in Hudson County," Sacred Heart, North Bergen, is located on a small side street in a residential area, rather than on a main road. Its popularity spreads by words of mouth. Founded on its current location in the "Hudson Heights" section of North Bergen in 1929, Sacred Heart was the "love vision" of the Polish immigrants who worshiped at the original site on the cliffs known as Shadyside, overlooking the Hudson River.

While situated in Hudson County, Sacred Heart Church is also closely bordered by the Bergen County towns of Cliffside Park and Fairview. Originally established as a Polish parish, today Sacred Heart also ministers to many Croatians, Hispanics and Filipinos. However, the common denominator is the English language, and uniting the parish is a love for the Sacred Heart of Jesus.

St. Brigid, North Bergen

In 1900 a wooden building was constructed and St. Brigid Roman Catholic Church was established.

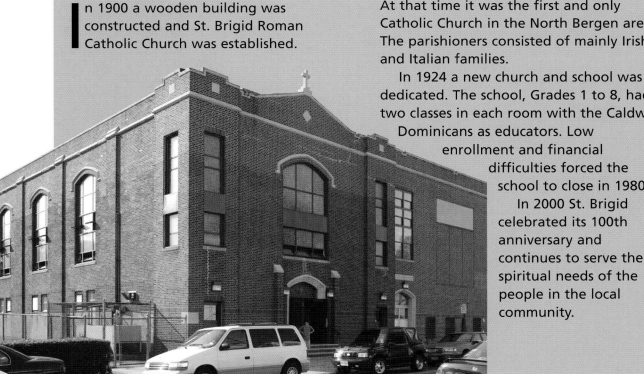

At that time it was the first and only Catholic Church in the North Bergen area. The parishioners consisted of mainly Irish and Italian families.

In 1924 a new church and school was dedicated. The school, Grades 1 to 8, had two classes in each room with the Caldwell Dominicans as educators. Low enrollment and financial difficulties forced the school to close in 1980.

In 2000 St. Brigid celebrated its 100th anniversary and continues to serve the spiritual needs of the people in the local community.

Holy Family, Union City

I n 1857 German parishioners of Holy Family, Union City, wanted to have religious services in their own native tongue. Later immigrants from Ireland and Italy came to the parish and the first Mass was celebrated in June that year. When the flock at Holy Family began to grow, a house on Patterson Plank Road was used only for religious services. Soon the Passionist Fathers sent a priest each Sunday for Mass

In 1884 a new era began with the arrival of Fr. Joseph N. Grieff, who served the parish for almost three generations. (1884-1941). He erected the church in 1887, the school in 1897, the Lyceum Clubhouse and the rectory in 1906 and Park Theatre in 1931. The high school opened in 1925. Passion Play productions began in 1915 and have enjoyed an unbroken string of yearly performances.

The parish school was destroyed by fire in 1943. A new school was dedicated in October 1944 and a convent for the Sisters of St. Francis was completed in 1948. The Parish Council was founded in 1971 and became a driving force for the future of Holy Family. The high school closed in 1972. During the '70s the parish attended to the needs of an ever-growing Hispanic community.

The '80s and '90s brought the closing of Holy Family Elementary school and the transfer of the administration of the Park Theatre to the Performing Arts Center. The parish and area continued to grow with the arrival of many immigrants from Central and South America. The parish and the new Centro Guadalupe, an Archdiocesan Pastoral Center and Institute of Formation for Hispanics, were entrusted to the Augustinian Recollects in 1997 under whom Holy Family looks forward to continued growth and grace.

St. Anthony of Padua, Union City

S t. Anthony of Padua was established in 1899. For more than half a century, to 1950, the church at the intersection of Morris Street and Tournade Lane served the Italian people of the then West Hoboken section. The church, at first considered a chapel of St. Michael Monastery Parish run by the Passionist Fathers, was dedicated on August 13, 1899, by Bishop Winand Wigger, Bishop of Newark.

In December 1916, St. Anthony Church was organized as a separate corporation. In 1919 the Chapel of Our Lady of Lourdes opened at 502 Palisade Avenue to minister to English-speaking Catholics. In 1938 the upper floors of the Chapel were adapted as a convent for the Filippini Sisters who began to work with the children.

In 1939 Fr. Caesar Rinaldi purchased property at the intersection of Central Avenue and Eighth Street, and construction of the new church and rectory began in 1941. Bishop of Paterson, Thomas Boland, dedicated the church on August 12, 1950. A new school was opened in September 1962 with Sr. Angelina Pecoraro, M.P.F., as the first principal.

With the arrival of the first Hispanics to the area, the parish experienced a great transformation. In 1965 a Spanish Mass was offered to accommodate its many Spanish-speaking parishioners. Today St. Anthony is a multicultural community open to the New Evangelization. It is constantly confronted by the advance of the sects and the collapse of Christian values that never have been challenged: family, religion, love, forgiveness. The parish is becoming a community of communities, a Christian village.

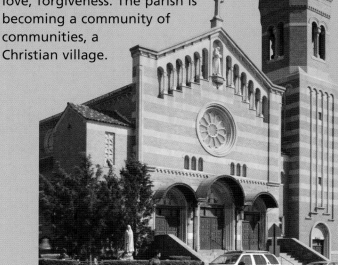

St. Augustine, Union City

In 1890, Reverend Augustine M. Brady named the parish he founded, St. Augustine, after his patron saint.

The original white wooden framed church faced Gardner Street, now 39th Street. The present church on New York Avenue, which won an award for design and creativity, opened under Msgr. Healy in 1958.

The Irish and the Germans, who worked in the local lace factories of this "embroidery capital of the world," were the first parishioners of St. Augustine parish.

In the late 1960's the first Cubans who moved to Hudson County were drawn to St. Augustine. Spanish culture has contributed to the economic and cultural status of both the city and the parish. Today, St. Augustine is one of the largest multi-cultural parishes in Hudson County.

In September 1881 a two-story brick school was opened to admit 100 students. Because of poor health among students, however, it was discontinued temporarily, and reopened in 1887. Today St. Augustine School, the first school in the Archdiocese to be accredited by the Middle States Association of Colleges in Schools, is registered as a Multiple Intelligence School at Harvard University. The entire parish community takes pride in its students and faculty.

SS. Joseph and Michael, Union City

The present-day SS. Joseph & Michael Parish is the merger of two parishes— St. Joseph and St. Michael the Archangel. St. Joseph Parish was established in 1889 to attend to the needs of the growing German population. The parish community expanded to the point that 10 years later, they had to build the much larger church that stands today. The parish distinguished itself by the flourishing of its many associations, but above all, for Veronica's Veil. This play gave name to the great Veronica's Veil Theater, which for more than 80 years presented the well known and well attended Passion Play.

St. Michael was the fruit of the missionary effort of the Passionist priests who arrived in West Hoboken (today's Union City) in 1861. Almost at once they began the construction of St. Michael Monastery and St. Michael Church. In 1982 a decline in Passionist vocations forced the community to close the monastery and the two parishes merged. Amidst many challenges, the new parish continues its commitment to evangelization, in which its parochial school, Mother Seton, plays a significant role.

In 2003 a long-awaited renovation of the Church was accomplished. The church was repainted and redesigned to follow the liturgical renewal of Vatican Council II.

St. Rocco, Union City

St. Rocco, Union City, was officially inaugurated and dedicated on July 14, 1912. The first pastor, Fr. Sinisi, led the parish from 1912 to 1922, when he was replaced by Pallottine Fr. Grisciotti. The Pallotines remained until 1984.

The first rectory was on the second floor of a wooden cobbler shop while the first floor became the church to which a small belfry was added. In 1923 a one-family wooden house on Liberty Street was purchased for use as a rectory. The present rectory was dedicated in 1951. The original wooden church burned down in 1924 and rebuilding of the existing buildings began. The many relics saved from the flames were housed in them.

In the 1950s, St. Rocco welcomed families from many nationalities. The first Spanish Mass was celebrated in 1968. Parishioners are grateful for the spiritual and material contributions of the Pallottine Fathers from 1922 to 1984 as they are for the archdiocesan priest who staff St. Rocco today.

St. Lawrence, Weehawken

Because of its tremendous accomplishments since its founding in 1887, St. Lawrence, Weehawken, has been called "The little church with the great big heart." The parish has gained recognition by putting Christian charity into action and reaching out to help others. Many of today's parishioners travel from many areas of Hudson County and beyond to this little church. At the present time, a new Parish Center is being built to accommodate the increasing number of students in the Religious Education Program and the many new ministries that parishioners have joined

through the drive for Stewardship. One of the main goals of the parish Pastoral Council is the empowerment of lay ministry in the parish through Small Christian Communities. There is new life at St. Lawrence because of the enthusiasm, generosity and loving spirit of the parishioners, pastor and staff of this little church in the shades of Weehawken.

Our Lady Help of Christians (St. Mary), West New York

The cornerstone for a combination church, school and sisters house was laid in 1895 for German-speaking Catholics in West New York. The site was the highest point in West New York, thus the later designation, "Lighthouse on the Hill." Within three months the buildings were completed and dedicated to Our Lady Help of Christians. The following month the school was opened with 76 children who were taught by Franciscan Sisters.

At the turn of the century the seating capacity of the church was doubled, stained-glass windows were installed, the sanctuary was painted, classrooms were added to the school, an auditorium was built beneath the church and a new and larger convent was built. The parish grew. In 1915 the cornerstone of a new church was

laid. The new church building was completed in 1927 and soon thereafter, a rectory. In the '70s one of the first team ministries (dual pastors) in the Archdiocese was started, bringing about a vibrant community of spiritual activity and stewardship. Soon after, the sisters no longer served the school, which eventually closed. Our Lady Help of Christians became one of the few parishes with Spanish-speaking members. People from all over the New York-New Jersey metropolitan area now attend. In 1983 the school and old convent were repaired, the rectory was renovated and the church was redecorated. In 1998 an old embroidery factory adjacent to the church was acquired for use as a Parish Center dedicated to Saint Padre Pio.

Our Lady of Libera, West New York

The history of Our Lady of Libera goes back almost a century to the emigrants of the little village of Campobasso Province in Italy. Those who came to the shores of America to settle in the towns of West New York and East Dunham saw Our Lady of Libera as the ancient protectress of all that they held dear and they relied on her to continue in this new land what she had done so well in the old country.

In 1903 the parish of Madonna della Libera was established and dedicated on November 12, 1905. The construction of the new church was begun in 1931, but had to be suspended for six years because of the Great Depression. The new church was finally dedicated in June 1937. The convent and sexton's residence were completed in that same year. The original wooden church became the Parish Hall. The Maestre Pie

Filippini were assigned to teach catechism and to direct the choirs.

On September 21, 1959, the new school building was opened and occupied by 204 children in five grades and a kindergarten. In the aftermath of Vatican Council II, liturgical changes were made to accord with the Council's directives, and after the Cuban Revolution, in addition to Spanish-speaking groups from America and South America, a large number of Cuban exiles swelled the community.

The parish formed a bilingual Parish Council, established parish trustees, and formed lay catechists and pastoral workers. In 1992 a Pre-Kindergarten was started, which, along with the Grammar School, flourishes today. Lay administrators and instructors now serve in the school.

Our Lady of Libera continues to grow in its mission to bring the message of Jesus to all.

A Wider World

FOLLOWING IN THE TRADITION WHICH ARCHBISHOP GERETY HAD
ESTABLISHED, THE FOURTH ARCHBISHOP OF NEWARK, THEODORE E.
MCCARRICK, WROTE A WEEKLY COLUMN FOR THE ARCHDIOCESAN
NEWSPAPER, *The Catholic Advocate*. ENTITLED "THINKING OF YOU,"
THE COLUMN WAS AN IMPORTANT WAY FOR THE ARCHBISHOP TO SPEAK
PERSONALLY TO HIS PEOPLE, TO SHARE INSIGHTS ABOUT THE GOSPEL,
AND TO TEACH IMPORTANT TRUTHS OF THE FAITH.

Archbishop Theodore E. McCarrick, a great communicator

Often these columns were framed with personal stories, not just from what was happening in the Archdiocese of Newark, but also in China, Latin America, Africa, Eastern Europe, and beyond, for the needs of the universal Church would often call upon the gifts of Archbishop McCarrick.

Theodore McCarrick

These gifts were indeed many. Theodore Edgar McCarrick, the only child of Theodore Egan McCarrick and Margaret McLaughlin, was born on July 7, 1930, in New York City, at the beginning of the Great Depression. Theodore McCarrick's father was a merchant sea captain from Norfolk, Virginia and had served as a helmsman in the United States Navy during the First World War. Unfortunately, he had contracted influenza in the great pandemic at the end of the war. Millions died during the outbreak, and tens of millions were left weakened by their sickness. McCarrick recovered, but his health was seriously impaired. In the fall of 1933, when his only child – a little son – was just three, Theodore Egan McCarrick

died after being infected with tuberculosis. Theodore Edgar's mother Margaret was left with the responsibility of being a single mother, caring for her son in the profoundly difficult economic times of the 1930's. Still, she was a woman of faith and of hard work, and went to work in an auto parts factory in the Bronx, while her mother helped to take care of the youngster. While the McCarricks were able to get by on Margaret's factory salary (often supplemented by commissions from photographers and artists, for Margaret McCarrick was a strikingly beautiful woman) poverty was a real fact of life for the childhood of Theodore McCarrick.

This faith in adversity was something Margaret passed on to her son. Their Church of the Incarnation, on St. Nicholas Avenue in the Washington Heights section of Manhattan, bustled with life, under the direction of Msgr. Joseph Delany, five curates, and the Sisters of Charity who cared for the bursting parish grammar school that Theodore McCarrick would attend. Even as a young boy, McCarrick had already begun to think about the priesthood. Graduating from Incarnation, he went on to study at Fordham Prep and then to Fordham University. Theodore McCarrick did not complete his studies there. Rather, he decided to travel and study in Europe for almost a year and a half, as he contemplated what course his life should take. Returning to the United States in 1952, he decided to enter St. Joseph's Seminary and study for the priesthood for the Archdiocese of New York. It was there that he completed his bachelor's and master's degrees.

As a young boy, Theodore McCarrick began to think of priesthood.

St. Joseph of the Palisades, West New York

HUDSON COUNTY

St. Joseph Church was dedicated in 1865 and placed in the charge of Passionist priests from St. Michael Monastery. In 1876 a diocesan priest took over as pastor and within the next 15 years, a new frame school with residence for the Franciscan Sisters of Peekskill, New York, was built. In 1896 St. Joseph of Guttenberg Church was built for German Catholics in the area that would become West New York. On September 13, 1903 the Guttenberg Church was transferred to the Slavic-speaking Catholics and St. Joseph of Guttenberg became St. Joseph of the Palisades, West New York.

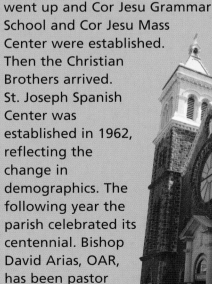

A new three-story school with sisters' residence opened in 1910 and three years later, a new church was completed and dedicated. Eleven years hence a grammar school on Palisade Avenue was added,

which by 1929 enrolled 1200+ children. The school at 20th Street was turned into a high school, which, within three years, had 280 students. In 1958 a new high school went up and Cor Jesu Grammar School and Cor Jesu Mass Center were established. Then the Christian Brothers arrived. St. Joseph Spanish Center was established in 1962, reflecting the change in demographics. The following year the parish celebrated its centennial. Bishop David Arias, OAR, has been pastor since 1994.

Little Flower, Berkeley Heights

Little Flower Parish in Union County is in the southwest corner of the Archdiocese with borders contiguous with parishes in two other dioceses--Paterson and Metuchen. The parish facilities, which include the Little Church, the Auditorium Church, the Parish Center and a rectory, are located on 24 acres of forested and flood-plain land.

It is not unusual to see deer on the front lawn in the morning, although Berkeley Heights has an overall population of 12,912 and the parish has grown to 1540 families. Efforts have been made to involve parishioners in parish ministry and to provide various small communities for personal spiritual enrichment.

A parish handbook describing the life of the parish is provided to all parishioners and is included in the welcome packet for new families in the parish. New parishioners are also welcomed personally by fellow parishioners.

One sign of the deep spiritual commitment of the parish is the great number who participate in two daily Masses. The arrival of many young families in the area has made the parochial elementary Religious Education Program an unusually large and active one, comprising some 600 children and 85 catechists.

Overall, the people of Little Flower are a diverse group--some with roots that go back to when the parish was a mission, while others have moved into the parish more recently. In any case, a desire for spiritual growth is characteristic of those who make the parish their faith community.

His academic talent was recognized by Cardinal Spellman, and, soon after his ordination to the priesthood on May 31, 1958, Fr. McCarrick was sent to the Catholic University of America, in Washington, DC, to complete a second master's degree and a doctorate in Social Sciences. While completing his degrees, McCarrick also served as an assistant chaplain at Catholic University, Dean of Students, and Director of Development. McCarrick's capacity for work, for balancing a wide array of different jobs, and juggling both administrative and pastoral tasks – which would become legendary – began early. From the Catholic University of America, Fr. McCarrick was sent to the Catholic University of Puerto Rico, where he would serve for four rewarding years as the president of that institution.

Bishop McCarrick

Returning home to New York in 1969, McCarrick (now monsignor) went to work as Associate Secretary for Education for the Archdiocese of New York, taking up residence at Blessed Sacrament Church on West 71st Street. He was able to work there for only two years, before Cardinal Cooke asked McCarrick to serve as his secretary. Serving for almost six years with Cardinal Cooke would give McCarrick great insight into diocesan administration, as well as the example and friendship of a devout and humble bishop. In 1977, Pope Paul VI named Msgr. McCarrick as one of three new auxiliary bishops for Cardinal Cooke. The Cardinal asked McCarrick to serve as his Vicar for East Manhattan and the Harlems. Responsible for the care of a number of parishes, McCarrick worked hard, using his personal dynamism and skill in languages to assist the priests of the area in serving an ever-widening array of ethnic groups. His availability, drive, unfailing memory for names, gifted capacity for work, and natural pastoral sense when preaching to and working with ordinary people, all assisted McCarrick in this labor.

Using his personal dynamism and skill in languages, Archbishop McCarrick assisted his priests in serving an ever-widening array of ethnic groups.

The expansion of suburban New Jersey had brought greatly increased numbers of Catholics to the central part of the state. Providing effective pastoral care for these Catholics became an increasingly important need. On November 19, 1981, Bishop McCarrick was appointed by Pope John Paul II to undertake an important new task – organizing an entirely new diocese, that of Metuchen, New Jersey, and serving as its founding bishop.

Drawn from the Diocese of Trenton, the Diocese of Metuchen comprised four counties of New Jersey, with half a million Catholics. It contained 93 parishes and was served by over 200 priests and almost 600 religious. This diocese would be organized and shepherded by Bishop McCarrick for the first five years of its life. Organize he did: it seemed that Bishop McCarrick was everywhere at once, celebrating, in a veritable whirlwind, Mass at a number of parishes each weekend, while visiting schools and religious houses, hospitals and institutions throughout the diocese. The priorities for this new diocese would be drawn from Bishop McCarrick's personal experience: outreach and care for the

poor, attentive service to ethnic communities, fostering of priestly vocations, and finding the resources to ensure that these priorities could be fully addressed. Unfortunately for the Bishop and people of Metuchen, McCarrick's time there would be all too short. Others would have the opportunity to reap what he had sown, for on June 3, 1986, a little more than four years after being installed in Metuchen, it was announced that Bishop McCarrick was appointed as the fourth Archbishop of Newark.

Archbishop McCarrick with children during a CCS visit, June 1989

Archbishop McCarrick on visit to the Bergen County Jail in 1988

Archbishop McCarrick at a Boy Scout Mass, Harrington Park, 1989

Seventh Largest Archdiocese

Under the leadership of Archbishop Gerety, the Archdiocese of Newark had continued taking up the reforms of the Second Vatican Council begun by Archbishop Boland. One of the great charges which would face the new Archbishop was to bring those reforms to greater and lasting maturity, coming to grips with both the changes that were occurring in the population of the Archdiocese and an increasingly secular

Dedication of the chapel in the Chancery

American culture. The wider Church, under the leadership of Pope John Paul II, was taking up these challenges, and they needed to be addressed in the Archdiocese of Newark. The Archdiocese of Newark, by this time the seventh largest in the United States in terms of population, had almost one and a half million Catholics. While the Archdiocese had had its share of post-Conciliar difficulties, it did not have to grapple with some of the problems that other dioceses in the United States faced. The Archdiocese of Newark had an educated laity who were taking ownership in the life of the Archdiocese, hardworking priests and religious in sufficient numbers, many vibrant institutions, an ample number of churches, and a fully-developed infrastructure to serve the poor and disadvantaged.

Together with other locations, Archdiocesan offices were housed in the old Chancery at 31 Mulberry Street until offices were centralized on Clifton Avenue, Newark.

What was needed was a shepherd to draw all of these elements together, shrewd enough in the ways of the world to try to understand 1980's America and wise enough in the things of God to try to transcend them. Pope John Paul II entrusted this role to Theodore E. McCarrick.

As in Metuchen, Archbishop McCarrick's first priority was to try to get to know his people by visiting as many parishes as possible. Pressing each weekend for time, McCarrick would visit all 240 parishes in the Archdiocese in his first year as Archbishop. Indeed, he would make it his custom to try and visit all the churches of the Archdiocese at least once every three years of his whole tenure. McCarrick pushed himself hard, eschewing days off or personal

A glimpse of the modern interior of the pastoral center

The Archdiocese has an educated laity who take ownership in the life of the local Church.

St. Agnes, Clark

On July 6, 1961, St. Agnes Parish was established, the first Mass being celebrated in Charles H. Brewer School on Westfield Avenue, Clark. As the congregation rapidly grew, it became necessary to hold Sunday liturgies at Arthur L. Johnson Regional High School. On August 15, 1963, four Caldwell Dominican Sisters arrived to teach the parish school children, for the first year, conducting classes at Union Catholic High School, Scotch Plains. The next September the children were happily settled in their new school on the parish grounds. The joy and pride of parishioners was evident at the new church and rectory completed in 1964. The school is currently under the direction of the Religious Teachers of St. Lucy Filippini of Morristown,

while the Chestnut Hill Sisters of St. Joseph conduct the present Religious Education program (CCD) for more than 520 public school children.

vacation time, taking an active interest and active hand in every aspect of the ministries of the Archdiocese. Seemingly overnight he knew the names of all his priests, the assignments where they had served, and their personal histories. Diocesan offices that had grown quiescent were shaken up. A vast amount of correspondence flowed out of the Chancery. New programs were established, from drug prevention, to assisting those who suffered from AIDS, to ministry for women and men in need of post-abortion healing. The poor and immigrant, union workers, unwed mothers, inner-city school children all found an understanding advocate in Archbishop McCarrick.

It is hardly surprising then, that Archbishop McCarrick's brother bishops, the Pope, and many other organizations recognized his energy and ability and decided to call upon his services. Few professional diplomats or politicians could match the Archbishop's

Archbishop McCarrick greets students at St. Aloysius Elementary and High School

stamina, his gift for languages, his ability to set people at ease while astutely judging and weighing situations fraught with difficulties or navigating through them.

Girl Scouts get to see the Archbishop at their Scout Mass.

St. Michael, Cranford

On October 2, 1872, Fr. Gregory Misdziol celebrated Mass for 58 adults and 61 children in the home of Terence Brennan, and thus the parish community of St. Michael, Cranford, was established. In 1877, through the generous donations of parishioners, the first church was built. When a tragic fire destroyed the building on February 22, 1901, the congregation immediately began plans for a new and larger church, to be located in the downtown area. The cornerstone was laid later that year and the doors of the new church opened in 1902. The building served the community until 1948, when, with the increasing growth of the congregation, it was demolished to make way for the present church. On November 26, 1950, the cornerstone for the current church with its soaring bell tower was laid. In 1995, the doors were once gain shut as a massive restoration project was undertaken to modernize the church interior. In 1997 St. Michael celebrated its 125th anniversary. It presently serves 3,500 families.

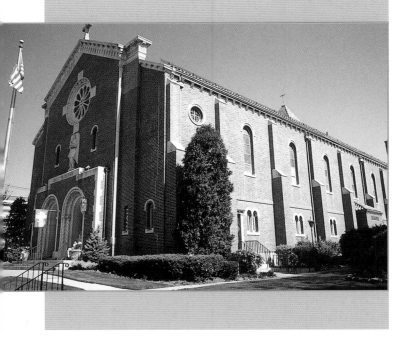

Leadership Roles

The United States Conference of Catholic Bishops elected him to head its Committee on Migration in 1986, the first of many undertakings they asked of the Archbishop. He would go on to serve on many committees of the NCCB, including those for International Policy and Aid to the Church in Central and Eastern Europe. The Holy See asked Archbishop McCarrick to work with the Pontifical Council for the Pastoral Care of Migrants and People on the Move as well as the Pontifical Council for Justice and Peace. He would be appointed to the

While working for International Religious Freedom for places like the Philippines and South Korea, Archbishop McCarrick welcomed all peoples in his own Archdiocese.

Helsinki Commission and to the United States Commission for International Religious Freedom. Never content to advise from afar, Archbishop McCarrick would make it a point to travel to wherever he was asked to go, to survey humanitarian or religious needs in person. So it was that the Archbishop witnessed some of the most noble accomplishments at the conclusion of the twentieth century, such as the transitions to democracy in the Philippines and South Korea and the rebirth of so many ancient Christian communities from behind the Iron Curtain. He also witnessed some of the greatest tragedies at the conclusion of the twentieth century, such as the grinding poverty of the

Church in Latin America, genocidal strife in Africa and Bosnia, and desire for freedom of the people of Cuba, China, and Tibet. It would be no idle compliment when, as the new Archbishop of Washington, McCarrick was welcomed by his predecessor James Cardinal Hickey as, "truly a citizen of the world."

The obligation to travel so frequently meant that when the Archbishop was back in the Archdiocese, his schedule had to be filled all the more. Indeed, McCarrick was able to arrive after a long flight following a significant international mission and drive directly to a rapid succession of parish events or weekend Masses, seemingly none the worse for wear. Archbishop McCarrick's travels also brought a steady stream of important international visitors, both ecclesiastical and lay, to the Archdiocese, who wanted to update him about events abroad and visit the Archdiocese of which McCarrick had spoken so often. His travels also gave the Archbishop a strong sense of what was happening in the wider Church, and often would supply him with a variety of ideas that might be tried in the Archdiocese of Newark.

Although involved in international movements, Archbishop McCarrick did not neglect his mission of proclaiming the Gospel in his home Archdiocese. He focused especially on developing vocations to the diocesan priesthood by word and example.

Blessed Sacrament, Elizabeth

On January 9, 1922, the 48 families who began Blessed Sacrament Parish gathered with their pastor, Fr. Anthony Goebel, OSB, in a small wooden church bought from a congregation in Ocean Grove and transported in sections to the

recently purchased property on North Avenue to celebrate their passage from a Mission of Sacred Heart Parish to full status as a parish.

Four years later the Benedictine Sisters welcomed 300 students to the new Blessed Sacrament School. By 1933 a convent for the sisters was built, and the church was expanded to accommodate the rapidly growing congregation. Four years later, in the mid-1940s, the bowling alleys in the school basement became classrooms to accommodate an ever-growing enrollment, and more property was purchased to create space for a larger church.

In 1964 the proud parishioners of Blessed Sacrmant gathered with their pastor, Fr. Claude Micik, OSB, to worship in a beautiful new church. Currently Blessed Sacrament, now staffed by Archdiocesan priests, offers services to not only the English-speaking community of the parish, but also its ever-growing Hispanic and Brazilian communities.

Development of Religious Vocations

While overseas, Archbishop McCarrick was able to keep in close contact with home through telephone, fax, and e-mail. One area of work in the Archdiocese however that he always made a point to concentrate on while home through personal witness and invitation was the development of vocations – particularly to the diocesan priesthood. Tirelessly, at all parish visits,

In the Archbishop's eyes, young people were the hope of the church.

Each individual seminarian was of special concern to Archbishop McCarrick.

Archbishop McCarrick sounded this theme, often asking the young people whom he greeted following Mass to consider becoming a priest or sister or brother and asking everyone to pray for vocations. McCarrick took a very active hand in the seminary formation program of the Archdiocese, attentively watching over the progress of each seminarian, and striving to be available personally to their needs. Though it did not return to the numbers of the 1950's and 1960's, gradually the enrollment of Immaculate Conception Seminary expanded.

Archbishop McCarrick also was instrumental in establishing a new missionary seminary for the Archdiocese, *Redemptoris Mater*, dedicated to seminarians formed in the Neo-catechumenal Way.

UNION COUNTY

Immaculate Conception, Elizabeth

Immaculate Conception Parish had begun as a Mission of St. Mary Parish in May 1904. In 1907 a building was purchased at what today is 1000 N. Broad Street, Hillside. In 1909 the property that now houses Immaculate Conception Church was purchased and the cornerstone of a new church laid the next year. Building continued until the new building was ready for use. It was dedicated in May 1913.

Following the pastorate of almost 40 years by Fr. William S. Condon, Fr. Thomas J. Donnelly built a new church alongside the existing rectory, a parish hall attached to the church, a new convent to replace the 100-year-old frame building,

a re-modeled school and a completely remodeled rectory.

As a result of demographic changes, Immaculate Conception is now a parish comprising various cultures with Hispanics in largest number.

Eight sisters of St. Joseph of Peace celebrate Golden Jubilees in 1993, as the religious who entered in the years of prolific vocations to religious life in the mid-fifties began to age.

Archbishop McCarrick was instrumental in establishing a new missionary seminary for the Archdiocese-- Redemptoris Mater, dedicated to seminarians formed in the Neocatechumenal way, which deepens faith through intense catechesis and small group support.

A renewal movement begun in Spain, the Neocatechumenal Way seeks to deepen and form the faith of marginal Catholics through intense catechesis and small group support. Young men from Neocatechumenal communities around the world come to study for the priesthood in the Archdiocese of Newark, serving in parishes within the Archdiocese, and then working as missionaries abroad.

Through the continual prayers of the faithful of the Archdiocese, the personal initiative of the Archbishop, and the new missionary seminary, Theodore McCarrick, during his time of service in Newark, was in fact able to ordain more priests than any other bishop in the whole United States.

Seminarians participate in a Cathedral ceremony with their archbishop.

Lay Formation

As important as vocations and seminary formation were to the Archbishop, he did not let that eclipse the equally important work of lay formation. The Archbishop invited all of the parishes of the Archdiocese of Newark to participate in "Renew 2000," an updating of the Christian small faith community formation program that had been developed and borne such fruit under Archbishop Gerety.

Lay people are called to greater involvement. A lay minister leads the congregation in song.

Likewise, he directed that all parishes in the Archdiocese undertake "Stewardship," an initiative to ask the faithful of the Archdiocese to consider their use of time, talent, and treasure and, through this examination, to increase the number of lay people who would be committed to working in ministry on a parish level. For those who had grown away from the Church during the post-Conciliar period, the Archbishop encouraged "Reconciliation 2000," a weekend dedicated to the Sacrament of

Penance, during which confessions were held continuously throughout the Archdiocese. To prepare for this, a media campaign was undertaken and priests staffed phone banks to answer callers' questions, both about the Sacrament and about all aspects of Catholic life. Beyond these programs, one of the most important ways that Archbishop McCarrick sought to encourage and promote greater involvement of lay men and women in the life of the Church of Newark was through holding an Archdiocesan Synod in 1994.

Clergy Synod

The last Synod that the Archdiocese of Newark had held was in 1941, under the direction of Archbishop Walsh. At that time, it was a gathering of the clergy of the Archdiocese to discuss and recommend policies concerning various aspects of liturgical, rectory, and priestly life to the Archbishop. The Synod of Archbishop McCarrick was, however, to have different

UNION COUNTY

Immaculate Heart of Mary, Elizabeth

The mission of Immaculate Heart of Mary since its establishment in the Elizabethport area has been to care for the spiritual needs of its Spanish-speaking parishioners. Perhaps the most remarkable feature of the parish is its physical appearance and location. Except for the stony cross that tops the structure, the church could easily be bypassed. Located on a second floor, originally Immaculate Heart was built as a physical therapy center. In the mid-1940s, when the complex was up for sale, the Archdiocese acquired it for the fast growing immigrant population. The Spanish-speaking Franciscan Fathers, T.O.R. were invited by the late Archbishop Walsh to meet the spiritual needs of the immigrants, mainly from Central and South

American countries and the Caribbean Islands. The parish strives to provide help, orientation and counseling to its people and so to encourage them in their strong Catholic faith, family bonds and spirit of friendly cooperation.

Our Lady of Fatima, Elizabeth

Our Lady of Fatima, Elizabeth, was established by Archbishop Thomas A. Boland for the Portuguese-speaking people on May 14, 1973. After worshiping for several years at St. Patrick on Court Street, Portuguese immigrants met at Immaculate Heart of Mary, Jersey Street, for their services. On December 23, 1973, a Methodist Church on First Avenue, with a capacity of 250, was purchased and remodeled.

When the parish outgrew the building, thought was given to building a new church. However, the Archdiocese was not receptive to the idea. Meanwhile, Bishop Dominick A. Marconi, Episcopal Vicar for Union County, contacted Our Lady of Fatima Parish Council, mentioning the possibility of merging with Sacred Heart Parish at Spring and Bond Streets. Under the leadership of Mr. Joseph Vancio of the Diocesan Planning Office, the two parish councils began meeting.

It took two years to agree on the terms of the merger. The most sensitive issue was the change of name from Sacred Heart to Our Lady of Fatima. The official merger took place on June 26, 1983, under Fr. John S. Antao, who had been the guiding force from the beginning.

focus. It was to be a gathering of representatives of all the faithful of the Archdiocese of Newark: laity and religious women and men, as well as diocesan priests. The agenda of the Synod was not to be worked out by Archdiocesan officials, but meant to grow by means of a series of assemblies held throughout the Archdiocese to listen and draw together a wide variety of concerns. At the actual Synod itself, held on the campus of Seton Hall University, these matters were examined more fully and formulated into a series of recommendations for Archbishop McCarrick to consider, particularly promoting lay ministry and outreach to young people.

The Neocatechumenal community of St. Peter Claver, Asbury Park, Trenton Diocese, participates in a joint celebration with members of the Archdiocese of Newark.

Concern for the Poor

While the 1980's and 1990's were very good times economically for many Americans, a number of people, particularly in the Archdiocese of Newark, did not share in the material prosperity of the country. A new wave of immigration to the Archdiocese of Newark, from Latin America, Africa, and Asia, also brought thousands of Catholics to New Jersey who were in need of material and legal assistance, language and work training, as well

as health and pastoral care. Catholic Community Services, the successor to the venerable Mount Carmel Guild, and Archbishop McCarrick – who understood from personal experience what it was like to be poor – worked hard to try to raise awareness on the local, state, and also federal level about the genuine needs of so many and to provide for all of these needs. Unhesitant and unabashed in asking for the needs of his people, the Archbishop was able to raise considerable amounts of resources from the materially blessed of the Archdiocese for their poorer brothers and sisters.

Before the completion of his time as Archbishop of Newark, McCarrick could proudly pay tribute to the concern and generosity of his people, "We [in the Archdiocese of Newark] are the largest provider of shelter for the homeless and feeder of the hungry in the state of New Jersey."

Catholic Community Services, the successor to the Mount Carmel Guild, continues to serve the poor of the Archdiocese.

Groundbreaking for St. Michael Hospital is a joyful occasion in the fall of 1980.

Under the compassionate care of Archbishop McCarrick, the Archdiocese of Newark became "the largest provider of shelter for the homeless and feeder of the hungry in the state of New Jersey."

St. Adalbert, Elizabeth

UNION COUNTY

In May 1905, a young pastor from St. Stanislaus Church in Newark rode his bicycle from Newark to an area of Elizabethport. It was in this area that he was to meet a group of people from Poland. He was amazed at the crowd of more than 1000 faithful that awaited his arrival. They pressed him to request the building of a church for the Polish people in Elizabeth. It was to be named after the Apostle and Patron of Poland. St. Adalbert (Wojciech).

Within one short year, their dream became reality. By August 11 a parcel of land on Third Street was purchased from the city of Elizabeth. The foundation work began by October 25 and the cornerstone was blessed on December 17, 1905. Finally in June 1906, St. Adalbert Parish Church was dedicated.

In the years 2005-2006, St. Adalbert Parish will celebrate its 100th anniversary.

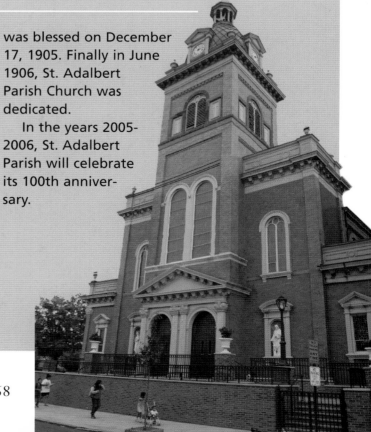

Our Lady of the Most Holy Rosary and St. Michael, Elizabeth

German immigrants founded St. Michael Parish in 1852, a year before the Archdiocese was established. By 1886 another parish was formed to accommodate the increasing number of non-German immigrants, and so Our Lady of the Most Holy Rosary Parish was established. Both parishes built elementary schools, St. Michael in 1885 and Holy Rosary in the early 1900s. The parishes flourished throughout the first half of the Twentieth Century. Holy Rosary built a new school in 1959. But the Sixties brought about rapid changes in the area with many of the older parishioners moving out and an influx of new immigrants from Latin America. By the early 1970s, Spanish Masses and Spanish-speaking priests were added at both parishes. In 1976, St. Michael offered a French Mass for the increasing number of Haitian immigrants.

Although there were many new immigrants, the overall Catholic population of the area declined. This necessitated the merging of the two parishes that had separated 99 years earlier. In 1986 the last Mass was celebrated in the Holy Rosary building and St. Michael School was merged with Holy Rosary. By 1993, this situation was deemed unworkable and Holy Rosary School was also closed. These painful experiences have left scars, particularly on those who belonged to Holy Rosary Parish. Currently the parish is a wonderful mix of cultures and faith expressions. It is predominantly Hispanic, but also serves a large Haitian community and a dedicated English-speaking community who glorify God with great energy and love.

St. Anthony of Padua, Elizabeth

As early as 1875, Italian immigrants, drawn by the prospect of steady jobs, came to Elizabeth. As their numbers grew, they sought a national parish of their own. In 1893 the first Italian families banded together and were given the use of St. Michael Chapel on Smith Street. This chapel kept shrinking and volunteers campaigned for funds to buy the German Methodist Church in their neighborhood. The rapidly growing Italian community became a parish on December 27, 1905.

New life in the parish came with the advent of the Salesians of St. John Bosco. In 1927, the new St. Anthony, built in Romanesque design with a 70-foot steeple, was dedicated, seating more than 700. Christian Doctrine classes for children and young adults eventually proved inadequate. A new school, convent and rectory were completed by 1964. In 1968 renovations were undertaken and the school was expanded with dedication taking place in 1970.

As the parish continues to flourish and new families move in, the Salesians are dedicated to continue the tradition of zealous service to God and Church in Elizabeth, where parishioners pass on the torch of faith to their children.

St. Genevieve, Elizabeth

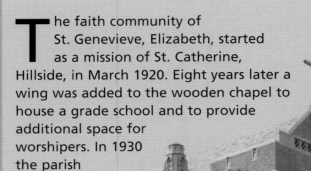

The faith community of St. Genevieve, Elizabeth, started as a mission of St. Catherine, Hillside, in March 1920. Eight years later a wing was added to the wooden chapel to house a grade school and to provide additional space for worshipers. In 1930 the parish erected the larger Church / School complex that stands today.

Ground was broken June 4, 1931 for the present wood frame convent to house the Benedictine Sisters who were to comprise the teaching staff of the new school.

The present rectory was built in 1957.

In 1994, in preparation for the 75th anniversary of the parish, the church was renovated to its original beauty and an elevator was installed. A series of pastors, with Msgr. Hugh A. O'Donnell as present pastor, led the congregation through the years, transmitting the faith to each new generation.

St. Hedwig, Elizabeth

More than 75 years ago, St. Hedwig Church was founded in Bayway for the ever-growing Polish community. The first pastor was assigned August 20, 1925, and 19 lots were purchased from The Standard Oil Company at a cost of $19,000. In 1926, dedication of the new church and school took place. Seven Sisters of the Immaculate Conception of New Britain, Connecticut, were assigned to staff the school, which had seven large classrooms with accommodations for about 400 children.

The rectory was completed in the spring of 1939 and the convent, in 1953. When land across 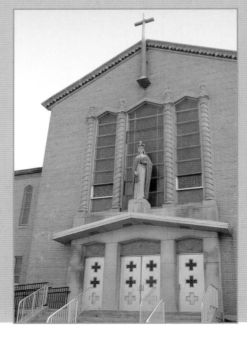 the street from the church was available, the present church of modern Romanesque design with a prominent modern tower and a seating capacity of 1000 was built and dedicated on October 15, 1960. Within a span of 50 years, St. Hedwig was blessed with three vocations to the priesthood and 16 to the sisterhood. The parish now has 750 families, but prior to the construction of major highways in the Bayway area, reached a total of 960. The school is presently attended by 231 children.

St. Mary of the Assumption, Elizabeth

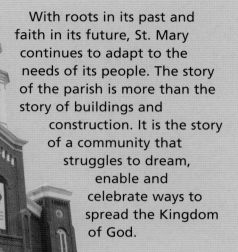

St. Mary of the Assumption Church is the oldest Catholic Parish in Elizabeth and in Union County. It predates the founding of the Archdiocese of Newark and the formation of Union County.

Established in 1844, it originally served a French and Irish immigrant population. Long identified as an Irish parish, it has served the needs of a number of waves of immigrants from European countries and, more recently, from Latin America.

St. Mary School is more than 150 years old. The parish high school was opened in 1930.

With roots in its past and faith in its future, St. Mary continues to adapt to the needs of its people. The story of the parish is more than the story of buildings and construction. It is the story of a community that struggles to dream, enable and celebrate ways to spread the Kingdom of God.

St. Patrick, Elizabeth

St. Patrick Parish was founded in 1858 to serve the blue-collar population of Elizabethport. In 1877 a building campaign was started by Fr. Martin Gressner, fourth pastor of the parish. The church structure is styled after the Cathedral of Cologne, Germany. The cornerstone was laid in 1887 and the completed building was dedicated in 1899. Built of Maine granite, the church is Gothic in style with geometric tracery and twin spires.

Its interior measures 180' by 60'; the height of the ceiling at its central point is 90'; seating capacity is 1600. Originally the church had a "lower church" seating 1300. This area is now used as a meeting hall, school cafeteria and social center. The main church itself has remained much as originally designed.

The Elizabethport area of Elizabeth was and remains a community composed of many ethnic immigrants. Originally St. Patrick ministered to the Irish population, but since the 1960s has attracted a multi-Hispanic community from Cuba, Puerto Rico, Peru, Columbia and other Central and South American countries.

St. Patrick has always been a nucleus for community-related activities. Currently it provides services to AA/NA groups, a Peruvian Culture group, a Spanish Club, CCD and support services for homeless pregnant women and a community pantry.

SS. Peter & Paul, Elizabeth

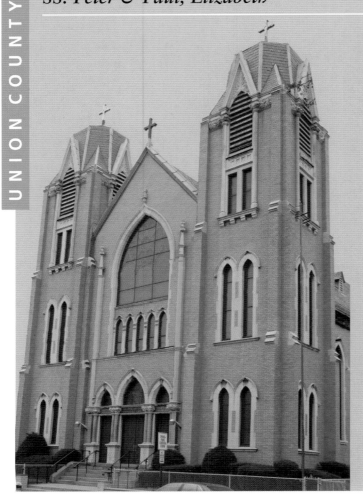

Lithuanian families settled in Elizabeth around 1878. During the years that followed, they celebrated Mass and religious services at St. Patrick, Elizabeth. By 1891 Lithuanians in the area increased considerably, and in 1893 permission was obtained from Bishop Winand Wigger to solicit funds for a new parish. On June 28, 1895, a small store on Bond Street was chosen as a temporary worship space with a Lithuanian priest. The next August the parish was officially established as SS. Peter & Paul, and the cornerstone of the new church, presently the parish hall, was laid on October 6, 1895.

The Lithuanian emigration to Newark increased so rapidly that Holy Trinity on Adams Street and parishes in Bayonne, Jersey City and Paterson were organized for the immigrants. The increase in Elizabeth's Lithuanians necessitated the building of a new brick, Gothic style church seating 1000 in 1910. It stands today.

Church of St. Anne, Garwood

On October 24, 1925, the parish of St. Anne, Garwood, was incorporated by Bishop John J. O'Connor and Fr. James F. McDonald was named first Mission Pastor. Five years later the parish was formally established and Fr. John M. Walsh became the first pastor.

On September 10, 1951, St. Anne Elementary School opened with the Bernardine Sisters staffing it. Beginning with 180 students, school enrollment reached more than 600 in the 1960s.

Declining enrollment forced the school's closing in 1986. In 1996 the building was rented to the Deron School and the convent has been transformed into a parish Education Center. Presently the parish registers 1450 households and 300 students attend religious education classes.

Christ the King, Hillside

Christ the King Church, Hillside, began as a Mission of St. Catherine, Hillside, on November 8, 1931. The congregation that worshiped in the little white wooden structure became a separate parish on June 16, 1948. As early as 1932 the Holy Name, Rosary/Altar Society, Young Ladies Sodality, Junior Holy Name Society and CCD were formed.

Fr. DeWitt, pastor since 1948, broke ground for Christ the King School, which opened with 530 students from K to Grade 6 in 1953 with the Dominican Sisters as teachers. In October 1954, the convent was completed. As of 2003 all the teachers are lay under Dominican principalship.

In the 1970s CYO, Prayer Group and the High School CYO took hold and the parish began to flourish. The Home School Association was also founded. When Fr. Richard D. Carlson became pastor in 1988, groups such as Couples for Christ, Handmaidens for Christ, AA, Portuguese Community and Small Prayer Groups began meeting at Christ the King. Since July 1, 2002, under the pastoral care of Fr. Venantius M. Fernando, parishioners have become actively involved as Eucharistic Ministers, Ministers of Hospitality, Readers, Choir Members, Parish Council Members, Stewardship Committee members and Rosary Society participants.

St. Catherine of Siena, Hillside

The largest church in the community for many years and the first within the future township's limits, St. Catherine of Siena was founded in May 1904 for the community of Hillside. Prior to its organization, residents journeyed to St. Mary of the Assumption in Elizabeth. With Fr. Thomas F. Canty as pastor, construction of the present church began on January 7, 1926, the cornerstone being laid in May. On February 12, 1928, the Weymouth granite church, of old English Gothic design, was dedicated.

Steady population increase soon made a parochial school necessary. In 1920 the Gilhooly estate in Elizabeth was purchased and altered for school purposes. The new building for 450 children, costing $492,000 was opened April 2, 1951, to replace the original school housing 350 children. The Caldwell Dominican Sisters supplied the teaching staff. Following the departure of the Dominicans in 1981, the Daughters of Charity of St. Vincent De Paul ran the school until 1996 when

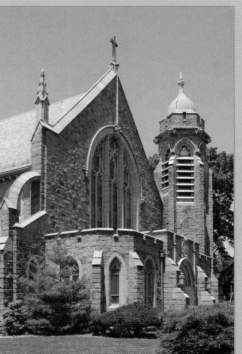

a lay principal was appointed. In 1997, the Franciscan Sisters of the Immaculate Heart of Mary of India established their first foundation in the U.S. in the convent, serving as nurses and teachers.

The shortage of priests prompted the Finance Board and Trustees to advise the pastor, Fr. Villanova, to appoint Sr. Margaret A. Scarpone of the Sisters of Mercy of the Americas as Pastoral Associate. The parish is also served by Deacon Osiris Molina. Amidst 80 years of change, St. Catherine has been constant in her mission: to preach and teach the Good News of Jesus Christ.

Papal Visit

The greatest tribute that was paid to the faithful of the Archdiocese of Newark during this time did not come from Archbishop McCarrick, but from His Holiness, Pope John Paul II. This Pontiff, who with his personal example of genuine holiness, joyous teaching of the Gospel, and tireless apostolic journeys, has done a tremendous amount for the renewal of the whole Church. The Pope was able to visit the faithful of the Archdiocese of Newark. Archbishop McCarrick, who had issued an open invitation to the Pope, was delighted to tell the people of the Archdiocese that the Pope had accepted, and would be coming to Newark in 1994.

The excitement and vast effort that the papal visit generated was turned to disappointment when the Pope's health would not permit him to undertake the trip. Pope John Paul II did not forget about the Archdiocese of Newark, and after he had recovered, made the journey to New Jersey in October of 1995.

Soon after his arrival in the United States, on October 4th, at the Cathedral of the Sacred Heart, Pope John Paul II celebrated Evening Prayer with the people of the Archdiocese, challenging them to become living stones "to build up the Church in faith, hope, and love." For the thousands of faithful – including all of the cloistered religious of the state, who had been invited to the Cathedral at the special

Newark Welcomes Pope John Paul II

Catholics of the Archdiocese of Newark and from all of New Jersey gathered en masse to present a warm welcome to the Holy Father in Giants Stadium in 1995.

Modern technology is employed to welcome the Holy Father.

The Holy Father greets the crowds in New Jersey from his Popemobile.

Celebrities like President and Mrs. Clinton graced the occasion.

The Holy Father ignores the drizzle to bless the assembly.

The Holy Father blesses the people.

Archbishop McCarrick greets Mother Teresa of Calcutta who visited her sisters serving in the Archdiocese.

St. Theresa, Kenilworth

Kenilworth was established as a mission of St. Michael Church, Cranford. The first Mass in Kenilworth was celebrated on October 4, 1936, in the Kenilworth Fire Headquarters. Increasing Sunday Mass attendance (abut 800 families) led to the

request of Archbishop McCarrick – civic leaders, and special guests, it was a moment of tremendous grace. The President of the United States of America, Bill Clinton, was present that evening, making Evening Prayer at Sacred Heart Cathedral the first time ever that an American President and the Pope participated in a prayer service together. The Holy Father too was moved by the evening and raised the Cathedral of the Sacred Heart to the dignity of a minor basilica. The following day, after his historic address to the General Assembly of the United Nations, Pope John Paul II returned to the Archdiocese of Newark and celebrated Mass with tens of thousands of the people of the Archdiocese, who braved driving rains at Giants' Stadium in the Meadowlands, to be with him. Asking them to live ever more deeply their faith in Jesus, to labor on behalf of the forgotten, and to protect the unborn, the Pope reminded the faithful of the Archdiocese of Newark that Catholics sometimes have to witness to Christ by challenging the dominant culture with the Gospel. As Pope John Paul II concluded his visit, the Archbishop expressed the feelings of all,

purchase of a building, which was renovated to a chapel where the blessing and first Mass were celebrated on November 1, 1942. By June of 1949, the mission was elevated to parish status. Fr. Sylvester P. McVeigh, the first pastor, announced plans in 1953 to build a school, convent and combination auditorium/church. These buildings were dedicated on October 25, 1954. Within six years, school attendance rose to more than 675 and space for classrooms was leased from the Borough in 1962. Grounds were broken for a school addition in 1962, and work was completed in 1964. The next year construction began on the new church and rectory, which were dedicated on March 18, 1967. Today St. Theresa Parish serves more than 1000 families with approximately 300 children enrolled in the school and more than 500 in the religious education program.

Holy Family, Linden

Founded in 1955 as a mission church of St. Joseph, Elizabeth, Holy Family Parish is a rich blend of the American-Slovak cultures characteristic of the people nestled in a secluded "old-fashioned" neighborhood of Linden. While many of its parishioners live in the tight-knit local community, others come from more than 30 different cities in the New Jersey / New York environs. Holy Family Parish is unique in offering a Sunday Liturgy in the Slovak language.

From its inception under the guidance of its first pastor,

Msgr. Michael Komar to today under its present pastor, Fr. Eugene Diurczak, the small parish forms a family that blends the traditions and history of its bilingual societies with steadfast Christian values.

St. Elizabeth of Hungary, Linden

The history of St. Elizabeth Parish mirrors the history of Linden and, beyond Linden, of America.

Ethnically diverse, the parish reflects the multicultural backgrounds of St. Elizabeth parishioners, many of whom are descendants of the waves of immigrants who flocked

to the United States in the late 19th and 20th centuries.

This year St. Elizabeth celebrates the 50th anniversary of its present church and in six years will mark its centennial as a parish.

The Benedictine Monks of St. Mary Abbey, Morristown, who staff the parish, began serving the people of Linden shortly after the parish was established.

Since opening in 1927 our school, originally staffed by the Dominican Sisters of Caldwell has now entered into a co-sponsorship with St. Mary's Parish in Rahway. Sts. Mary and Elizabeth Academy provides an excellent foundation in the faith for its children from Pre-K through 8th grade.

The Missionaries of Charity of Calcutta assemble in the Cathedral at the advent of their General Superior Mother Teresa.

St. John the Apostle, Linden

saying that the Church in New Jersey, "will never be the same."

Certainly his experience while in Newark made a lasting impression on the Holy Father as well. During the Great Jubilee of 2000, the Pope asked Archbishop Theodore E. McCarrick, now 70, to become the Archbishop of Washington, DC. Serving the Archdiocese of Newark had been the longest assignment that Archbishop McCarrick had had in his priesthood, yet, like Bishops Bayley and Corrigan before him, when called upon, McCarrick placed his gifts at the service of the wider Church.

Ever first a priest, Archbishop McCarrick conducts a ceremony honoring the Blessed Sacrament with great reverence.

The lights are--literally--always on at St. John the Apostle, Linden / Clark. At Perpetual Adoration of the Eucharist more than 600 people pray perpetually for vocations, family life, young people, the sick and a greater respect for human life. Morning Prayer from the Divine Office precedes the 7 A.M. daily Mass. Confessions follow the 7 P.M. Mass every weekday evening. Benediction is celebrated each Monday evening, charismatic prayer, every Wednesday.

St. John School enrolls 475, introducing students from Pre-K to Grade 8 to the latest technology. However, religious education is the focus of school life. Processions, the Living Rosary, Stations of the Cross, Advent Wreath devotions and special school Masses are important events in the students' lives. High test scores result from a strong academic environment and the dedication and hard work of the teachers.

More than 600 youngsters fill the elementary Religious Education classes, while on Tuesday evenings, teenagers meet to share faith and fellowship. The 7 P.M. Sunday Mass for youth has standing room only. Scouts, CYO, athletic teams and cheer leaders fill the gymnasium almost every afternoon and evening, while Scripture, RCIA classes and C.F.M. classes provide adult religious education.

Forty-five different groups meet in the parish. Among them are Rosary Society, Holy Name Society, Neo-Catechumenate, Prayer groups, Mothers Circle, AA, Grief Counseling and Couples for Christ. St. John's busy, prayerful and welcoming parishioners also engage in outreach programs. Three times a year the parish hosts a group from the Coalition to the Homeless. The St. Vincent de Paul Society and Social Concerns Organization help people in need.

St. Theresa of the Child Jesus, Linden

Fr. Edward S. Kozlowski was appointed pastor of a new parish, St. Theresa of the Child Jesus to serve the spiritual welfare of the Polish people of Linden. Twenty people celebrated the first Mass in 1925. Organizing several societies, Fr. Kozlowski fanned the flame of faith. Groundbreaking for a new church and school took place in 1926. The Sisters of Nazareth, who at first ran the school, were replaced in 1952 by the Felicians.

Through the early Forties, St. Theresa Church experienced additional growth. By 1954 ground was once again broken for a new church, separate from the school. With many renovations and expansion through the years, blessings continued to be showered upon St. Theresa Parish, but on Thanksgiving morning 1970, a fire struck the church, leaving heavy smoke damage and requiring the new organ to be dismantled and cleaned. As the decades rolled on, further renovations and additions were made to accommodate a flourishing membership. The Little Servant Sisters of the Immaculate Conception joined the staff who from the beginning ministered to the school and parish. With hope and confidence and reliance on St. Theresa, the parish is looking forward to its centennial.

Our Lady of Lourdes, Mountainside

Since its inauguration on December 13, 1958, the community of Our Lady of Lourdes has been special to the Catholic residents of Mountainside. It is special--

- because of the founding pastor, Fr. Gerard McGarry, who guided the parish for 20 years through his love and devotion to the Blessed Mother.
- because of Sr. Gertrude Agnes, the first school principal, and all the sisters and lay people who provide Catholic education to the youth.
- because of the people who visited every Catholic home in Mountainside during fund drives that built the church buildings.
- because of the volunteers who share their time and talent: Eucharistic ministers, Altar servers, ushers, choir, CCD teachers, the Holy Name Society, the Rosary Society, CYO groups, the Knights of Columbus.
- Because of the church's social activities: Bingo, Fashion Shows and Card Parties, Dances, Picnics and plays that bring the parishioners together as family.
- because of all the parishioners who give an hour of adoration in the Perpetual Adoration Chapel, open 24 hours a day every day of the year.
- Above all, because all are one in the Lord. Thank the Lord for 45 years of Your love!

Our Lady of Peace, New Providence

On a Sunday morning in February 1919, four benches of former parishioners of St. Theresa, Summit, and St. Mary, Stony Hill, gathered in the Old

Council Chamber of New Providence Borough Hall for the first Mass of a new Mission. Since World War I had recently ended, the Mission became known as Our Lady of Peace. On December 21, 1919, the first Mass in the little church built on Springfield Avenue was offered.

Until 1942, Our Lady of Peace remained a Mission of churches in Stirling and Summit. In June 1952, Fr. Peter J. Doherty, the second pastor, acquired land for a combined church and school and an auditorium and convent. By October 1954, the first Mass in the new basement church was celebrated, and a month later, the church complex and convent were dedicated.

By June 1965, funds had been raised to begin work on a new church and rectory at the South Street location. Ground was broken on June 27, 1965. More than 1000 people braved deep snow to celebrate the first Mass in the innovative church-in-the-round at midnight, Christmas 1966. In April 1975, Msgr. Paul J. Hayes was appointed pastor of Our Lady of Peace, serving for 20 years. His successor, Msgr. Joseph P. Plunkett, returned to his work in the inner city in 1997 and was followed by Fr. Sean Cunneen.

St. Bernard of Clairvaux, Plainfield

The mission church of St. Bernard of Clairvaux was opened in May 1915. In 1921 St. Bernard was separated from its mother parish and given a pastor, Fr. Joseph M. Kelly. Ground was broken for a combination school, religious and meeting center in March 1925. The next month Mass was celebrated in the new building and the school was ready two years later. The present church building was opened and blessed in 1952. Subsequent years saw the construction of a rectory, convent and addition to the school.

Over the years a parish that was once pre-dominantly composed of Italian immigrants has been transformed into a mosaic of nationalities and cultures from all over the world: Europe, Africa, the Caribbean, Central and South America and Asia.

In June 1986 the Sisters of St. John the Baptist, who had served the school for many years, withdrew. In September 1986 St. Bernard School merged with St. Mary School becoming incorporated into one building under the name of Holy Family School, which closed in June 1995. The priests were relocated to St. Mary Rectory and the convent and rectory were rented to Renew International. On April 1, 2000, Fr. Frank Rose became the tenth pastor of St. Bernard of Clairvaux.

St. Mary, Plainfield

By 1847 about 100 Catholic German immigrants living north of Plainfield established a small chapel, which they called St. Mary, Stony Hill. It became St. Mary, Plainfield, in 1851. On September 8, 1880, a new church was dedicated as St. Mary of the Assumption. The first school of St. Mary Parish, staffed by the Convent Station Sisters of Charity, served the children from 1899 to 1971.

The debt relinquished, St. Mary was dedicated September 30, 1900. Two parishes have sprung from St. Mary- -St. Bernard and St. Stanislaus. The current St. Mary School opened in 1932 through the efforts of the parishioners who dismantled the old school and broke ground for a new building on March 5, 1931.

In 1947 Fr. Harold V. Colgan founded the Blue Army of Our Lady of Fatima. It rapidly grew into a national and international movement, spreading to more than 57 countries with national headquarters established in Washington, New Jersey, and an international headquarters at Fatima, Portugal.

During the period of civil unrest in the late 1960s, St. Mary parishioners helped to form and guide Mobilization of Churches, a city-wide organization of all faiths working to bring understanding, peace and harmony among all peoples.

Following Vatican Council II, St. Mary's first Lay Advisory Board was formed, and in 1971 the school was staffed by an all-lay faculty and administration. St. Mary Convent became The Ark, a youth meeting center. From 1983 to 1991 the church was beautified and restored, and St. Mary was recognized as a historic building. In 1988 Fr. Mirandi invited the Missionary Sisters of the Blessed Sacrament and Mary Immaculate who served the parish until 1998. At the same time the contemplative branch of the Missionaries of Charity, founded by Mother Teresa of Calcutta, took up residence in the convent. The school closed, consolidating with St. Bernard to end 101 years of instruction for students in grades 1 through 8.

In 1995 the church exterior was restored even as the interior was also refurbished. The Neo-Catechumenate flourished, the number of involved people growing to nine communities, the largest group on the East Coast.

In 1996 St. Mary opened a soup kitchen, providing more than 20,000 meals over a five-year period. Today St. Mary Church embarks on journey into a new century supported by the solid foundation and firm commitment of faith inherited from those who have gone before.

St. Stanislaus Kostka, Plainfield

In response to the Polish people who settled in the Plainfield area and wanted to organize a parish, permission was given in 1920 to establish St. Stanislaus Kostka Parish.

Fr. Edmund Uminski celebrated Mass for them in St. Mary Church Hall. Two years later, the first St. Stanislaus Kostka Church was dedicated.

Between 1934-1949 improvements were made to the rectory and the mortgage was burned. Then in 1949, a new rectory was built and permission was given to build a new church, where on Easter Sunday 1972, the first Mass was celebrated.

From 1985 the parish was reduced from more than 500 families to about 150. The English-speaking community dwindled to a handful of faithful parishioners and in 2000, the parish received an administrator.

New Horizons

It was a considerable personal challenge, after 14 years in the Archdiocese of Newark, for Archbishop McCarrick to pull up the roots that he had grown here and to start anew in an archdiocese that had a people, a clergy, and a character all its own. In fact, he was the first Ordinary of Newark to be moved since Bishop Corrigan nearly 120 years before. How to begin again, learning and serving the strengths and the needs of a new community of faith? If perhaps the fifth Archbishop of Washington approached his new office with some trepidation, he could take some solace in the fact that the fifth Archbishop of Newark, John Joseph Myers, was quite probably experiencing those very same emotions.

John Joseph Myers

Born in Ottawa, Illinois, John J. Myers is the oldest of seven children of Jack Myers and Margaret Donohue. Growing up in the 1940's and 50's, John and his three brothers and three sisters experienced on his family's farm a sort of life which had become all but extinct in the Archdiocese of Newark. If, however, farming had become scarce in the Archdiocese of Newark, the Myers family's life was otherwise very similar to many Catholic families throughout America at the time. The entire family regularly attended Mass at St. Theresa's Church, where John would be an altar server for several years. Early on, he developed a fascination for science fiction – a fascination that he shared with his boyhood friend Gary Wolf, the creator of the character Roger Rabbit. To this day, both have remained close friends, and have collaborated on a proposed science fiction novel.

After receiving his education in local public elementary and high schools, John Myers began attending Loras College in Dubuque, Iowa. There he felt a strengthening in his call to the priesthood, and transferred to the school's seminary program. After graduating from Loras in 1963, John Myers began studies for the priesthood in Rome, and was ordained a priest for service to the Diocese of Peoria at St. Peter's Basilica, Rome, on December 17, 1966. During this time of study in Rome at the Pontifical North American College, Father Myers received a licentiate in Sacred Theology from Gregorian University. However, one of the most important events in his life and that of the Church occurred during his training for the priesthood – the Second Vatican Council.

"To be a Catholic then," the young priest once said, "was exciting and a little bit unsettling because of all the depth of possibilities for renewing the faith of people of the Church. But to be there, studying in Rome while the Council was taking place, was something else. There was always some news, some activity, that drove our conversations about how we as Catholics and priests would face the future." The depth of the Council's actions and new direction for the Church has always been uppermost in this future bishop's life, as evidenced by the framed front page of the October 11, 1962 edition of Vatican newspaper *L'Osservatore Romano* announcing the Council that hangs in his office in the Newark Archdiocesan Center. Despite the tumult and excitement of the Council, Fr. Myers returned to his home diocese of Peoria, Illinois, where he began fulfilling his promise to serve the local Church. As an assistant pastor and associate pastor in two parishes, he entered into the daily

St. Mark, Rahway

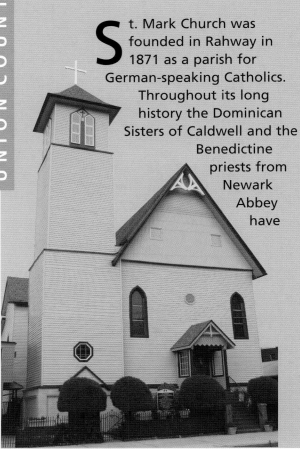

St. Mark Church was founded in Rahway in 1871 as a parish for German-speaking Catholics. Throughout its long history the Dominican Sisters of Caldwell and the Benedictine priests from Newark Abbey have served the parish in various capacities.

From 1941 to 1978 the Parish purchased and renovated its hall annex, acquired additional parking and rebuilt many sections of the wood-frame church building. During this time, family membership multiplied more than 10 times. Liturgical renovations, the Renew program and the Neo-catechumenate were introduced after Vatican Council II.

Throughout its 132-year history, St. Mark has been a vibrant parish with many active organizations. Its religious education program serves grades one through middle school. It has a well respected choir, a vital St. Anne Society, a hard-working Holy Name Society, a youth group and a social action committee that does everything from visiting the sick to making sandwiches for the St. Joseph Service Center in Elizabeth. Now a culturally diverse parish, volunteers serve the church in the Altar Society, as altar servers, adult acolytes, Eucharist ministers, lectors and ushers.

St. Mary, Rahway

Years before the City of Rahway Seal was cut St. Mary's R.C. Church was already incorporated. In 1845, priests from St. Mary of the Assumption in Elizabethtown, NJ, started to come to Rahway for church services. In 1854 the Church of St. Mary's was incorporated. Baptism registers date back to 1853 calling the parish St. Mary's Church of Rahway and Amboy. The first marriage in the Marriage Register is November 10, 1853. The original church (wooden) was replaced by a stone structure, unique in its architectural genre, in 1888 and its interior renovated (1980's) in accordance with the norms of the Second Vatican Council. The Rectory building (1888) with later additions was also renovated in the mid 1980's. The original St. Mary's School (late 1800's) with a later addition still stands and a new building was dedicated in 1925. The Dominican Sisters of Caldwell staffed St. Mary's School for over 100 years until the 1980's.

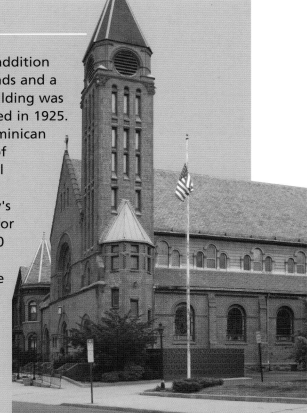

St. Joseph the Carpenter, Roselle

In the early 1890s the Union County Catholic population was rural and scattered. In 1877 the Bishop of Newark, Michael Corrigan, decreed that Westfield, Cranford and Roselle should be one parish with Fr. W. J. Wiseman, centered at Cranford, as pastor of all three communities. Mass was celebrated for the Roselle Catholics on Christmas 1882.

The ever-growing population soon had to meet for worship in the Masonic meeting rooms on Chestnut Street. In 1895 Bishop Wigger incorporated St. Joseph as a separate church. With the purchase of the Moore Estate, the first wooden church was begun in 1997 and dedicated the following year.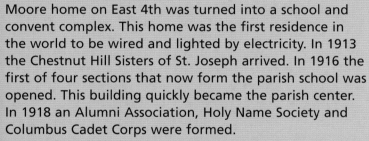

In 1903 Fr. John A. O'Brien, the first resident pastor, finished the rectory, started CCD classes and organized various parish societies. Subsequently the Moore home on East 4th was turned into a school and convent complex. This home was the first residence in the world to be wired and lighted by electricity. In 1913 the Chestnut Hill Sisters of St. Joseph arrived. In 1916 the first of four sections that now form the parish school was opened. This building quickly became the parish center. In 1918 an Alumni Association, Holy Name Society and Columbus Cadet Corps were formed.

Fr. Edward G. Murphy was to guide the parish for almost 37 years. He inherited a debt of $45,000 as well as a rapidly growing parish. The debt was paid and in 1930 and 1952 additions were made to the school. In 1957 a 20-bedroom convent was opened and a drive for a Catholic Boys High School was launched. Eighteen rooms were added to the elementary school in 1963 and Roselle Catholic was made a regional school. Girls Catholic High School opened in 1964 in the old grade school and after Vatican Council II, the changes called for by the Council were implemented. In 1971 Fr. Anthony Chu came in residence to further his education and assist the poor of the parish. Fr. John Dowling, the tenth pastor, consolidated the parish and invited fuller participation in decision-making. He established the Parish Council, the Parish Cabinet, the Board of Education, Renew and a parish census. For more than 40 years Fr. Dowling has witnessed the Old Testament blessing of seeing his "family" to the third and fourth generations.

Assumption, Roselle Park

Church of the Assumption was incorporated on January 15, 1907, after several Italian Catholic families in Roselle Park expressed their desire to practice their faith in their native language. As their demands for a priest grew stronger, Rev. Cataldo Alessi arrived to serve the spiritual and cultural needs of the people as their first pastor. The first Mass was offered in a small church built and owned by one of the founding parishioners.

As the parish grew, so did the need for a larger church. On October 12, 1911, the Most Rev. John J. O'Connor, then Bishop of Newark, dedicated the new church. In 1916 and again in 1922, the church was remodeled and more Masses were added to the schedule to accommodate the need of the expanding parish community. Today, the original church serves as a Religious Education Center and meeting hall for the parish

The people of the Church of the Assumption continue to try to live out their parish mission: *We are dedicated to building up a praying, loving and caring community which will proclaim the Good News of Jesus Christ by example, service and witness and to deepen our commitment to the Lord through the guidance of the Holy Spirit and the intercession of Mary, the Mother of God.*

Immaculate Heart of Mary, Scotch Plains

In June of 1964, Bishop Thomas A. Boland, Archbishop of Newark assigned Fr. George Byrne to establish a new parish in Scotch Plains. The first Mass of Immaculate Heart of Mary Parish was celebrated on June 21, 1964, at the Union Catholic High School auditorium.

Groundbreaking for the present church took place on July 23, 1967, with the first Mass offered on January 18, 1969, in the new church. More adaptation has taken place since then, including additions to the rectory and the construction of the Nazareth Center. Since 1964 the parish has grown to more than 1800 families who are bound together by common beliefs and who journey together toward lasting peace with the Lord of all.

St. Bartholomew, Scotch Plains

St. Bartholomew the Apostle Parish was established in 1948 by Archbishop Thomas J. Walsh. Fr. John S. Nelligan was appointed pastor.
The first Mass was celebrated on June 20, 1948, at Scotch Plains-Fanwood High School, now Park Middle School. The first Mass in the church was July 9, 1950. The parish school opened in September 1950.

A narthex was added and inside renovations to the church were completed in 1993.

The parish today has about 2000 families with a very large CCD program for the parish children.

faith life of the people and eventually began relying on their insights and concerns to shape his thinking about issues affecting Catholics. During this time, Fr. Myers started several lay study groups to examine Scripture and its relevance to people's lives. Questions raised often became the basis for Father's homilies.

A few years after entering parish life, Father Myers was sent to Washington, DC to pursue studies for a doctorate in Canon Law at Catholic University of America. Upon completion of this studies, he returned to Peoria and began serving the Church of Peoria in a number of administrative as well as pastoral posts, including Administrator of the Cathedral, diocesan Vice-Chancellor and ultimately Chancellor, Director of Vocations and Vicar General.

He was appointed Coadjutor Bishop of Peoria on July 14, 1987, with the right of succession, and acceded as Bishop of Peoria in 1990.

While serving as Bishop of Peoria, Bishop Myers again resurrected his idea of lay involvement in the development of the issues of the day. With the assistance of members of his diocesan pastoral council, Bishop Myers developed pastoral letters that addressed a range of topics of concern to the people of Peoria, among them the role of fathers, the sanctity of life, educating children and adults in the faith, and the Eucharist.

When Bishop John Myers received the call on July 4, 2001 stating that Pope John Paul II had named him to lead the Church of Newark as its new Archbishop, he said, "I am profoundly humbled." Later, when his appointment was made public on July 24 and he was questioned about the differences between Peoria and Newark, he said both have "good people who have a deep faith and a deep love for the Church. It will be a great adventure as we follow the Lord with trust into the 21st Century. Surely He will help us to do the part He intends for us in His great plan for the human family."

St. James the Apostle, Springfield

St. James the Apostle Parish was founded in 1923 when a delegation from St. Rose of Lima, then located in Springfield, made a plea to the Bishop of Newark expressing its desire to create a second parish in the town. On December 23, 1923, Fr. James T. Brown celebrated the first Mass in Municipal Hall. Shortly thereafter a new church that now houses a bank on Morris Avenue was constructed.

The parish grew rapidly as people from Millburn and Union joined the church. Then in 1950, 26 years after the first church was built, construction commenced on the current campus. Because after World War II many military grant homes became available to veterans, the design for the church was a wrap-around style with the school encircling the worship space. The 12 churches in the Archdiocese built from this design were named "Apostle Churches." In 1950 the church was established in what was to be a school gymnasium. After some renovations, the parish was still worshiping there in 1973.

In 1999 a capital campaign was launched and ground broken on June 16, 2001 for the new church, which was dedicated on June 6, 2002. Under the present and tenth pastor, Fr. Robert B. Stagg, the parish membership consists of 1700 families with 200 students in the parish school and 450 enrolled in the Religious Education Program. St. James the Apostle is celebrates its 80th anniversary as a parish in 2003 and the school its 50th.

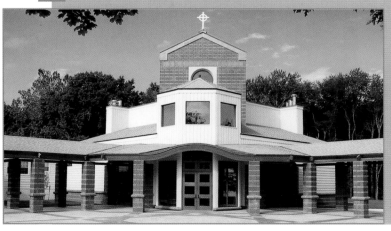

St. Teresa of Avila, Summit

A deed recorded in the office of the Union County Clerk, dated June 8, 1863, records the transfer of land owned by the George Manley family to the Diocese. On this land the cornerstone of a tiny stone building honoring St. Teresa of Avila was laid in 1863.

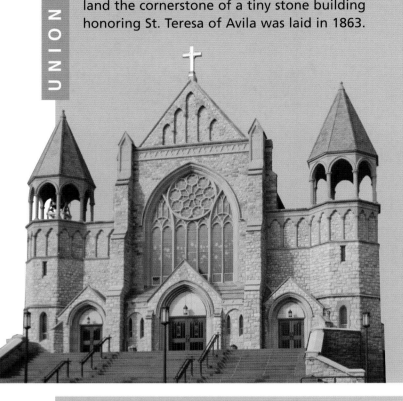

A Mission for 10 years, the Church was incorporated on October 15, 1864 with Fr. W. M. Wigger, later Bishop of Newark, as the first resident pastor.

One of the first acts of Fr. Wigger was to purchase a lot at Chestnut and Park Avenue for a small school building staffed by the Sisters of Charity from Convent Station in 1881. The rectory, which remained in use until 1962, also went up at this time. In 1886 the cornerstone was laid for the second church, with the parent church annexed and used as a sacristy. Fr. Giovanni Vassalo, pastor for 30 years, officiated.

A brick school, now the Education Building, was built in 1905 and the previous school moved to serve as the convent. The cornerstone of the third and present church was laid in 1924 with Fr. Michael J. Glennon as pastor. The second church was moved and is presently known as Memorial Hall. When the Sisters of Charity withdrew in 1973, a lay teaching staff oversaw the school until it closed in June 1982. The Felician sisters joined the Religious Education staff in 19082 and remained until 1997. The school reopened in September 2001 with a Pre-school followed by the addition of Kindgergarten the next year.

Holy Spirit, Union

Holy Spirit Parish had its inception when Archbishop Thomas A. Boland S.T.D. canonically erected it, on June 14, 1963. The new parish was to be built on the Archdiocesan-owned four and a half acre tract of land at the intersection of Morris Avenue and Suburban Road.
It was, for the most part, to serve those Catholic families attending St. Michael's Church in Union, Christ the King Church in Hillside, and St. Genevieve's Church in Elizabeth, and living within the newly defined boundaries.

On June 28, 1963, Rev. George D. Drexler was appointed the first Pastor.

Holy Spirit's second

Pastor, Msgr. John H. Koenig, was appointed on June 30, 1978. Under his direction the Parish grew in numbers of the faithful and in many new organizations and apostolates. At age seventy-five Msgr. Koenig retired.

On January 31, 1992, Msgr. Vincent J. Doyle was appointed as the third Pastor of Holy Spirit.

Again, the Parish Family has grown to some 2500 families with some thirty-two Ministries of the Word, Worship, and various Service Ministries of hospitality for the homeless and poor. There is a School for some two hundred children from Pre-K through eighth grade, with about five hundred Children in the Religious Education Program. Holy Spirit is a very vibrant and flourishing Parish.

St. Michael the Archangel, Union

Rapid population growth in Union brought St. Michael the Archangel into existence in November 1928. For the next few years, Mass was celebrated in Union Theater, but work on a church / school combination building was started almost immediately on a block of land donated by the Kelly Family in memory of their son, Michael, the first citizen of Union to die in the First World War.

The school opened in 1931, staffed by the Dominican Sisters of Caldwell. Very soon, the men of the parish built the first convent, replaced in 1952 with a building capable of housing 22 sisters. It now serves as Parish Center.

The church, in the middle level of the building, was the place of worship until 1954. Union grew rapidly from a farm town into a suburb during the Great Depression. After World War II, the original buildings became woefully inadequate. The present church was completed and dedicated in 1954. Within three years it could not accommodate the huge numbers of worshipers, and the basement was turned into a Lower Church. In the early 1960s, Holy Spirit became a daughter parish of St. Michael, alleviating the overcrowding. In the late 90s, St. Michael was renovated according to Vatican Council II.

St. Michael has had 17 men ordained as priests and many more young women professed as religious. Always a dynamic and ever-changing, St. Michael mirrors its locale. A predominantly German / Irish population in its early days welcomed Italians, Poles and Hungarians post-World War II. The advent of Portuguese, Filipinos, Hispanics, Africans, Indians and other ethnic groups has turned Union and St. Michael into one of the most diverse places in the state and Archdiocese. It is hoped that the parish will always imitate Christ on the Cross whose arms were outstretched in love for all people.

Holy Trinity, Westfield

A corporation president who read the book, *Men of God*, was so impressed that he ordered 375 copies for his employees. The book's Chicago distributor responded, "We do not have 375 Men of God in Chicago. Try Los Angeles!"

Holy Trinity Parish, Westfield, has far more than 375 men and women of God whose hearts, in imitation of the God of love, reach out over and over to God's hurting children. Their prayer is abundant and joyful, their hope, undiminished by the powers of darkness, their spirits, proud of and grateful for the 130-year heritage of faith in the parish, as they labor mightily to pass on the gift of faith to the next generation.

Faithful and generous stewards of their gifts of time, talent and treasure, the far more than 375 men and women of God of Holy Trinity seek to be ever more, as their mission statement proclaims, "a servant community of welcome and hospitality, of reconciliation and forgiveness, of compassion and hope."

St. Helen, Westfield

Thirty-five years after its modest beginning, St. Helen's Parish community has become an active and multi-faceted community known for its many outreach efforts, its vibrant liturgical celebrations and its various programs for children and adults.

The current church, completed in 1972, provides a warm and supportive environment for liturgical celebrations and is often filled with parishioners who now number approximately 3800 families. The parish center, constructed in 1984, was expanded in 1988 and named after the founding pastor, Msgr. Thomas Meaney. It provides office space for clergy and lay staff, limited meeting space and a gymnasium.

Over the years, the programming for education and social outreach has diversified and now includes elementary, middle-school/Confirmation, and youth ministry pro-

grams. This year, the Catechesis of the Good Shepherd will bring together three and four year-olds. Small faith-sharing groups, groups for separated and divorced Catholics, opportunities for individual spiritual direction, as well as other faith-development and retreat opportunities enrich the faith-life of St. Helen's members. Helping Hands and Hearts groups a wide variety of outreach efforts. A counseling project begun in 1985 continues to offer support to families and individuals. The parish, along with Holy Trinity (Westfield) and Our Lady of Lourdes (Mountainside), supports sponsors a growing Catholic elementary school using facilities at Holy Trinity and Our Lady of Lourdes.

Over the years, the parish community has benefited from the many staff members - clergy and lay who have given their energy and talents to support the growth of the community under Msgr. Meaney until 1990, Msgr. James A Burke until 2000 and Msgr. William Harms, the current pastor. Central to the spirit of the parish has been the continuing commitment of parishioners to give real meaning to St. Helen's mission - "We are committed to bringing the Good News to others in our community and beyond. United in prayer, we understand that it is our calling to use our time, treasure and talents for the benefit of all."

The First Challenge

Hardly had those words stopped echoing in the halls of the Newark Archdiocesan Center than the faith of the people of the Church in Newark was tested by the September 11 attacks on the World Trade Center and Pentagon. Archbishop-designate Myers, still in Peoria because of the federal government's ban on air travel, immediately reached out to the people of his new home by phone through the diocesan administrator, Bishop Paul Bootkoski, because so many people living in New Jersey were affected both directly and indirectly by the attack. In a general statement, the new Archbishop said, "Even as I am taking leave from my family and friends here in Illinois, I pray for those in my new family who are suffering in

whatever way. I am grateful for and proud of the many ways that the parishes, hospitals, social services, schools, and other institutions of the Archdiocese of Newark have found to offer help and support."

The new Archbishop reached Newark in the first week of October, and immediately he and Bishop Bootkoski visited Ground Zero at the World Trade Center to pray with and console the rescue and relief workers. "I was visiting with a woman at the Port Authority Temporary Headquarters," Archbishop Myers said after the visit. "She said something which struck me as very wise. She said, 'Archbishop, I understand that you are coming from the Midwest into a new and different situation. But, you know we are all in a new and different situation, too. Maybe we have more in

Shortly after his arrival to Newark, Archbishop-elect John Myers (with then-Vicar General and Archdiocesan Adminstrator Bishop Paul Bootkoski) toured Ground Zero at the World Trade Center.

common than we once imagined!' And I thought, 'She is right. We are all in this new situation together!'

"Another women came up and said that she hadn't prayed since the attack. I told her 'That's okay. I'll pray for you.' I gave her my Rosary and we prayed together."

Although still smarting from the attack, the Church of Newark welcomed its new Archbishop on October 9, 2001, in an installation ceremony at the Cathedral Basilica of the Sacred Heart that was broadcast by television throughout the state.

In the days and weeks that followed, there were many other opportunities to reach out to try and heal the hurting. At special Masses and funerals, Archbishop Myers commended police and fire officers who perished, and thanked the many emergency service workers, police, chaplains and hospital staffs and volunteers who rushed into action after the attack. The new Archbishop also sought to address the spiritual needs of the Catholic people of Newark through a new pastoral, *If God Is For Us, Who Can Be Against Us?*, issued one month after the attack, that addressed in question-and-answer format the range of emotions felt by everyone.

Also during his first weeks, Archbishop Myers began to "get acquainted" with the full scope of the institutions and services of the Archdiocese.

Several days were spent visiting with the staffs and clients of many Catholic Community Services agencies serving the homeless, refugees and AIDS patients. He toured Cathedral Health Care hospitals to see how the Church is meeting the health needs of inner city residents. And he visited several schools and parishes as well.

By the end of 2001, Archbishop Myers had issued his second pastoral letter, *A Reason For The Hope That Lies Within Us.* Again employing the question-and-answer format, this new pastoral was a true teaching document, expressing for the people of Newark the relationship of the local Church to the Universal Church, and outlining a vision for individuals to participate fully in the faith. The timing of this new pastoral was coincidental to a significant crisis in the Catholic Church in the United States.

Scandal and Confusion

Between December 2001 and early 2002, a growing number of media reports about a case of serial sexual abuse of minors by a priest in the Archdiocese of Boston spawned a growing revelation of past and present offenses by current or former Catholic clergy. This revelation quickly developed into a scandal that overtook the country

Catholics in the Archdiocese are strong in their commitment to promoting the sanctity of life. Archbishop Myers prays the rosary at a March for Life on Good Friday in Englewood.

Lay participation at parish and archdiocesan levels in setting policy and programs are part of the life of the Church of Newark.

and the Catholic Church in America. The Church in Newark also began to feel the pain of this scandal, as information about events alleged to have taken place both currently and well into the past began to reach the Archdiocesan Center.

As these events unfolded, Archbishop Myers quickly instituted a series of steps to strengthen the already strong processes in place in Newark for such actions. The Archdiocese already had a review board of laypeople with expertise in investigation, law enforcement, law, medicine and psychology in place and operating since 1993, to review cases for the Archbishop. Additional volunteer members were added to the board. Archbishop Myers publicly announced that no priest would serve in ministry if the review board found an allegation credible. And the Archdiocese would continue to provide counseling and other support services to victims.

In the following months, a number of priests in the Archdiocese left ministry while the review of allegations – often 20, 30 or more years old – continued. The Archbishop took on an additional assignment from the US Conference of Catholic

Bishop – as member of the Ad Hoc Committee on Sexual Abuse. In this role he helped draft the Charter for the Protection of Children and Young People.

As part of the Charter, Newark and all other dioceses were charged with instituting "safe environment" programs to increase awareness of the problem of sexual abuse. The Archdiocese had been involved in the development of a program -- *Protecting God's Children* – and had already introduced it to the Archdiocese's Youth Ministry program. During 2003, it would be implemented at all levels of the Archdiocese for anyone working or volunteering in programs serving children or adults. In addition, a Victim Assistance Coordinator was added to the process to assure that people with allegations of abuse would receive appropriate counseling as soon as possible. The

Archbishop also asked a retired New Jersey Supreme Court Justice to serve as a consultant to the Review Board to assure that all appropriate and available steps are taken in every case of misconduct.

During this time, some Catholics and others were questioning the scandal in terms of its sexual nature. Archbishop Myers sought to address some of these questions within the context of the teachings of the Church and Pope John Paul II's earlier work on the theology of the body in a third pastoral letter, *And the Word became Flesh – a Theological Reflection on the Human Body*.

At this point, the Archdiocese has reviewed most of the allegations brought to its attention. Several priests remain on leave during this process while the cases move toward a tribunal under the Canon Law of the Church. Civil authorities have tried two cases under current law. Archbishop Myers has continued to assure all that any victim of abuse will be heard, and all allegations will be investigated, in order to restore trust in the Church of Newark.

Financial Problems Return

In 2001, early signs of financial troubles for the Archdiocese – troubles not seen since the time of Archbishop Gerety – began to surface. Growth and income from investments of the Archdiocesan endowments, which had for many years allowed the Church to expand in order to meet growing and changing needs, were disappearing. The Church was falling victim to the same economic forces that were plaguing businesses and individuals throughout the country. The overall financial downturn also had an adverse effect on giving at the parish and archdiocesan levels. With less coming in, it became apparent by 2002 that some dramatic changes were needed in the structure and operation of the Archdiocese.

At the same time, a number of demographic shifts in all of the four counties of the Archdiocese began to indicate that many of the programs, operations and institutions of the Archdiocese may not have been meeting the needs of Catholics and others they serve.

Archbishop Myers took the unpopular but necessary step of requesting all parishes, schools

In spite of significant demographic and economic change in the Archdiocese, support for Catholic education remains strong. Archbishop Myers joins in song with students from one of the Archdiocese's more than 160 schools during the annual Scholarship Fund for Inner-City Children fundraiser.

and Archdiocesan institutions to reexamine their current operations to see where expenses and programs could be changed to address the reality of having to do more with less.

At the same time, he charged two independent task forces – one for parishes and one for schools – to develop guidelines that will enable these critical sources of Catholic teaching and worship to remain vital into the future.

As this book is nearing publication, these two task forces are preparing to deliver their recommendations on the future life and operation of parishes and schools. "No places touch our lives more than Church and school," Archbishop Myers says. "They speak directly to the heart of my role as bishop – that of teacher and spiritual leader. They also speak to the commitment that we, as people of faith, make to the Church we love and serve. In many ways, we remain a mission church like in colonial days. Over the last 150 years, the people of this Archdiocese have supported many amazing and beautiful buildings and important programs as expressions of their love for God and His Church. We must be innovative and ready to adapt to what the world presents to us today."

In the days and weeks after the September 11 attacks, many sought help and comfort from the Church, and came to mourn the men and women who perished.

As the people of the Archdiocese of Newark enter the Third Millennium, we are committed to follow in the tradition of those who came before us to proclaim in faith and love the mission of Christ the Redeemer.